British Imperialism

Histories and Controversies

General Editor: Jeremy Black

Histories and Controversies introduces key questions and debates surrounding major historical themes and events.

Robert Johnson
British Imperialism

Further titles are in preparation

British Imperialism

Robert Johnson

First published 2003 by
PALGRAVE MACMILLAN
Houndmills, Basingstoke, Hampshire RG21 6XS and
175 Fifth Avenue, New York, N. Y. 10010
Companies and representatives throughout the world

PALGRAVE MACMILLAN is the global academic imprint of the Palgrave
Macmillan division of St. Martin's Press, LLC and of Palgrave Macmillan Ltd.
Macmillan® is a registered trademark in the United States, United
Kingdom and other countries. Palgrave is a registered trademark in the
European Union and other countries.

ISBN 0–333–94725–8 hardback
ISBN 0–333–94726–6 paperback

This book is printed on paper suitable for recycling and
made from fully managed and sustained forest sources.

A catalogue record for this book is available
from the British Library.

Library of Congress Cataloging-in-Publication Data
Johnson, Robert, 1967–
    British imperialism / Robert Johnson.
        p.   cm.—(Histories and controversies)
    Includes bibliographical references (p.) and index.
    ISBN 0–333–94725–8 (cloth)—ISBN 0–333–94726–6 (paper)
    1. Great Britain—Colonies—History.   2. Imperialism—History.
    I. Title.   II. Series.

DA16 .J65 2002
325′.32′0941—dc21

                                                                        2002026768

10   9   8   7   6   5   4   3   2   1
12   11   10   09   08   07   06   05   04   03

Printed and bound in Great Britian by
J. W. Arrowsmith, Bristol

Contents

Preface

This book aims to explain some of the histories of and controversies about British imperialism. It offers an introduction, critical analysis and overview of some of the debates that surround
the British Empire from its origins to the return of Hong Kong
to Chinese rule in 1997. The historiography of imperialism is
vast, and the subject matter is on a global scale, so it is increasingly difficult to obtain a firm grasp of the major issues, from
'Informal Empire' to 'colonial discourse'. Moreover, there has
been a sharp division between those who claim to practise
Imperial History and those who challenge the very basis of its
methods, such as post-colonial theorists, subaltern studies scholars,
and the large group inspired by Edward Said. Part of the
reason for the lively debate between these groups is that the history of imperialism continues to exert a strong influence on the
present, and moral judgements of its worth are made with reference to the shadow that empires have cast over the world.
Another no less contentious and current debate on 'globalisation' is rooted in a far older controversy about international
finance, 'Great Power' influence, and poverty and instability in
the poor nations of the world. Moreover, it is sometimes argued
that the cultural system of imperialism is still with us. Three
areas, it is argued, appear particularly imperialist: our language
that harbours concepts of power, stereotypes that fuel 'institutionalised racism', and the patronising air of the affluent West.
Ranged against this negative verdict are those who argue that
imperialism was a typical episode in history (the world was full of
empires in 1900), and believe that the British Empire was a
modernising influence which bestowed democracy and free institutions when it liberated its colonies after 1945.

Imperialism is a concept now universally condemned in
Britain and the world. It is regarded as morally bankrupt, even
though barely 100 years ago, it was thought the British Empire
could bring benefits to the rest of the world. Some of the British

were proud of their Empire, although exhibiting enthusiasm for it (outside of jubilees or *durbars*) was regarded as vulgar. The Empire passed away without much of a fanfare, converting itself, as it had always done, as the circumstances changed. It was, as the world's largest empire, enormous in extent. It is estimated that perhaps as many as one-quarter of the world's inhabitants lived under the British flag. However, British imperialism affected many millions more, since British *influence* spread beyond the regions under direct rule. The extent of this influence, and how historians might measure it, is problematic. Moreover, the motives for this influence are also debatable. It is sometimes argued that there was some kind of ideology of imperialism. In its simplest form, this could be defined as a will to exert power and influence (financial, political, military or cultural) over other peoples without consent. The history of the Empire is apparently shot through with this motive, from slavery to finance capitalism.

Most of the states in South Asia, Africa and the Middle East experienced colonial rule by one or two of the European powers. Europeans drew up the borders of many African states regardless of ethnic boundaries, producing a terrible legacy in Congo, Burundi and Rwanda. The memory of the colonial period is often a painful one, a national humiliation of conquest, military occupation and subservience. Independence was frequently greeted as a celebration of liberation. But there was a pattern of modern Western imperialism that can be traced back to the fifteenth century, and which culminated in the late twentieth century. Britain's imperial expansion ebbed and flowed within this period, resulting in an assemblage of different states. Each one was at a different stage of 'development' and was fitted with a tailored political system, ranging from democratic self-government to the benign dictatorship of a colonial governor. Nevertheless, the British endeavoured, wherever they could, to hand over a colony with an established democratic system in the hope of continued partnership.

Imperialism was, of course, a far older phenomenon. The Romans, like many of the classical civilisations, had been adept at the subjugation and incorporation of other peoples. They had extended their system of law, their politics and their military power across Europe and the Mediterranean, but they had supplemented existing religions and merely incorporated the original trading network. The British impact was also selective, but the extent of its influence was far greater than that of the Roman Empire. In 1910, in his *Ancient and Modern Imperialism* Lord Cromer wrote: 'The great imperial problem of the future is to what extent some 350 millions of British subjects, who are alien to us in race, religion, language, manners and customs, are to govern themselves or are to be governed by us. Rome never had to face such an issue as this.'

However, the Europeans were not the only imperialists of the modern period. The Ottoman Empire, built up to its greatest extent in the sixteenth century, continued to exert its influence on Europe's southern and south-eastern flanks. The Chinese Qing dynasty controlled East Asia, including Manchuria and Kashgaria, whilst the Russians held Central Asia and stretched across Siberia to the Pacific, where in 1858–60 they expanded their long-established presence. In Africa, the Fulani had ruled large parts of West Africa, while in 1900, the Abyssinians possessed an empire of many nations, rivalling the extension of Egyptian control over the Sudan and Equatoria. Of all these world empires, those of the European powers were remarkably short lived. Decolonisation, when it came, was also a rapid process; most of Africa achieved independence in a period of 20 years. Whilst space does not permit a more detailed comparison of empires, this context must not be forgotten when examining British imperialism.

This book will offer an evaluation of the motives and the methods and examine some of the effects of British imperialism in three parts. The first section, Chapters 1–4, will highlight the definitions of imperialism, the nature of British imperialist rule from its Angevin origins to the early nineteenth century, imperialist thinking and the notion of 'New Imperialism'. The second section, Chapters 5–9 will examine a number of themes in the heyday of British imperialism (*c.*1870–1914), such as the commercial and financial foundations of imperialism, the effects of migration, the limits of imperialism, the collaboration of 'sub-imperialists', and resistance. There will also be discussion of four areas that have attracted interest in recent years: namely the role of cultural imperialism, the strengths and weaknesses of post-colonial theory as a tool of analysis, the gendering of imperialism, and racism. The third section, Chapters 10–14, examines the continuities of imperialism after 1914, the British responses to nationalism and decolonisation, the Empire in the world wars, popular culture, questions of development, and the impact of imperialism on Britain itself.

This book is concerned with controversies in imperial history, but offers only an introduction to this vast subject. It is not a history of the British Empire, since the emphasis is on imperialism and its controversies. Therefore, readers will find more coverage of the *debate* on the economic motives for imperialism, for example, than perhaps on the actual economics of Empire. Moreover, selected events that have attracted attention are included in more depth, such as the shootings at Amritsar in 1919, even if they were untypical of the British Empire's handling of civil disturbances. The book also touches on some imperial myths. Some of the results are surprising and challenge the simplistic model of imperialism as a system of oppression and exploitation by the colonisers over the colonised. The vast numbers of collaborators amongst indigenous peoples suggests opportunities arose as often as they were stifled. Programmes of development and investment changed social systems, even where they did not improve them. Frequently, the British themselves were profoundly affected by the expectations of the Empire. They found they had to 'fit the mask' of overlords. They had to respond appropriately to conflicting local interests. The difficulty of this will be appreciated when one considers the handover of power in India in 1947, and the sectarian violence that accompanied it.

The book is framed on a series of questions, chosen for their relevance, significance and popularity. Many of them will be of interest to readers outside of imperial history, such as the relative importance of British imperialism to the process of globalisation. Others will be eager to know what motivated British imperialists, and whether economic, political-diplomatic or military factors were paramount in imperial expansion. Of some importance is the question whether the imperialists wittingly, or unwittingly, constructed 'supremacist paradigms' through knowledge, ideology, propaganda and language. This is considered, bearing in mind the more fundamental question: Do post-colonial theories assist historians or mislead them? There will be discussion of how far the full extent of collaboration has really been acknowledged. Moreover, there will be consideration of whether imperialism could 'pay its way', whether it was a financial burden, and whether or not it can be measured in moral terms. In addition, Britain itself has been included in order to analyse why it was that a liberal and parliamentary state embarked on an enterprise of conquest and world influence, and how it applied the same values to ensure, through decolonisation, that it left behind democratic institutions.

This book serves as an introduction to British imperialism rather than a history of the British Empire, since there are many excellent works already available, including the recently published *Oxford History of the British Empire*. It does not give any more than an outline in some areas (such as the partition of Africa), and much has been left out simply because of restrictions on space. However, it will be a useful starting point for anyone trying to ascertain how some of the historiography of British imperialism has changed, showing the strengths and weaknesses of different historical interpretations. To assist the reader, the book follows a thematic approach, but is also broadly chronological. This framework will help to convey the idea that the British Empire was a global entity which emerged in a piecemeal fashion over a long period of history. It is not surprising therefore that viewed in hindsight, British imperialism was continuously evolving, was somewhat incoherent and even contradictory.

There are many people who have helped in the writing of this book and it is hard to do justice to their efforts in a paragraph. Professor Jeremy Black of Exeter University kindly supported my first steps, and has been a generous friend and advisor ever since. Professor Andrew Porter of Kings College, London, freely offered his advice and very kindly assisted with the compilation of the bibliography. Dr Iain R. Smith of Warwick University, who captured my interest in South African history with his engaging seminars, and challenged my parochial ideas, has continued to be my mentor and an example to me. He was able to point me in the right direction on numerous occasions. There have been helpful questions posed by students, friends who have endured enthusiastic debate, and relatives who have gracefully accepted my absences in order to read, draft and redraft this book. Nevertheless, any errors are entirely my responsibility.

Rob Johnson

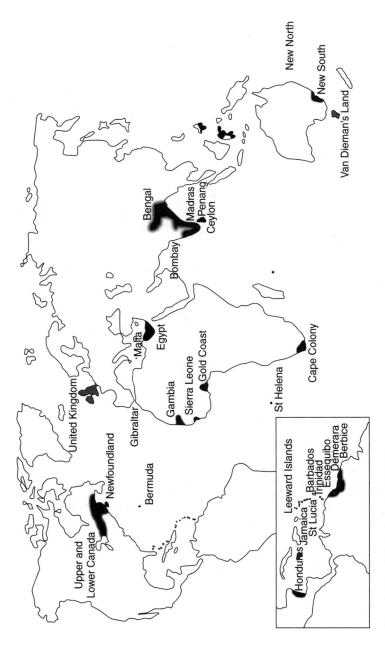

Map 1 The British Empire in 1815

Map 2 British India, *c.*1757–1947, adapted from Norman Lane, *Mastering British History,* 3rd edition (Palgrave Macmillan, 1998), p. 144.

Map 3 European possessions in Africa 1914, adapted from Norman Lane, *Mastering British History*, 3rd edition (Palgrave Macmillan, 1998), p. 244.

1 Introduction: what was British imperialism?

The British Empire seems, at first sight, to merit a straightforward definition. United by the British Crown, and governed from London, the vast array of territories and seas that fell under British military and economic control was the Empire on which 'the sun never set'. However, historians and social scientists have grown dissatisfied with the idea that the Empire was some monolithic entity exclusively and firmly under British government direction throughout the 300 years of its existence. In 1900, the British Empire covered one-fifth of the globe and governed 400 million subjects of many faiths and ethnic groups. There were 60 dependencies covering 3.2 million square miles, and British India consisted of a further 2 million square miles and 322 million subjects. In addition, Britain possessed five dominions covering 7.6 million square miles and 24 million people. As the hub in a system of trade, financial services, communications, migratory patterns, naval and military power, Britain had become, as Makinder once put it, 'the centre of the world'.

British control over its sprawling collection of lands and peoples was flexible. In some places, it was a 'benign despotism', in others, it was exercised through the voluntary association of local rulers with the Crown. Large numbers of imperial subjects had very little direct contact with the British, particularly in India or in Burma where the terrain meant that rural populations were not easily accessible. Moreover, whilst the territorial extent of British rule is clearly documented, the *influence* Britain exerted was far greater, but rather more difficult to quantify, and is the subject of intense debate. In South America, the Middle East and China, trade, finance and currency were significant features in their relations with Britain. British imperialism can thus be defined as the exercise of power over the domains Britain controlled, but any definition must take account of the degree of influence it had beyond the imperial borders.

The term 'imperialism' generates considerable controversy and has a tortured historiography. Whilst imperialism is often still discussed in no more than Marxist economic terms, historians would point out the limitations of this definition to explain far older periods of imperialism or colonisation. Benjamin J. Cohen argued that imperialism could not be explained by the maturity, or otherwise, of capitalism at all.[1] He believed that the anarchic nature of relations between independent and sovereign states made them strive for improvements to national security. In order to achieve improved security, states sought to dominate or influence others, and to reduce levels of dependence. This dominance was never absolute because of the costs and risks involved. Cohen wrote:

> It follows that if a state is to enhance its national security, it must, to the extent possible, try to use its foreign policy to *reduce* its dependence on others . . . it must try to enhance its net power position by *increasing* its own influence on others – that is to say, its *dominance* over them. This means that *imperialistic behaviour is a perfectly rational strategy of foreign policy*. It is a wholly legitimate and logical response to the uncertainty surrounding the survival of the nation.

This definition would help to explain why British expansion had its origins in the pre-capitalist early modern period. Taken broadly, the term 'imperialism' might describe political domination, economic exploitation and military subjugation. It might also include aggrandisement of a policy through the colonisation of a territory by settlers or invaders. The term can describe the process of how an empire grows; it might also refer to the method by which an empire maintained itself and the influence it exercised.[2] Theories about 'why' and 'how' it developed have provoked discussion on the relative importance of specific economic aims (raw materials, markets, investment opportunities and employment), strategic objectives (national security), the timing and importance of these aims in different regions, and the degree to which these were officially or privately sanctioned.

Above all, imperialism is a concept of power and influence, but it has often been used as a term of abuse. In the 1840s, imperialism entered the English political language to describe, with loathing, a potentially aggressive foreign policy in France by Prince Louis Napoleon.[3] By the 1870s, it was being used to describe the unpopular and aggressive aspects of Disraeli's policy in Zululand and Afghanistan. However, the *Spectator*, referring to the defence of Canada, tried to redefine imperialism as the 'consciousness that it is sometimes a binding duty to perform highly irksome and offensive tasks'.[4] In 1878, the Earl of Carnarvon envisaged an imperialism which bound together 'a great English-speaking community' and delivered 'wise laws, good government, and a well ordered finance . . . a system where the humblest may enjoy freedom from oppression and wrong equally with the greatest; where the light of religion and morality can penetrate into the darkest dwelling places. This is the true fulfilment of our duties; this, again, I say, is the true strength and meaning of imperialism.' Therefore imperialism was seen by some of its practitioners as a set of values that were essentially benign. This was not propaganda or window-dressing; the benevolent mission was a genuine belief for the overwhelming majority of imperial administrators and for many of the settlers too.

In Britain, there were many, in a brief 'popular' period in the late nineteenth century, who saw imperialism as a vehicle for enlightenment and an advertisement of civilisation to be proud of. Studies of this form of imperialism have suggested that it was designed to be a 'social cement' that would offset the growth of radical politics, but it was only partially successful in that endeavour.[5] Imperialism was never clearly defined, and it was never one monolithic idea or process: ultimately, the British Empire meant different things to different people. Imperialism is thus a term that offers more flexibility for an account of all the controversies and debates than a conventional 'history of the British Empire'.

The trajectory of British imperialism does not fit precisely any single 'model' of economic, cultural, military or political theory.[6] The Empire was built up over a long period of time, and territories were acquired for quite different reasons. The Empire also developed in an uneven way, with some colonies achieving a measure of self-government as a means to retain their co-operation with Britain, whilst others did not. In the sixteenth century, following the centralisation and consolidation of political power in the metropole, England followed in the footsteps of the Spaniards and Portuguese in a search for new wealth. In the seventeenth century, coastal outposts developed into flourishing colonies in North America and the West Indies, but the desire to establish trade with the Asian markets drove the process on.

The whole Empire was internally dynamic and it continued to evolve throughout its history. Centrifugal forces within Britain meant that migrant communities were established and reinforced in settler states, mission stations, plantations, mines and trading posts. It was also subject to external pressures, such as foreign rivals, wars, revolts or economic change. By the 1800s, faced with the economic challenge of industrialised competitors in Europe and America, and the military-naval challenge of hostile powers, Britain redefined its imperial role. It sometimes appeared to be consolidating and on the defensive, yet in the last 30 years of the nineteenth century, it acquired 5 million square miles and 88 million new subjects. Strategically valued regions became the focus of intense diplomatic interest or of military operations. When European powers began to rival Britain's widely flung possessions, the existing toeholds became springboards for expansion into the interior of Africa and Asia.

The First World War was the first great test of the Empire in the twentieth century, but after the war, there was a determination to preserve imperial rule by reference to the continuities of previous periods. It wasn't until after the Second World War that the old assumptions were abandoned. However, decolonisation was accompanied by a desire to create mutually beneficial relationships that would survive independence. The British were eager to leave behind them democratic institutions in the hands of approved political elites, and to encourage continued voluntary association in the Commonwealth. The best that can be said is that the British were determined to hand over control to representative bodies modelled in their own image, although this view is sometimes disputed.[7] It is certainly clear that Britain tried to maintain continuities with colonies in Malaya and West Africa, and with the Sterling Bloc economic zone, purely in its own interest.

The way the Empire 'worked' also defined imperialism. The territories of the British Empire were protected by the world's largest navy. Its sea-lanes, the arteries of trade, were filled with a vast merchant fleet. The exchange of goods on this global scale was supported by a financial system based in the City of London. Administering the Empire was a hierarchical bureaucracy, and monitoring its external and internal security was the British Army. Supplementing these relatively small agencies were colonial administrations, and the quite considerable colonial armed forces. In India, for example, the government was a cabinet of British personnel with their headquarters in Calcutta and later Delhi (and Simla during the hot season) which sought the approval of London in its decision-making. In 1917, its Indian Civil Service was small, with little more than 1300 staff (about half of whom were Indian) serving a population of 300 million. British rule in India was backed by the Indian Army which, in peacetime, numbered 300,000 men.

The British managed the imperial workforce through an oligarchy of political officials, soldiers, police forces and businessmen. Revenue to pay for this administration was raised through taxation of the indigenous people whenever possible, but sometimes Britain was forced to contribute too. Local labour extracted and farmed the mineral and agrarian wealth of the colonies, and goods were transported to Britain and other destinations through a network of shipping, railways and land carriage. The counter-flow of finished products, manufactured in Britain's industrial workshops and factories, was distributed on the same network. The whole system was supervised by British banks, insurance and joint stock companies, and promoted by entrepreneurs whose activities generated a dynamic of development. The English language was the mode of communication, information being transmitted through a global telegraph, postal, and eventually radio and telephone service. Astride this vast network was the British government, and in support were the legions of other professionals: academics, journalists, publishers, religious leaders, engineers, architects, educators and much of the British public too.

Military force played a part in the acquisition and maintenance of the British Empire. The British armed forces were deployed to protect the colonies from outsiders, but also to maintain internal security. This was achieved not simply by the exercise of military power by fighting, but also through the presence of garrisons. Local police forces, of varying quality, augmented military forces throughout the empire. Colonial troops and locally raised levies were used in most colonial campaigns. For example, in the 1893 Matabele Rebellion, the column of imperial forces consisted of 700 volunteers from the British South Africa Company, 225 Bechuanaland Border Police (a paramilitary police force) and 2000 levies from the Bechuanaland Protectorate. This fact demonstrates the extent of collaboration in the British Empire, and the way in which local people formed the bulk of the manpower for the imperial enterprise – with or without British direction. There were complex layers of loyalty in imperial society.

British imperialism can also be examined through the impact, or the global influence, that it had. The degree of actual British direction or influence in the world surfaces in a long-standing debate on 'Informal Empire'. This term refers to British access and interference, mainly economic in character, in territories not formally governed by the British in Asia, the Middle East, South America and Latin America.[8] The debate has been reopened recently because of a concern about globalisation. The issue is whether the origins of this phenomenon can be traced not just to formal imperial control, but also to the development of Western economic domination and influence. However, 'influence' is difficult to measure and there is considerable doubt about the extent, or effects, of Informal Empire. Economic penetration was dependent on local conditions, and on resistance. In China, for example, there was a long history of opposition to Western influence and British merchants were dependent on Chinese *compradors* (intermediaries) who frequently stifled their enterprise.

The issue of Informal Empire also raises questions about British trade itself. If Britain embraced free trade, it did so because it was a leading player in a global system of trade that, to some extent, already existed. As the smaller trade networks, such as those within Africa, became linked to a global system, Britain was able to benefit. However, foreign competition forced Britain to consider 'pegging out' its future in formal possessions. In some cases, the breakdown of informal relationships or economic setbacks might necessitate formal annexation, but equally, formal rule could be extended where there was economic success (such as in South Africa) to reinforce Britain's influence there. By contrast, in the settler states like Australia, the economic success of the colony meant that Britain dismantled its formal control in an effort to cut costs.

British imperialism could affect economies and populations in dramatic ways. The West Indies, one of the most important economic zones of the Empire at the end of the eighteenth century, accounted for 17.6 per cent of British trade in 1815 (£15.4 million) and its population grew from 877,000 to 2 million in the period 1815–1911. This growth was due to the natural increase in a population that, from the late seventeenth century, had been shipped out of Africa as slaves, a process that had reached its peak in the 1790s when 420,000 were transported in just one decade.[9] A rather different migration affected British North America (Canada), whose population grew from just 550,000 in 1815 to 18.9 million in 1911. Canada's trade, together with the other colonies where settlers had established new states, accounted for 16.5 per cent of British trade in 1913. After the Second World War, Canada's industry had expanded dramatically, and it possessed the world's third largest navy. However, the consequences of colonisation for some local populations were catastrophic: an estimated 750,000 Aboriginal Australians were forcibly displaced and many were killed, whilst the Tasmanian population of between 4000–6000 was decimated, largely by disease.[10] British India, the most prized of all imperial possessions, had a population of 140 million in 1815 which rose to 305 million in 1921, and its trade with Britain increased from £8 million to £120 million (35 per cent) by 1913.[11] However, in 1947 the partition of India and Pakistan led to the migration of 11 million people and the deaths of approximately a million people in inter-communal violence. The African colonies, confined to coastal strips in 1815, consisted of 40 million subjects by 1911 and accounted for £44 million (13 per cent) of imperial trade, although £30 million of that came from South Africa alone.[12] Beneath these broad figures were shifts within the local economies, with significant consequences for the workforces.[13]Whilst there is agreement on the changes, including the effects of railway construction, the availability of cheap goods and the impact of British capital investment across the Empire, the verdict is often entirely negative. It is sometimes suggested that the net result of British imperialism was the 'arrested development' of the colonies.[14] Nevertheless, as with globalisation, the picture is a complex one.

The British claimed the credit for a number of achievements in the colonies: economic growth, law and order, government free of corruption, free institutions, civil liberties, an end to tribal and communal warfare, the development of infrastructure, all of which attracted British and foreign investment. However, it was impossible for the British to be consistent in developing every part of the Empire even where they tried, because some regions were more important to British interests than others. There have been criticisms from Indian historians, such as S. Gopal, that India's industry was sacrificed in the interest of British companies, rendering her a client state, but David Fieldhouse argues that the Indian case is by no means universal.[15] He contends that the British were economically conservative, developing some industry where it was viable to do so, but avoiding development where it could not be sustained.

A study of imperialism must also now acknowledge the wider social and cultural aspects of British rule, but also its limits. Imperialism led to the spread of English as the language of the educated and political elite, and also of commerce.[16] Nevertheless, it was a language that evolved its own characteristics, for example, in the West Indies and South-East Asia. Imperialism was a catalyst for migration and colonisation, which led to the dispossession of indigenous populations. However, migration was not limited to the white colonists. Migratory patterns were generated within the colonies, with, for example, Chinese labourers working in Canada, indentured Indians settling in Natal, or Sikh policemen serving in Hong Kong and Malaya. The study of cultural imperialism still tends to focus quite heavily on the flow of Western influences out into the world, and rather less on the counter-flow, or on the transfer of languages, cuisine and ideas.[17]

The hegemony of British imperial influence was limited in other respects. British trade, for example, was never as dominant as it seemed. It was dependent on local conditions, such as the availability of resources. The volume of trade was also dependent on the demand for British goods.[18] In South-East Asia, internal trade networks were already well developed before British intervention, and the demand for British products was low. Moreover, despite considerable attention recently on the growth of the British financial system, the City was less influential than it appeared.

British imperialism was also subject to changes in the diplomatic relations of the Great Powers, or the emergence of the super-powers after 1945. France, which had frequently tried to solve domestic tensions by recourse to an aggressive foreign policy (from Napoleon to the Third Republic), posed a challenge to British supremacy in the Mediterranean, North Africa and South-East Asia for much of the nineteenth century. Not only did French interests lay astride British trade routes, but her geographical proximity to Britain made her a significant threat. Russia, too, was a power that clashed with Britain in the eastern Mediterranean and in Asia. The decay of the Ottoman Empire, Persia and China, along with the vulnerability of Afghanistan, drew Britain into a prolonged effort to prop up these states against Russian incursions, from Persia in 1826 to China in 1901. Russia's communist ideology added another dimension to the 'Great Game' struggle in the twentieth century. The emer-gence of Germany, Italy and the United States as Great Power rivals, and the combination of Russia and France as allies in 1894, created a threatening situation for Britain at the turn of the century. There were three solutions to these problems: first, diplomacy, local treaties and alliances; second, consolidation and federation to strengthen colonial allies; and third, conquest for improved security.

Local conditions on the periphery often affected British impe-rialism. Diseases, climate and access, as well as resistance, influ-enced British policy. In West Africa, the high costs of colonisation and the threat of malaria meant that despite some interest in palm oil from the 1820s, there was little incentive to pursue trade or conquest in the region. Foreign competition, the threat that France might annex the area, and resistance by African states combined to overcome the inertia.

More generally, conquests were reactive and unplanned, and frequently the British tried to influence regions through local residents and consuls, using diplomacy and compromise rather than occupation. The key to understanding this process was the balance between potential benefits and cost, a theme that ran throughout the period of British imperialism.[19] Frequently, there were concerns about the acquisition of new colonies because it was so expensive, and there were sometimes calls for the aban-donment of colonies on the basis of cost alone.[20] However, the real financial crisis Britain faced in the 1930s, together with the cost of a war against the combined power of Germany, Italy and Japan, proved too great a challenge for the British Empire. It was fatally weakened by a loss of prestige and military power in the period 1940–5.

After the Second World War, local nationalist movements undoubtedly hurried the British into relinquishing power, a factor that combined with the continuing financial difficulties Britain faced after 1945 and the new geopolitical balance of the Cold War. It appears that the main concern was that retaining the colonies would cost Britain more in the long run, from a financial, strategic and moral point of view.[21]

Identities were also affected by British imperialism. National identities in Asia and Africa were often shaped by the achievement of independence from colonial rule. Despite the deposing of Kwame Nkrumah by Ghanaians in 1966, his successors still use his name and party identity to legitimise their own parties. Robert Mugabe similarly makes use of the language of independence as a form of legitimacy against his political opponents in Zimbabwe. These identity issues were not confined to the formerly colonised, but also affected the settler societies and Britain too.

There is some doubt over what is meant by the 'Britishness' of the Empire. Irish, Welsh and Scottish migrants, driven perhaps by unemployment at home and new opportunities overseas, populated the Empire in large numbers, often preserving their own brand of Celtic identity. However, the colonies of settlement contained migrants from Eastern Europe, Scandinavia and Asia too. The French-speaking Quebecois maintained themselves in population and culture in spite of 'British' administration, a feat also achieved by the Afrikaners of South Africa. British identity was a totem for settlers in a strange land, and they claimed to represent British values more enthusiastically than the British still at home. The ideals of fair play, modesty, self-sacrifice, duty, endurance, resourcefulness, protection of women and the vulnerable, integrity and cheerfulness were not always realised, but they were the salient features of a British settler identity. Identity was also based on separateness from the native community, and whilst there were acts of generosity and benign paternalism, there was also brutality and exploitation, reinforced with views of native inferiority.[22]

Imperialism was accompanied by racism. The categorisation, even dehumanising, of the 'black' or 'yellow' races from the second half of the nineteenth century, undoubtedly made it easier to justify British rule. Characteristics of inferiority were attributed to subject races, and the mantle of superiority exclusively British. Punishment was meted out, and discrimination and exclusion reinforced through a set of ideas, which, some would argue, are still unwittingly held by the British today. However, the British Empire used racial categorisation, perhaps not consciously as a tool of oppression and division, but to assist British officials faced with a bewildering variety of peoples, customs, cultures and ideas. It allowed the British to separate warring factions, to pacify antagonised subjects and to thwart decades of exploitation by one group over another. Racial identities were based on a sense of pessimism that imperial subjects were incapable of improvement, but they were also the result of trying to make sense of the fact of European domination at the end of the nineteenth century. This suggests that the theoretical constructions of imperialism were not imposed according to some central paradigm, but, in fact, *followed* the practical experience of imperialists. Nevertheless, the condescending nature of British assistance, guidance and rule was a humiliation to many indigenous peoples. John Nottingham, a District Officer in Kenya, recorded: 'I don't know how you define racism, but being patronising, being paternal, being nice but being very tough are all part of this pretending that the people you're dealing with are children.'[23]

Can a working definition of British imperialism be established? The Empire was a complex entity, and definitions have shifted in the ebb and flow of debate about its purpose and its effects. It evolved through a period of 300 years, it covered a number of climatic zones and geographical areas, as well as a very wide variety of peoples and cultures at very different stages of development. It was fitted to local circumstances in politics. It could contain at the same time the contradictions of democratic and constitutional government at home, the self-government of its dominions, and the idea of 'responsible government' in India, but also the despotic whilst benign governorship of small Pacific territories. British 'influence' was widespread and took many forms, such as trade, culture, diplomatic leverage or alliances. British 'rule' was evident but in some regions it was rather loose, and, in a pragmatic fashion, it depended on local agents. That rule was backed by military force, but it was force that was rarely used. It had no defined central ideology beyond allegiance to the Crown, although this too was changed to 'association' when, after the Second World War, republics joined the emerging British Commonwealth of Nations. The British Empire depended for its survival on its flexibility and its ability to adapt, concede and develop.

British imperialism combined a host of peripheral, local and metropolitan influences. It is a term that encompasses the desire of states to dominate for reasons of national security, the exercise of direct power or the extension of influence, or economic and military hegemony. Imperialism can also be used to incorporate the imposition or spread of cultural values and ideas. It can be used as a term to assess British power or influence, the process of how the British Empire worked, and the impact it had on Britain and the wider world. British imperialism was not an unlimited phenomenon, and responses to it must form part of its history. By these means, perhaps, the term can be extracted from its merely pejorative sense and used more effectively.

2

What was the nature of imperialism in the early nineteenth century?

Continuities and change

Vincent T. Harlow introduced the idea of 'two British Empires'. The first began with the foundations of the settlements in America in the seventeenth century, the establishment of British power in the West Indies, exploration in the Pacific, and the development of trading networks in Asia and Africa. The 'second British Empire' dated from 1783 and reflected the nature of imperialism that came after the American War of Independence.[1] Whilst this change conveys the idea of a turning point for Britain in America, no account was taken of the continued growth of a considerable British overseas empire elsewhere, particularly in India, which took place between the 1750s and early 1800s. A focus on the Americas also obscures the long-term economic influence of the industrial revolution, which can be traced back to the early eighteenth century.

Harlow was challenged by Ronald Hyam and Ged Martin who stressed that the 'Second' British Empire could *only* be understood with reference to the period before the loss of the American colonies.[2] The American War of Independence, and later the Napoleonic Wars (1793–1815), had created an illusion of difference because of the special conditions thrown up by these conflicts. There was little change, for example, in the land revenue systems of India, and no appreciable difference in the Atlantic slave trade in the late eighteenth century.

However, a turning point after 1783 could still be valid. New ideas about the Empire emerged, government apparatus changed (the Colonial Office was set up in 1801), and there was greater international economic integration. Harlow suggested a 'Swing to the East', a shift of emphasis in the Empire as Britain became a major Asian power, and this new status was illustrated

13

by the deployment, for example, of Indian troops in Egypt in 1801. Whilst Harlow's criteria are debatable (since they ignore, for example, the attempts to influence South America at the beginning of the nineteenth century), the spread of formal rule into Asia and Africa throughout the 1800s was a significant development.

The events of the last decades of the eighteenth century had a considerable impact on the direction imperialism took in the early nineteenth century, but not because, as Harlow suggested, Britain faced a setback in America. The successes of British forces in the Seven Years' War in Canada (1756–63) and conquests in India (1798–1804) expanded the imperial dominions, and removed the threat of its chief rival France.[3] The loss of the American colonies, whilst a serious blow to Britain's prestige in 1783, in fact did little lasting damage to British trade. Indeed, British commerce soon revived in that continent. Whilst the old West Indies colonies, which had been built on the profits of mercantilism and slavery, went into relative economic decline, the Caribbean islands were still a lucrative enterprise until the 1830s.

In the Napoleonic Wars, the continental blockade (the embargo of trade imposed by France across Europe) made little difference to Britain, providing evidence of Britain's economic strength. Indeed, manufacturing exports increased. With peace in 1815, European manufacturers recovered and were able to supply their own impoverished markets, which led to a downturn in British exports to the continent. However, despite the historical interest in manufacturing, which was to develop so spectacularly in the mid-nineteenth century, Britain's economy in 1815 was still predominantly agrarian. These fluctuations in Britain's economy perhaps defy models of economic development or 'capitalist take-off'. Certainly, they cast doubt on the direct connections, so often drawn, between economic growth and imperialism.

Slavery and anti-slavery in the West Indies

Perhaps the most debated aspect of imperialism at the end of the eighteenth century was slavery. The question most frequently posed is: how could the British, who had established democratic institutions and whose society was based on the principles of Christianity, have perpetuated the trade in humans? The answer is to be found in the juxtaposition of liberal traditions and commerce in Britain's history. Although Englishmen believed their rights were enshrined in Magna Carta, they acknowledged that this extended only to the king's subjects.[4] In the West Indies, slaves were not regarded as subjects: they were 'commodities'.

Only slaves could create a profit in the labour intensive industries of the Caribbean. Paid labourers could not do the back-breaking work of tobacco and sugar harvesting profitably on the scale required. It was simply a case of the value of West Indian produce, compared with the costs of production.[5] The system produced three significant outcomes:

1. African labour sustained the economy of the West Indies, and had a significant effect on the wealth of individuals, which, ultimately, flowed back into Britain.
2. African people and their descendants populated large areas of the West Indies and the Americas, but were left with the stigma of never having been royal subjects.
3. Africa suffered a massive haemorrhage of manpower with internal consequences which are still hardly understood.

Sugar was the basis of British interests in the West Indies, and the labour force for the production of sugar was almost entirely made up of black slaves until the ban on their transport in 1807 and the abolition of slavery in 1833. The reason for the use of black Africans was twofold: they were thought more suited to toiling in the tropical climate and labour costs were minimised.[6] The slaves were purchased from African merchants and the agents of African states all along the west coast, and they consisted either of members of their own clans or they were the prisoners of rival states.[7] In the 1790s, it is thought that 420,000 were transported across the Atlantic, but 13 per cent died *en route* (twice the normal rate for paying passengers), and, in the first three 'seasoning years', a further 20 per cent died of disease, poor diet or exhaustion.[8]

The progress towards the abolition of slavery in Britain and her Empire was not a smooth one, and the legacy of the trade in human labour has produced a variety of historiographical responses.[9] Despite the effective lobbying of parliament by the Abolition Society from 1787, and the issue of a bill for the abolition of the trade within 4 years in 1792, the Emancipation Act was not passed until 1807. The revival of French slaving in 1814, after the Anglo-French peace accord that year, re-energised the abolitionist movement and in 1823 a new group, the Anti-Slavery Society, dedicated itself to the complete removal of slavery across the world. In 1833, Parliament abolished slavery throughout the Empire, and its replacement, 'apprenticeship' (which demanded free work from former slaves for a certain period every day), was abandoned in 1838.[10]

The maritime nature of the British Empire had made slavery feasible, but it also gave Britain the means to be its most ardent opponent once the change had been made. The Royal Navy pursued slave vessels all over the globe, and the power of the British navy was such that it could compel other European powers to accept a 'seize and search' policy against their own ships. Only the United States refused to be pressured by the British, although it too banned the trade in slaves.

The pursuit of slave ships and slave centres naturally drew the British towards West Africa. There was a realisation that the development of free trade was a necessity to replace the profits that had been made by slavery. Lord Russell remarked: 'It is only by the establishment of legitimate trade that we may hope totally to eradicate the slave trade.'[11] There was some interest in the hardwoods of the area around Lagos, which would be ideal for the navy's ships, but up to the 1860s the absence of any threat meant there was no need to annex any territory and they relied only on local military action for security.

Until the 1960s, historians tended to concentrate on the study of the planters, the slave owners, and the work of the anti-slavery lobbyists. Often there was more than a hint of inevitability about the abolition of slavery in these works, and a great deal of emphasis given to leaders with a benign approach to their imperial subjects. Sir Reginald Coupland's work was a classic example of this.[12]

Eric Williams attacked this approach in 1944, when he stated that the slave trade was abolished only because, as a system that belonged to an antiquated form of mercantilism, it was no longer economically viable.[13] Prime Minister William Pitt the Younger (1783–1801, 1804–6), Williams argued, considered abolition when the British West Indies was failing to compete with the French plantations on San Domingo. Although San Domingo's production was disrupted by the slave rebellion of 1791, the recovery of this colony, new competitors (Brazil, Mauritius), and costly over-production necessitated a scaling down of the British plantations. This, in turn, meant the abolition of the slave trade. Williams then added an even more dramatic argument. The profits from the transport and working of slaves had provided the capital necessary for the financing of the industrial revolution. Hence, Britain's status, standard of living and wealth had all been based on the backs of black slave labour.[14]

However, Williams's view has been severely criticised. Seymour Drescher argued that, although in relative decline compared with the expansion of Cuban production, British sugar plantations still accounted for over 12 per cent of Britain's total trade.[15] In 1806, the islands' trade with Britain amounted to £13.5 million. In the last decade of the eighteenth century, slave trade profits and cargoes had been increasing. The capital value of the trade almost doubled in the period 1800–7. These figures tend to refute any idea of decline. Furthermore, the parliamentary committee report on the volume of sugar left unsold in Britain concluded that it was the result of attempts to block British trade on the continent by Napoleon, a temporary problem, and not any long-term over-production in the West Indies. J. R Ward took this one step further. Higher yielding cane varieties, more efficient crushing and refining technologies, and a more abundant supply of manure (from expanded livestock farming) made the sugar trade more profitable than ever. Half of Britain's long-distance shipping, and one-eighth of the exchequer's revenue, was derived from the Caribbean, suggesting that it was still an important source of wealth. Ward concluded: 'When abolition was finally enacted, British West Indian trade stood at record levels.'[16] Moreover, David Richardson found that profits from slaving voyages contributed less than one per cent of total domestic investment in Britain at that time. He concluded: 'Such calculations do not suggest that the slave trade was vital to the financing of early British industrial expansion.'[17]

The issues which have been the subject of recent investigation include the mortality of Africans in the slave trade, but also the variations in the trading conditions in Africa which shaped the structure, if not volume, of the traffic in slaves.[18] David Eltis has also recently examined the slave trade as part of the history of the 'Atlantic world', bringing in the nature of European slave trading and revealing that the traffic in humans notwithstanding, Africans were by no means the weaker partners in Afro-European relations.[19] Eltis also argues that it was the African capacity to resist colonisation that forced Europeans to adopt the far more costly enterprise of shipping thousands of slaves across the Atlantic to the West Indies.

The exploitation of resources, and African people, was not the only method of generating wealth in the empire. Whilst the West Indies was an economic system based on the production of sugar, cotton and coffee, British rule in India was based on the collection of revenues via Indian intermediaries or British officials, and, in 1815, land taxes were worth £3 million. Like much of the Empire, it was a political system based on the principle of minimum interference. This meant that, at first, there was no attempt to introduce British institutions. However, this was a period of evolution in British imperialism. It was not, perhaps, the decisive turning point as Harlow suggested, but could be seen, as C. A. Bayly put it, as an 'Imperial Meridian'.[20]

The imperialism of free trade

Ronald Robinson and John Gallagher adopted the expression 'imperialism of free trade' to argue that Britain extended its influence *beyond* its old colonial possessions in the nineteenth century. This extension, to uphold British paramountcy, was 'by informal means if possible, or by formal annexations when necessary'.[21] By a combination of commercial penetration, investment and military force, China, South America, the Ottoman Empire and parts of tropical Africa were as much subject to British imperialism as Australia or India. Whilst British influence is now seen to have been much more ambiguous, fluid, and mutually permeable in these regions, the concept of informal empire/influence remains an integral part of the historiography of British imperialism.[22]

The robust defence of trade was considered vital to Britain's economic future: in 1739, William Pitt the Elder (later, the Earl of Chatham) declared: 'When trade is at stake it is your last entrenchment: you must defend it or perish.'[23] In 1760, 40 per cent of Britain's trade was colonial and consisted of a bewildering variety of manufactured goods for export. Earlier mercantilist legislation, such as the Navigation Acts, had given Britain a monopoly of exchange with its colonies, and the East India Company possessed total control of all trade with East Asia until 1813. In the Seven Years' War (1756–63), Britain had shown it was prepared to fight to maintain its supremacy against its chief commercial rival, France, in what Tom Pocock calls 'the very first world war'.[24] Yet the loss of the American colonies in 1783 did not produce a major setback for the wealth of Britain and the empire. Trade with the United States rose from £14 million in 1784 to £40 million in 1800. Historians have also doubted the detrimental economic effects of the Napoleonic Wars, but there is little agreement on this.[25] Nevertheless, there can be no doubt that the defeat of its chief opponent left Britain with undisputed mastery of the seas, and consequently in a position to dominate maritime trade in the decades to follow.

It was anxieties about the security of commerce, the requirements of administration and organisation, and the reactions to perceived threats, that tended to draw governments into 'formal' rule. At times, defensive alliances were sought, often in response to the French threat, which resulted in the extension of British influence without annexation. However, a series of military expeditions ejected the French from the rim of the Indian Ocean. Arthur Wellesley (later the Duke of Wellington) had conquered vast sections of the Indian subcontinent to protect Britain's commerce, and its strategic position. The land revenue system acquired paid for the expansion of the army of the East India Company in a form of 'military-fiscalism'. Yet Wellesley was also eager to avoid unnecessary fighting, or the extraction of frequent tributes, lest it cause resentment. He was eager to preserve a military hegemony, and to avoid any chance of defeat, which might lead to the 'loss of our reputation'.[26]

In 1815, the East India Company was making considerable profits from its monopoly. In addition, the British domestic demand for tea, spices, saltpetre, tobacco and raw cotton was considerable. However, as David Washbrook points out, imports of British goods expanded up to the 1820s before levelling off at £3–4 million per annum.[27] The expansion of Britain's domestic cotton industry led to a loss in demand for Indian manufactures, and locally produced indigo turned out to be a poor substitute. This forced the company to look towards China, which eventually precipitated the Chinese Wars. In time, the desire to acquire the potentially rich Indus valley of the Punjab, and control of the trade routes to Persia and Central Asia, drew the British to annex the north-western provinces, such as Sind in 1843. Nevertheless, it could also be argued that the advance to the north-west was also driven by concern about the expansion of Russia across Central Asia. P. J. Marshall states that it was this concern that compelled the British to invade Afghanistan in 1838, although the occupation led to a military disaster in 1842.[28]

By the mid-nineteenth century, the mercantilism of the six-teenth and seventeenth centuries, with state restrictions on imports and control of exchange, had given way to free trade principles. In 1599, the Crown had been directly involved in the granting of chartered company status to the East India Company, and the Hudson's Bay Company was formed in 1670. These monopolistic ventures indirectly benefited Britain as a whole, but, by the mid-nineteenth century, their charters had all been abrogated in favour of free trade arrangements. Although chartered companies were resurrected in the late nineteenth century (as a means of controlling regions without the expense of direct rule) they were relatively short-lived.[29]

The promotion of free trade became a mantra amongst nineteenth-century radical MPs who represented manufacturing interests. It was thought that free trade would help other countries earn sterling through increased exports of raw materials and food to Britain. In return, Britain's manufacturing would be further stimulated by the increased overseas demand. The moral force of capitalism was just as important in mobilising support in Britain itself. Free trade would encourage the regeneration of backward economies, develop a work ethic, assist in the replacement of outdated elites, and therefore act as a mutual benefit to Britain and the rest of the world.[30] In 1839, Richard Cobden argued: 'Free Trade! What is it? Why, the breaking down of barriers that separate nations . . . I see in the Free Trade principle that which will draw men together, thrusting aside the antagonisms of race, creed and language, and uniting us in the bonds of eternal peace.'[31]

Cobden's expression of idealism and radicalism equated unshackled trade with freedom in a diplomatic and political sense. The optimism and modernity of liberalism offered a worldview where the oppressor would be overthrown wherever he was found, anywhere on the globe, just as the concept of slavery had been defeated before. Critiques of capitalism and imperialism, which stressed their exploitative and acquisitive nature, had yet to be developed. Therefore, in order to understand the mentality of nineteenth-century imperialists, it is crucial to recognise that there was a deep faith in the benefits of commercial penetration.

Martin Lynn points out that whilst British governments would support the freeing up of trade, they would not confuse public duty and private gain. The government was 'hostile to supporting individual bondholders or traders, and it was only prepared to intervene on behalf of British economic interests overseas where such interests reinforced existing British political concerns'.[32]

The Opium War (1839–42) is usually cited as a classic example of the British government using military and naval forces to lever open Chinese goods and markets (in this case for British Indian trade), but it is also an example of how events on the periphery could influence government or 'imperial' policy. The British government decided to act against the Chinese in response to a threat to the lives and property of British subjects and what they perceived as a slight to British prestige. After a short war, an 'Open Door' trade treaty was imposed, but there were no exclusive privileges for Britain. However, Lynn also notes that Britain's economic success, through its world leadership in finance and manufacturing, made it possible to dominate trade in the region almost by default. It was, as Lynn notes, a *de facto* policy of expanding British influence. The freeing up of trade certainly benefited Britain. Trade with China (imports and exports) stood at £4 million in 1830 and rose to £15 million in 1860.

Even though it was of obvious and immediate importance to the war with China, the commercial factor has sometimes been over-emphasised in interpretations of imperialism. Not least, because of the importance of trade in the British Empire in the nineteenth century, it has often been assumed that it played a consistent role in the imperial enterprise throughout its history, and in imperialist policies pursued by other European powers too. Nevertheless, it is clear that radicals like Cobden felt their country was engaged in something far greater than just a war for trade. Commerce was not always the most important consideration for British governments in their decision-making.

The deregulation of the domestic economy did not mean, however, that the state had no role to play in British commerce. A number of free trade treaties were concluded by the British government with Latin American countries to create the institutional frameworks to keep markets open. A treaty with Brazil in 1810 gave Britain preferential duties, and others reduced tariffs with Argentina in 1825 and Peru in 1834. By the mid-nineteenth century, Britain was firmly established as the main trading partner in the region. Before 1913, Latin America took 10 per cent of British exports and supplied 10 per cent of British imports. British investment in the area grew from £30 million in 1826 to £81 million by 1865.[33]

British commercial and political interests also coincided in the Ottoman Empire. Preservation of the Turkish Empire was thought an essential safeguard for British trade arteries to the east. Economic penetration was regarded as the means to regenerate the Ottoman domains, thus acting as a stimulus to modernisation and increasing strength. The free trade treaty of 1838, the Convention of Balta Liman, established a tariff regime beyond the Ottoman government's control, ended customs duties on internal trade and abolished state monopolies. The loss of state revenue forced the Ottoman government to seek foreign loans which could be used as a diplomatic lever. This, it was hoped, would be the means to bring to an end the abuses of Ottoman subjects that threatened to destroy the Turkish empire. The end of tariffs and increased trade stimulated Turkey's agriculture. Wheat and cotton exports increased and there was a sharp rise in the import of British textiles between 1840 and 1870. The first British loan was made in 1854, followed by 13 more over the next 20 years. The Ottoman Bank was set up in London in 1856 and from 1863 became responsible for the issue of the Ottoman currency. However, repayments on the loans caused higher taxation of local merchants and government bankruptcy in 1875.

The British government's promotion of free trade was not surprising since it advocated the purchase of raw materials at the cheapest possible prices, and freedom to sell manufactures at any price. Britain's domination of world manufacturing left it ideally placed to do this. Government endorsement was gradual, but reached its apogee in the repeal of the Corn Laws in 1846 and the 'free trade budgets' of 1853 and 1860. The key question was, since so much of Britain's trade was not with its own colonies, was it necessary to retain them? Moreover, why was it necessary to incur the expense of war to acquire 'formal control'? The concern was that other powers would restrict trade and impose tariffs (such as the USA in 1861), making British products less competitive. The resistance of the Chinese suggested that Indian rulers might also impose restrictions if granted their freedom. India's trade and markets were too valuable, and too much had been expended in the process of opening up India, to relinquish it so easily.[34]

British imperialism was not, however, only a manifestation of 'Mars and Mammon', or warfare and trade. As Marshall noted: 'Expansion' of the British Empire rather reflects the willingness of many sections of British society to seek opportunities for trade, plunder, land, office, knowledge – in short, advantages of all kinds . . . '[35] The 'imperialism of free trade' reveals that there was a convergence of impulses – moral, intellectual, commercial and military – that impelled the British into the wider world. Formal rule was expensive and the British frequently sought alternatives to it without sacrificing their interests in a region. What they wanted was 'empire on the cheap'. Free trade was the most important guiding principle of nineteenth-century imperialism, but it was not the only one.[36] There were often unwritten or accepted codes of behaviour derived from the backgrounds and education of the rulers. In the writings of politicians, soldiers, intellectuals, explorers, reformers and missionaries, it is possible to glimpse how contemporaries debated the nature of empire, and, above all, how they were concerned to balance its benefits and its costs.

3 What was the nature of British rule in India, c.1770–1858?

India was the most prestigious and populous of all Britain's imperial possessions and was regarded as the 'Jewel in the Crown' of the Empire. British rule in India emerged over many decades. British 'factories' (trading posts) had been established on the coasts with Indian approval in the eighteenth century, in order to cope with the huge demand for chintzes (washable decorated fabric), indigo, saltpetre, rice and sugar cane. The trading posts in India and Ceylon were important to the British because trade in the East Indies had failed in the face of Dutch competition. The resulting commercial revolution in pre-conquest India exposed the subcontinent to the penetration of British merchants to a far greater degree than in China. The enterprise or aggressive profiteering of individual merchants, the lack of accountability of the men in India, the difficulties in maintaining communications due to the distances between Calcutta and London, and a series of conflicts with the French and the Dutch, as well as the rulers of the Indian states, all served to drive the East India Company from trade to administration.[1] Although the process of acquiring intact a lucrative land revenue system was a long one, the defeat of the Marathas in 1817 is regarded as a watershed in the transition from commercial interest to formal rule. By 1834, this fact was recognised when the East India Company's monopolistic trading functions were abolished in favour of private ownership.

It is generally recognised that the extension of British power was dependent on the willing participation of Indians, either as allies, or by those employed as revenue collectors, merchants and sepoys. The decay of the Mughal's authority hastened the British success, as the powerful Maratha Confederacy descended into anarchy and Indian states stood as rivals to each other.[2]

Nevertheless, Percival Spear made a distinction between the process of annexation and the motive for it. He concluded that it was the decline of lucrative trade in India (and the costs of its army) that necessitated greater political control and the development of the subcontinent as a market. In addition, vested interests, such as cotton manufacturers, soldiers who sought Indian manpower, and the shipping companies, all promoted a scramble for greater control.[3] However, C. A. Bayly and Burton Stein have challenged the idea of Mughal 'decline'. Both argue that increasing prosperity fostered new political alignments that assisted in the construction of British rule.[4] John Darwin notes that, although the East India Company was constantly forced to seek military support from Britain, it had the means to pay for that help and the justification that military action was essential to thwart French designs.[5]

Imperial ideology and the 'Age of Reform': Orientalism and Anglicisation

To many company officials, maintaining peace and security in India was possible only with the minimum of interference in the lives of the people. Sir John Malcolm, the Governor of Bombay between 1826 and 1830, believed that 'reform' on Western lines was a grave error. He stated: 'Our great error in India appears to have been a desire to establish systems founded on general principles . . . In our precipitate attempts to improve the condition of the people, we have often proceeded without sufficient knowledge . . . I have been led, by what I have seen, to apprehend as much danger from political as from religious zealots [that is, British missionaries].'[6] British rule had, until the 1810s, generally integrated itself with Indian modes of government. Many British officials had become 'Indianised', adopting Indian dress and custom. Colonel Kirkpatrick, for example, the Resident of the Court of the Nizam of Hyderabad, dyed his beard with henna, married a Muslim woman and adopted the etiquette of a Muslim nobleman. The educational conservatives, or Orientalists, were a group of scholars of the late eighteenth and the early nineteenth centuries who went to India to study its culture, history, languages and society. From an early stage, they promoted a revival of India's past, and they shared a passion to record all that they found. Sir William Jones, who studied and translated ancient Sanskrit texts, was convinced that this ancient language was linked to classical Greek and Latin; establishing in 1786 the modern notion of the 'Indo-European' family of languages. He was regarded as one of those who had genuinely tried to promote Indian culture and avoid the imposition of the West.[7]

In contrast, the educational reformers, the Anglicists, were determined to change India. Scholars, such as James Mill, and the Law Member of the Governor-General's Council, Thomas Babington Macauley, believed that India was a fundamentally backward place. Its only opportunity for salvation, the Anglicists argued, was if the Indians could learn the English language and adopt English customs through an English education. Macaulay stated:

> It may be that the public mind of India may expand under our system till it has outgrown that system, that by good government we may educate our subjects into a capacity for better government; that, having been instructed in European knowledge, they may in some future date, demand European institutions. Whether such a day will come I know not . . . Whenever it comes it will be the proudest day in English History. To have found a great people sunk in the depths of slavery and superstition, to have ruled them as to have made them desirous and capable of all the privileges of citizens, would indeed be a title to glory all our own.[8]

Moreover, Utilitarians were eager to reform the political and legal systems, whilst Evangelicals aimed to see the subjects of British rule saved through Christ and they campaigned vigorously for access to India. In addition, Free Traders advocated the economic development of India through roads and railways.

The reformers were often successful in their demands. Evangelical and missionary movements began to make inroads into India from 1813, and their views are classically represented by James Mill's *History of India* (1817). The attack on *Suttee* (or *Sati*: the burning of widows) in 1829 and arrest or execution of the *Thuggee* gangs (bandits who prayed on travellers under a pseudo-religious philosophy) between 1829 and 1837 were measures accompanied by the imposition of English as the official and unifying language of the subcontinent, and reforms of the education system along English lines. Macaulay also carried out legal reform: the Indian Penal Code (1860), for example, was based on British law.

Despite these movements, the actual business of administration was a practical task that still made use of local elites and social structures, even if they were adapted.[9] The work of the idealists impacted on relatively few Indians. Coins used by the East India Company still bore the image of the Mughal emperor, courts still applied Muslim or Hindu law, and the British were responsible for the upkeep of some Hindu temples, despite the increase of missionary work. *Suttee* was abolished only with the consent of Indian reformers.[10] The 200 British schools catered for just 30,000 Indian children in 1850, although English was welcomed as a ladder to advancement. Above all, the administration of India was dependent on Indians, as British civil servants had little knowledge of local conditions.[11]

This pragmatic approach was familiar to old hands in India. It had been endorsed by Edmund Burke as early as 1775, when he called for rule through practical moral prudence rather than by doctrine.[12] Robert Frykenburg believes: 'The Raj itself, in its conquest, construction and control of India, could not be understood without reference to indigenous power structures. In day to day control, the Raj was an Indian institution.'[13] Judith Brown concluded: 'An age of reform existed in the minds of many of the British concerned with India: whether it ever existed in Indians' experience is doubtful.'[14]

However, as a result of Edward Said's work, the once common historiographical view that British Orientalists were merely scholars who translated ancient texts, examined India's history and championed a 'renaissance' among Indian intellectuals, has been seriously challenged. Said's view was that they were agents of colonisation.[15] The Orientalists, so the argument runs, proceeded to first establish and then perpetuate British hegemony in India by creating their own idea of what the Indian past had been. The differences between the Orientalists and the later Anglicists seemed to be irrelevant when the purpose of both was to maintain British power.[16] Indeed, this charge was therefore applicable to all the British in India: all were working towards a paradigm of stifling colonial rule, and seeking to 'divide and rule'.[17] Ranajit Guha and Gayatri Spivak were determined to investigate the downtrodden, to recover the authentic Indian voice and, although not stated, reveal the proto-nationalists. This desire inspired a whole new school of writers.[18]

Not surprisingly, Said's attack has produced a critical response. Whilst most pre-Said scholars have conceded that a major motivation for Orientalism was to assist the imperial rulers, they have insisted that there was a major difference between Orientalists, such as Sir William Jones or H. T. Colebrooke, and the Anglicists. Since the Anglicists effectively halted the study of Indian languages, culture and history, they appeared to be the only ones who warranted Said's attacks. It has even been argued that, had later scholars and administrators 'been like Jones and his most productive followers, the unsavoury quality of European political and cultural exploitation might never have developed'.[19]

There seems to be little chance of resolving these approaches. The British Orientalists will probably never be regarded as 'benevolent' because they will be associated with cultural imperialism. However, John M. MacKenzie concludes that, in assessing the work that the nineteenth-century Orientalists produced, particularly with regard to art, there is a danger of labelling all Western efforts as cynical and imperialistic.[20] Moreover, a narrow focus on intellectuals tends to produce the assumption that their impact was considerable when, in fact, their influence was probably quite limited.

Over-emphasis on the impact of British influence is not confined to cultural history. Since the call, by Edmund Burke, for an end to corruption and misrule in the regions under the East India Company's control, there has been considerable debate about the degree of economic impact on India. Burke was convinced that the company had destroyed the fabric of the Indian economy and society.[21] Rajat Kanta Ray echoes this sentiment, describing the economic system of the East India Company as a form of 'plunder', which amounted to a catastrophe for the old Mughal order.[22] Ray argues that it was the depletion of food and money stocks, along with the high level of taxation, that caused the famine of 1770 in which one-third of the population of Bengal died.

However, P. J. Marshall notes that the received wisdom of the British either inheriting a power vacuum left by the collapse of the Mughals, or creating a period of disruption them-

selves, has recently been challenged.[23] Patterns of Indian rule
continued under the company, and regional control was dele-
gated to local rulers, even after 1858. This compliance was
only possible with continued prosperity, at least in some
areas.[24] The British employed Indian bankers and collected the
revenue system in much the same way as before British rule
(rates remained the same, and accounted for one-third of the
produce of the Indian cultivators). The British therefore did
not 'conquer' India by force alone: their takeover was sometimes dependent on Indian co-operation. Moreover, the
decline of Mughal rule did not necessarily mean anarchy and
chaos, but its replacement by some stable authorities: the break
between the two periods was perhaps not as abrupt as previously thought.[25] However, the company, under Warren
Hastings (1773–85), took decisive steps to prevent the
exploitation and abuse of the administration by abolishing
power 'without responsibility', although the close co-operation
of Indian and British officials continued.

Two parallel and significant changes took place in the last
decades of the eighteenth century. First, Cornwallis, who succeeded Hastings, wanted to see Indian agriculture restored to its
former glory by a 'Permanent Settlement' of the land revenue
system, and he began to take steps to alter the existing system.
Second, the wars of expansion under the Wellesleys, the conse-
quent instability of the Marathas states, the raids of the Pindaris
and the invasion of British territory by the Nepalese drew the
company into retaliation and further annexation. However, these
changes were not without their limits. Warren Hastings was
impeached for 'oriental despotism', for 'having destroyed, for private purposes, the whole system of government' through bribery,
corruption, war, robbery and conquest.[26] It was a reminder that
imperial proconsuls were answerable to parliament.

The most significant cultural changes to India took place over
a long period of time. A discernable difference in attitude to
Indians developed with the rise of missionary influence after
1813. There had already been a mutiny of sepoys at Vellore in
1806 because of fears of forced conversion to Christianity, and,
although a mutiny at Barrackpore in 1824 was provoked by a
lack of equipment for the campaign in Burma, Douglas Peers
attributed it to: 'The sepoys' fear that the respect with which

they were held by the British was deteriorating, and, as a consequence, their service was . . . not as advantageous as it had once been.'[27] Moreover, the exclusion of Indian elites from the administration, particularly the civil service, was significant, for it marked the beginning of segregation. Fewer company officers took Indian wives, embraced Indian arts or made the conversion to Islam. Steam shipping made return journeys to England possible, families could join company servants from home, and thus permanent roots in India were unnecessary.[28]

There is continuing controversy over the effects of British rule on the Indian economy by the mid-nineteenth century. Contemporary British accounts stressed that India's economy was backward, agrarian and in decay when they took over, but there is evidence to suggest that there was some industrialisation in India prior to British rule. The focus of this idea is the Indian textile industry, which flourished in the eighteenth century even though the majority of Indian textiles were produced on handlooms, not machines. The imposition of tariffs to protect Lancashire's textile industry and the import of English goods appeared to have wiped out the embryonic Indian factories in Bombay.[29] In addition, free trade, according to Romesh Dutt in 1901, made little difference because India was forced to grow cash crops.[30] Investment in India, the construction of railways, irrigation canals and education, achievements of which the British were immensely proud, were also subsequently criticised. Investment profits were not spent on India, it was argued, and there was too much expenditure on railways and the Indian Army.[31]

Tapan Raychaudhuri argues that the British reduced the people to poverty and, when crops failed, they lacked the purchasing power to buy food even when it was available, causing famine.[32] But successive British administrations were eager not to add to the burden of taxation, which would have been necessary to develop India's industry, and they were cautious in their spending. The Indian Army was regarded as an indispensable force for operations beyond India's borders, as in China and Burma in the 1850s or for the defence of the North-West Frontier.

Muriel Chamberlain also refuted Raychaudhuri's assertion. She pointed out that, from the establishment of a jute-spinning mill by two Scots and an Indian in 1855, with power looms from 1859, industry *did* develop in India.[33] Cotton spinning was established in Bombay in 1854 and cotton manufacturing boomed during the American Civil War (1861–5). There was a suppression of the Indian textile industry through duties, but it is unclear if this was a concerted effort by the mill owners of Lancashire or Scotland to pressurise rival Indian factories, or simply an attempt to increase government revenue. Certainly, by the twentieth century, coal, steel (such as the great Tata steel works from 1907), cement, brick, paper, hardware and soap were all being produced in Indian mines or factories. Nevertheless, Neil Charlesworth argued that the lack of new industries and the limited extent of industrialisation held India back.[34]

If the impact on industry remained limited then the disruption in agriculture and rural communities was equally small. Eric Stokes's research produced a mixed verdict: some villages were affected; but others were not.[35] Local institutions survived even when power shifted. Thomas Metcalfe argued that, whilst villagers were relatively unaffected, the landlords in north India were disrupted to a much greater extent.[36] Ratna Ray, by contrast, believed that the position of the *Bhadralok* (Bengali gentry) was consolidated, not disrupted or reduced at all.[37] Indeed, in recent years, there has been some consensus that particular elites had prospered under the Raj.[38] The combination of prosperity (a result of the end of interstate warfare at the end of the Mughal period) and non-interference in the affairs of the rural community, or of consolidation and opportunity for the elites, helped ensure that the majority of Indians did not participate in the rebellion of 1857. This fact, although of great significance for the years 1857–8, is often overshadowed by the dramatic events of that bloody period.

The Indian Mutiny: rebellion or war of independence?

The Indian Mutiny/Rebellion marked a watershed in British rule in India, and shaped attitudes towards the imperial mission for decades. Despite attempts to re-title the Mutiny as the First War of Liberation, there can be little dispute that it began in the Indian Army as a mutiny. Rumours of ritual defilement by the use of animal fats on new greased cartridges coincided with fears that any disruption would meet fierce repression. Consequently, after the first outbreak in May 1857, the number of mutineers rose quickly. Land owners dispossessed by the British, peasants subjected to more thorough and comprehensive taxation than under previous rulers, and opportunist sepoys gathered in major towns in the North-West Provinces. Slow to react at first, the small and outnumbered garrisons of British forces were besieged while relief columns marched to their rescue.

Historians disagree about the nature of the rebellion. It suited some Indian nationalist historians to claim that this was a war for independence: V. D Savarkar was the first to produce such a view in 1909.[39] The Marxist approach also favoured the idea that this was a national war. But the claim rested on the notion that the mutineers called upon the old Mughal Emperor for leadership, and that the flavour of the revolt was specifically anti-British. However, this failed to persuade British historians who pointed out that the mutineers were divided, leadership was fluid and split between several princes and war-lords, the peasants' grievances were frequently different from the sepoys, and finally, and most important, was the sheer number of Indians who remained loyal to the British, even within the northern provinces.[40] Although the troops of Bengal had taken up arms, the armies of the two other presi-dencies, Madras and Bombay, were loyal and fresh troops from the recently annexed Punjab were raised for British service (through a combination of military tradition, mercenary opportunism and sectarianism).

Why was the rebellion limited to Bengal? David Omissi shows that recruiting in Bengal had been confined to a narrow social base and limited to one high caste (due to manpower shortages), unlike Madras. Grievances were therefore more likely to be shared and transmitted more quickly.[41] The suspi-cion amongst sepoys that the new British rifle cartridges were coated with pork and beef fat, the handling of which were offensive to Muslims and Hindus, was yet another essentially religious grievance, and although the British quickly issued new instructions which avoided soldiers having to bite the bullet end, the rumours of defilement had already been circu-lated.[42] Other than the cartridges affair, there was resentment at the loss of their field allowance for 'foreign' service (this included any operations distant from their home province), which had already caused unrest in the 1840s. Crossing the 'black water', leaving the shores of India, also implied pollution to high caste Hindus.

What made the Mutiny of 1857 different was the fact that British troops were depleted during the Crimean War and the reduced garrisons were concentrated in small pockets or still held in the Punjab. At Cawnpore (Kanpur), for example, there were only 200 European soldiers, many of whom were invalids of the 32nd Regiment. They faced 3000 sepoys equipped with small arms and artillery. Martin Gubbins, the Financial Commissioner of Oudh (Avadh) in 1858, concluded: 'All the causes, however, which have been enumerated, might have been in operation and yet would have failed to produce the Mutiny, but for the capital error which was committed, of denuding our provinces of European troops . . . there were none at Delhi, or at Bareilly; none at Fyzabad, at Mirzapoor, or at Benares . . . Throughout the entire province of Oudh, we possessed but one English battery of artillery.'[43]

Tom Metcalfe has argued that the civilian dimension to the Mutiny has too often been obscured, which may be a result of the dearth of written sources produced by civilians.[44] However, Eric Stokes has attacked Metcalfe's idea that there was a proportional link between land ownership, revenue collection and reliance on moneylenders that had led to rebellion.[45] Stokes carried out a study of one district (Saharanpur) and found that money lending was limited, land transfer from the traditional holders was marginal and, where it did occur, it was between wealthy landowners. What had determined peasant involvement, Stokes concluded, was the participation of the landed elites; they had provided the leadership. A. Dashe, the Collector and Magistrate of Kiyalpore, reported that, in his district: 'In the outlying posts, indeed, the people knew nothing of what was going on around them, and even in the towns resistance was not thought of until the prospect of immediate suppression of the mutiny disappeared.'[46] The proclamation issued by the rebels in Delhi on 25 August 1857 included a list of grievances by *Zemindars* (landlords), merchants, soldiers, public servants and artisans. Yet the only unifying themes are of self-interest and religion, which may tell us more about the authors of the document than the actual causes of the rebellion. The specific reference to the conflict was that: 'at present, a war is raging against the English on account of religion.'[47]

It is also difficult to argue, as it once was, that English reformers had provoked rebellion by their interference. Macaulay's legal reforms were brought in after the Mutiny, and were much amended by local circumstances. Education affected relatively few, as had been the plan, because it aimed to produce local administrators. Reform was also tempered with conservatism and took place over a long period of time. However, after the Mutiny, the search for an understanding of its causes, in order to avoid a repetition, meant that the reforms were blamed.[48] Lord Roberts, who fought in the Mutiny and won the Victoria Cross, wrote that one might prevent reoccurrence: 'By recognising and guarding against the dogmatism of theorists and the dangers of centralisation. By rendering our administration on the one hand firm and strong, and on the other hand tolerant and sympathetic; and last, but not least, by doing all in our power to gain the confidence of the various races, and by convincing them that we have not only the determination, but the ability to maintain our supremacy in India against all assailants.'[49]

Syed Ahmed Khan, a Muslim Company servant, believed that the rebellion had been a misunderstanding; the result of ignorance about government intentions and a complete lack of knowledge about the impact British rule was having on the people. Syed's solution was to establish bodies where Indian opinion might be consulted.[50] However, the Mutiny/Rebellion produced a British desire for segregation, not consultation, because they felt trust had been betrayed and they could not forgive the massacres the mutineers had perpetrated.

A special poignancy was created by the atrocities committed by both sides during the fighting. The massacres at Cawnpore for example, where British men were shot down after safe passage was promised on surrender, and British women and children were executed by 'butchers', aroused a profound desire for revenge amongst British soldiers.[51] To a culture that held women in a special position of vulnerability, the violation or murder of them was felt to be indicative of the lowest forms of barbarity. Released from the restraints of 'civilised rules of war', the British exacted a terrible price in return, although the notion that they had been betrayed by their own men also fuelled the desire to punish.[52] The battlefields of the Mutiny became shrines and symbols of the sacrifice the British had made for the 'improvement' of India. To the Indians, relations with their rulers became more distant; segregation and exclusion were normalised. For historians since, the emotiveness of the atrocities is hard to ignore for it coloured so much of the Raj mentality that followed: a combination of paternalism backed by military power, where social interaction was conducted at arm's length.

Judith Brown believes that the Mutiny should be seen in its proper context, as the largest in a series of longer term acts of resistance.[53] The reaction of civilians to the Mutiny, and the factors that determined collaboration and resistance, varied according to land settlement arrangements, levels of revenue demand, provision of facilities (such as education and irrigation), and the extent and longevity of reform programmes. Yet, in addition, the existing tensions within Indian society, such as the patterns of authority and power and of social bonds and divisions, were also distorted by the arrival and influence of the British, and these too could determine local responses to the Mutiny. Above all, assessments of the causes must take into consideration the great diversity of factors, and acknowledge that opportunism played a part. Spontaneous looting, for example, caused much of the destruction of property. Moreover, conspiracy theories, such as those put forward by Savarkar, seemed to have been finally laid to rest.

The significance of the Mutiny is also open to interpretation. Judith Brown notes that the great changes that led to India's modernisation and democratisation were yet to come.[54] The rebellion lacked a coherent ideology; the discontented were 'fractured in loyalty and intention, often looking back to a society and a polity that were no longer viable'. Raychaudhuri disagrees, and suggests that the raising of the Mutiny to the status of a war of independence, whilst a nationalist myth, reflects the views of the subject peoples.[55] He concluded: 'The Empire was nearly destroyed by the great rebellion of 1857 . . . [and it] created a legacy of racial hatred which permeated all aspects of the relationship between the ruler and the ruled.' These claims seem hard to justify. If the Bengal rebels had managed to erect some kind of unified political system, they would still have faced the same forces: the

British troops and their Indian allies. If the subcontinent had been overwhelmed, it is hard to see how this could have initiated the secession of the colonies of settlement. Even the charge that racial hatred pervaded all institutions seems difficult to justify in the face of so much collaboration.

Nevertheless, on the other hand, these ideas help to support modern nationalist sentiments. They excuse the failure of the rebellion to unite the masses by demonising 'the horrendous experience of British rule'.[56] Racial antagonism *was* a consequence of the rebellion, but it was created by a combination of British reprisals at the time and attitudes towards the 'natives' in the years that followed. However, treatment of Indians as inferiors had begun before the Mutiny/Rebellion, and British rule was successfully re-established. Therefore, 1857–8 probably marks a point in a continuum, rather than a turning point in history.

British rule in India: conclusions

British rule in India, like the rest of the British Empire, was shaped by continuities from preceding decades. However, changes in the character of British imperialism were also manifest by 1858. Annexation of territory had resulted from a combination of many factors, ranging from the strategic threat posed by powerful military states, to the desire to acquire the benefits of a valuable land revenue system. There may be differences of opinion on the relative importance of government direction, military considerations and the 'profit motive', but, once the British assumed control of large sections of the subcontinent or found themselves allied to the princely states, some degree of internal reorganisation was inevitable.

The British believed they were introducing modernisation by the abolition of slavery, *suttee* and thuggee, they were sustained by a strong faith in missionary work (which was reflected in a revival of the churches at home), and they saw benefits in the Anglicisation of education and in the opening up of Indian, South-East Asian and Chinese trade. The degree of influence the intellectuals had is now thought to be much less than suggested by the post-colonial writers, although there is little doubt that reform in government under Lord Dalhousie's administration did cause deep resentment in the central provinces in the 1850s.

Can the Mutiny and the civilian rebellion be seen as resistance to imperialism? David Washbrook notes that the rebellion was directed against religious enemies, but was triggered when Indians perceived a weakening of the military state.[57] The Mutiny and the rebellion were essentially backward looking and the Indians remained as divided as they had always been. Of equal significance, perhaps, was the loyalty of the majority of Indians, relatively undisturbed in their customs, sharing little sympathy with Bengal, and enjoying a degree of peace and prosperity. Ultimately, this rebellion to restore the *status quo ante* was ironic. After the great shock of the Mutiny, there were changes in commerce, in security requirements, and in the degree of centralised control in India (contrasting with devolved representation in the Colonies of Settlement), as well as in the nature of the ideas of leading philanthropists. These dynamics have attracted the interest of historians who have grappled with the problem of measuring the extent of the impact of the Raj on Indian society and the economy.

How could the military-fiscal state and centralisation be reconciled with British traditions of responsible government and liberal democracy? Warren Hastings had stated, whilst referring to India, that England's task was to use her 'sovereignty towards enlightening her subjects, so as to enable the native communities to walk alone in the paths of justice'.[58] Yet Macaulay had told the House of Commons in July 1833: 'Of all the innumerable speculators who have offered their suggestions on Indian politics, not a single one, as far as I know, however democratical his opinions may be, has ever maintained the possibility of giving, at the present time, such institutions to India.'[59] The reason, Macaulay argued, was the lack of education amongst the Indian people and the degree of influence from their lords that would make democracy unworkable, an argument also used in Britain.

Many contemporaries felt that India had to be 'managed' until sufficiently modernised before self-government could be contemplated. Even so, there were many in India who felt that even the mention of self-government would recreate the conditions of the Mutiny, or set in motion moves to independence that would cause the break up of the Empire and the loss of Britain's Great Power status, wealth and influence. This explains the nature of British imperialism after the Mutiny, that of firm control and cautious reform to avoid unrest. Warren Hastings wrote: 'It would be treason to British sentiment to imagine that it could ever be the principle of this government to perpetuate ignorance in order to secure paltry and dishonest advantages over the blindness of the multitude.'[60] Nevertheless, it was that very desire to educate, however tacitly, along Western lines that would give rise to calls for independence amongst the Bengali intellectuals later in the century.[61]

4 'New Imperialism' and 'Gentlemanly Capitalism': did the flag follow trade?

Interpretations on the extension of formal rule

Britain's formal Empire expanded dramatically from the late 1870s, with new colonies added in Africa and Asia. In the space of barely 25 years, the European powers together partitioned 10 million square miles in Africa and governed 110 million new subjects. South-East Asia was carved up, with France and Britain taking the lion's share. In the Indian Ocean and the Pacific, Britain, Germany and the United States acquired new territories and islands. In the second half of the nineteenth century, America and Russia stepped up the colonisation of their vast hinterlands. Even apparently moribund older empires such as Portugal and China renewed their imperialist drive, the Portuguese in Africa and the Chinese in Xinjiang. The world in 1900 was a world of empires.

What characterised this process as 'new' for Britain was the rapid extension of formal control, a growing awareness of new threats from other Great Powers and the concomitant growth of competitive capitalist economies in Europe. Put simply, Britain had both the means and the determination to assert itself more effectively than in previous centuries in defence of what it regarded as its essential 'interests'. Britain was already a vast imperial power before the late nineteenth century, and its existing colonies exerted an enormous influence on its subsequent development. John Darwin places considerable emphasis on these 'bridgeheads', which he regards as key to understanding the development of the empire in the Victorian period.[1] For example, Bechuanaland and Rhodesia were extensions of influence from Cape Colony, Burma was annexed as a branch of

India, and the hinterlands of Canada and Australia were colonised from the much older coastal settlements.

For decades it was thought that after a period of indifference to Empire in the early nineteenth century, Britain became more aware of the need to protect its existing colonial possessions and acquired vast amounts of new territory.[2] This expansion was accompanied, or perhaps followed by, a new enthusiasm for imperialism throughout British society. However, Britain's reluctance to annex or maintain expensive colonies, and its continuing faith in the ability of the foreign office to settle disputes with rivals, meant that it could, it was thought, acquire new territory without really intending to: 'in a fit of absence of mind' as Sir John Seeley put it.[3] There has been considerable controversy ever since, primarily between those who feel that Britain cannot have been as reluctant as it claimed, and those who feel that the British government was not always in control of events and was sometimes subject to the forces on the periphery of the Empire, or the vagaries of international power politics.

Three approaches can be discerned in the historical debate. The first is the 'metropolitan' interpretation where the motivations and policies of the British are examined with particular reference to economic forces and political decisions emanating from Britain. The second approach focuses on the 'periphery', taking account of the indigenous peoples and their reactions to the British, but also noting the role played by the 'man on the spot': missionaries, traders, local administrators and soldiers.[4] The third approach is to place the British expansion in a European and global context, looking at Great Power rivalry when diplomacy had reached a critical stage in the late nineteenth century. Some analyses offer syntheses of these broad approaches. John Darwin, for example, attempts to combine domestic pressures and decision-making by individual statesmen and leaders, within the context of international relations.[5]

Metropolitan core and periphery models of 'New Imperialism'

Economic explanations have dominated the metropolitan approach to New Imperialism. J. A. Hobson argued that the partition of Africa was deliberately planned by 'financiers, capital investors and unscrupulous politicians' who supported investment in new areas of the world rather than spending on high wages, or on projects that required inflationary expenditure on public services and housing for British workers at home.[6] The subsequent misdistribution of wealth gave the rich a surplus to invest overseas, but the suppression of the British workers' wages reduced the consumers' power in the economy and curbed the expansion of British industry. The Bolshevik leader Lenin felt that overseas investment and the subsequent acquisition of colonies was an inevitable stage of capitalism. He stated that imperialism could therefore only be understood by studying the economies of Europe. To Lenin, 'imperialism is monopoly capitalism', but – to fit the Marxist model – it was a period of crisis. Too many nations were chasing too few lucrative markets, which induced protectionism, stiff competition and colonial rivalry. Governments were therefore acting in the interests of 'finance capitalists' and 'monopoly companies' in order to secure raw materials. They were the 'puppets' of capitalism.[7]

Historians who promoted the 'periphery' approach were dissatisfied that the emphasis was at the centre, as if imperialism was generated only from Britain, or just London, and disseminated outwards. R. Robinson and J. Gallagher argued that the British really preferred to have 'informal control'; that is, economic influence without the expense of political control. Government offices, military forces, civil servants, public services and administration had to be provided in colonies, but informal spheres of influence were 'empire on the cheap'. In 1961, they argued that the event which had initiated the 'scramble for Africa' was the invasion of Egypt in 1882. The primary motive for this had been the desire to protect trade routes and British strategic ('national') interests when informal influence broke down, but it was a 'local crisis' initiated on the periphery of Empire. Throughout the imperial period, the British looked at their strategic role in the world rather than acting simply because of business lobbying or fluctuations in public opinion, but they had been overtaken from around 1880 by the development of a 'general crisis' in European relations with Africa and Asia. This made British imperial policy reactive and conservative.[8] The key decisions had been taken by the 'official mind', a term they used to describe a body of Foreign Office and Cabinet officials barely affected by external influences of the press, public opinion or lobbyists.

However, Robinson and Gallagher perhaps gave insufficient weight to those lobbyists (or indeed the entrepreneurs or the missionaries on the spot) and their contributions in encouraging intervention. J. S. Marais argued that, in South Africa, mine magnates had worked with the British government to challenge the Transvaal government and John S. Galbraith examined the role of chartered companies in extending British control in South and East Africa.[9] However, Iain Smith has shown that the businessmen, divided amongst themselves, vigorously pursued their own interests 'irrespective of the rather different interests of the British government . . . they were certainly not "under orders".[10]

Exceptional individuals on the periphery certainly played a part in the expansion of British rule in Africa.[11] Cecil Rhodes's companies developed diamond mining at Kimberley in British Cape Colony in the 1870s and gold mining on the Witwatersrand in the Transvaal in the 1880s, both of which attracted interest from the British government.[12] Rhodes advocated the annexation of Bechuanaland, independently annexed a massive territory he called Rhodesia in the vain search for more mineral deposits, and conspired to topple the Transvaal government in 1895 in favour of British rule (and with it, the end of punitive taxation on mine profits and resources). Rhodes also aimed to see the construction of a railway from Cape Town to Cairo, which would dominate the trade of Africa. Although no railway was built, Rhodes was an inspiration to other imperialists, and his patriotism ensured he could command the support of the English-speaking community in the Cape.[13] However, some of the missionaries and explorers, such as Livingstone, Stanley or Joseph Thomson, had also advertised the potential of Africa. In Thomson's case, he positively promoted intervention.[14] Together, they paved the way for later claims to British territories such as Kenya and Uganda, and they created a sense of exotic appeal through their writings, which went a long way in popularising imperialism.

Critics would argue that these individuals alone could not have been as important as the economic or military forces at work, but these explorers and missionaries did call on British government assistance, or, at the very least, financial support from home. A more convincing criticism is that individuals rarely dictated to governments, even if supported by lobbyists at home, and governments did not make decisions solely on the basis of events on the periphery.

John Darwin challenged the idea of a unified 'official mind' dominating the decision-making process in an unfettered environment, and places the emphasis instead on forces of 'chaotic, opportunistic, centrifugal imperialism'. He argued that the decentralised parliamentary imperial state was unfavourable to the authority or even coherence of an 'official mind'. Officials and ministers were engaged in 'unremitting struggle to retain some official control over the centrifugal forces that drove Victorian expansion'.[15] Darwin identifies five key impulses behind Victorian expansion. First, an aggressively interventionist ideology made up of deep faith in free trade, utilitarianism, evangelical Christianity and anti-slavery which could mobilise public opinion to support expansion. Second, a new culture of consumerism which created an appetite and interest in overseas activity. Third, economic forces which included inexpensive and long-term credit, cheap manufactures and a flow of migrants who took their capital, consumer tastes and productive capacity overseas. Fourth, increased maritime supremacy beyond European waters. Finally, the British presence in India was a springboard for further expansion in Asia, a source of manpower and Britain's entrepôt to the Asian world. Darwin concluded: 'The bridgehead was the hinge or "interface" between the metropole and a local periphery. It was the transmission shaft of imperialism and the recruiting sergeant of collaborators. It might be a commercial, settler, missionary or proconsular presence or a combination of all four.'[16]

In 1900, the British Empire was still the hub in the circulation of world trade and therefore the commercial element cannot be ignored. An industrial revolution meant that its low cost, mass-produced manufactures were carried across the globe. Flowing back to Britain, but also across the world and between the colonies, were a great variety of raw materials and semi-manufactured goods. However, David Abernethy notes that: 'The direction, composition and volume of trade . . . hinged upon the Industrial Revolution', which created a 'yawning chasm' between the wealth of industrialised and non-industrialised states in the nineteenth century.[17] Paul Bairoch also focuses on the effects of imperialism and estimates that whilst real per capita income in Western Europe rose by 222 per cent between 1800 and 1913, it rose by only 9 per cent in Africa and 1 per cent in Asia.[18] David Landes illustrated the disparity by noting that in Britain in 1810: 'the price of yarn had fallen to perhaps one twentieth of what it had been [50 years before], and the cheapest Hindu labour could not compete in either quality or quantity with Lancashire's mules and throstles.'[19] As a result, India imported 51 million yards of cotton fabric in 1830 and 2 billion yards in 1890. In 1830, Latin America, Asia and Africa still generated 60.5 per cent of the world's hand and machine manufactured goods, but by 1860 this had fallen to 36.6 per cent and in 1913 accounted for just 7.5 per cent.[20]

However, although the first industrialised power, Britain had been surpassed by both the United States and by Germany in coal and steel production by 1914, the existence of cheaper mass-produced goods meant that Britain faced increased competition from other industrialising countries. Its share of world trade declined although output continued to increase, a situation that was sustained by an increase in demand. The First World War meant that many of its rivals captured traditional British markets, whilst American economies of scale and lower wages in South and East Asia undermined the competitiveness of British labour. Britain's lack of natural resources had made her economy dependent on trade, despite exports of coal, and her manufacturing relied on the continued import of raw materials. Moreover, from 1900, about two-thirds of British food was imported and a growing population increased the demand annually.

Even so, Britain remained the financial capital of the world and, with its vast fleet of shipping, the premier merchant carrier. It was these invisible exports that supported the British economy. However, a point often overlooked in economic statistics of the Empire, is that in 1902 one-fifth of imperial trade was not directly concerned with the United Kingdom. This commerce between the dominions and other colonies, or with foreign powers, represented a figure of £254,342,000. Not only does this highlight the difficulty in measuring the value of the British Empire, and the importance that economic factors had on the changes within it, but it reminds us that Britain and the Empire were only one part of the global economy. This raises considerable doubts whether industrialisation and imperialism are really as closely linked as once thought.

However, it is the economic dimension of Robinson and Gallagher's controversial 1953 article entitled the 'Imperialism of Free Trade' that continues to attract attention. It stated that the idea of indifference to the Empire in the early nineteenth century was wrong; the mid-nineteenth century had been 'a decisive stage in the history of British expansion overseas.'[21] They justified this view on the basis that the Empire had continued to expand territorially and that it developed ways of dominating parts of the world through trade, but without annexation (a point noted before as Informal Empire). Nevertheless, this 'Informal Empire' was not totally without coercion. In South America, after a series of wars of independence against Spain, the British aim had been to use commerce to 'shatter the Spanish trade monopoly and gain informal supremacy'.[22] This pattern was repeated elsewhere: 'Once entry had been forced into Latin America, China and the Balkans, the task was to encourage stable governments as good investment risks, just as in weaker or unsatisfactory states, it was considered necessary to coerce them into more co-operative attitudes.'[23] Robinson and Gallagher seemed to have found a way to explain both the effects of the economic supremacy of Britain, and the reason for the series of punitive attacks (as in China), or wars of annexation, (as in Lower Burma, Sind and Punjab), or takeovers (as in Oudh, Hong Kong, and Kowloon). They concluded that the British government had sought to establish 'trade with informal control if possible; trade with rule if necessary'.[24]

D. C. M. Platt was critical of Robinson and Gallagher, particularly over the role of the British governments. Platt maintained that the British government aimed to remain impartial over trade, rather than intervening on its behalf. This was perhaps a misreading of Robinson and Gallagher. Informal Empire *could* be achieved without any involvement of the British government. However, the alteration of a local economy by the domination of British manufacturers would leave that economy 'dependent' on Britain (until other competitors reduced the monopolising effect of British trade). Platt did, however, criticise the pervasiveness of British trade in the so-called Informal Empire with greater justification. Local resistance to British goods, Platt argued, and the absence of any goods of value to local requirements prevented British influence from spreading in China and Latin America.[25] The synthesis of the Robinson-Gallagher and Platt approaches suggests that British governments did not seek to secure exclusive trading rights, but equally they might not permit 'British Interests' to be completely excluded either. The degree of interference might depend on either the extent of resistance or the limits to their control. In some cases, local agents of imperialism acted where the British government would have urged restraint.

There are additional problems with Robinson and Gallagher's general theory. South America provided a boom for British exports after its independence in the 1820s, with 12.6 per cent of the total trade going there, which supports the idea of Informal Empire. However, this had fallen to 8.8 per cent by the 1850s. In China too, the percentage of trade fell so that by 1900, it provided £2.5 million imports, £5.5 million exports and a capital investment of £30 million which equated to only 1 per cent of Britain's total overseas investments.[26] Perhaps Robinson and Gallagher overestimated the extent of Informal Empire?

The *Oxford History of the British Empire* makes a useful contribution to the debate on Informal Empire and its influence on current notions of globalisation. Wm Roger Louis notes that Robinson and Gallagher brought about a conceptual 'revolution' in the historiography of British imperialism because they promoted the idea that even before the 1880s and the scramble for Africa, Asia and the Middle East, British free trade had established a global empire of dependency and influence, and this marked the emergence of a capitalist world economy.[27] They identified continuities between the nineteenth and twentieth centuries, and attacked the traditional view that the explanations of British expansion lay in the metropolis. At the time they wrote this piece, Louis observed, Robinson and Gallagher were greatly influenced by the Cold War. They were especially concerned that the American programme for the economic revitalisation of Europe in 1945, the Marshall Plan, would reduce

Britain to the status of an American satellite. They argued that a country did not have to be conquered militarily to lose its independence: the same could happen through trade and investment from a more powerful economy. They also supported the idea that capitalism was a world system controlled by the dominant ruling elite, a view shared by critics of globalisation.

However, despite the survival of the concept of Informal Empire, there are critical reappraisals in the *Oxford History*, particularly for the period before 1880. P. J. Marshall argued that Robinson and Gallagher underestimated the political and economic obstacles to effective domination. In South America, it was only in Brazil that the British found pliant political collaborators. In the United States after 1776, Britain could exert no political influence, although there was a population long habituated to British goods and able to pay for them through large exports of primary produce. Over much of Asia, Marshall argued, indigenous political systems were still largely beyond the reach of British diplomatic influence or even the threat of British warships and Indian troops, while intercontinental trade had little influence on most Asian economies. Despite being the most powerful European 'formal' power in Asia, British economic influence at the end of the eighteenth century, Marshall claimed, had been exaggerated: 'Concepts of informal empire are even more difficult to apply to Asia, outside the Indian subcontinent, or to Africa, than they are to the Americas.'[28]

Martin Lynn also devotes a persuasively argued chapter to the same thesis. He says that the idea seriously exaggerates both the British government's willingness to intervene overseas before the 1880s and its success in establishing more than a superficial paramountcy over parts of the wider world. Lynn points out that there are conceptual limitations to the use of terms such as 'Informal Empire' or 'Informal Control' to understand, or measure, Britain's relations with these areas. The terms distort what was actually a more ambiguous and fluid form of influence and are unhelpful in implying that this influence was all one way, from Britain to the outside world, rather than a 'mutually permeable process'. Lynn concludes: 'That Britain established a commercial or financial presence in a region did not mean, necessarily, that she gained either economic or political paramountcy over it. Only at the highest level of abstraction can Latin America, China, Ottoman Turkey, and Africa in the mid-nineteenth century be described as parts of a British informal empire.'[29]

Robinson and Gallagher considered the importance of resistance, and therefore of financial risk, in their assessment of Britain's Informal Empire. Fear that control of the Suez Canal by hostile powers would seriously affect the volume of British trade from the East (which amounted to 13 per cent in 1882, or put another way, British trade accounted for 80 per cent of the total trade carried through the canal), and prompted by competition from newly industrialising nations in Europe and the influx of cheap grain from north America, Britain felt compelled to secure its trade and protect its arterial routes to maintain its global economic leadership. Consequently, in 1875, when Egypt faced a financial crisis and the Khedive put up for sale shares in the canal, the Prime Minister, Benjamin Disraeli, acquired the lion's share of holdings worth £3.25 million. Financial weaknesses in Egypt led to an increase in foreign loans, and by 1881, foreign control of state revenues. Corruption within the tax collection system meant that the burden fell heavily on the *fellahin* (peasants) and compelled the state to consider cuts in public services, including the army. A portion of the Egyptian Army under Colonel Arabi Pasha rebelled, provoking disturbances in Cairo. This made the British fearful that a nationalist revolt would jeopardise the security of the canal. The British therefore intervened militarily in 1882. The occupation of Egypt initiated the scramble for Africa, and sustained it 'until', Robinson and Gallagher believed, 'there was no more of Africa left to divide'.[30] The French annexed parts of West Africa, Robinson and Gallagher contended, in the belief it would compensate them for the loss of influence in Egypt (which they felt they exercised from the 1830s). They felt it would, perhaps, even compel the British to leave the Nile valley. Robinson and Gallagher explained Salisbury's decision (as Prime Minister and Foreign Secretary, 1885, 1895–1900) to maintain British rule in Egypt, and his subsequent extension of influence over the Sudan and Uganda as a means to secure the headwaters of the Nile on which Egypt's prosperity depended. This, they claim, acted as the spur to the further partition of Africa.

Robinson and Gallagher's theories, showing economic forces in concert with other factors, altered thinking about the nature of imperialism in Africa, but once again, their views have been challenged since. Their argument that the British invasion of Egypt in 1882 led directly to the scramble in West Africa because the French, angered by the British unilateral action, abandoned the 'gentleman's agreement' (whereby the two powers had agreed to respect each other's spheres of influence) is not supported by the evidence.

According to A. G. Hopkins, French annexations in West Africa *preceded* the invasion of Egypt. For example, the decision to take Porto Novo, which lay between the British colonies of the Gold Coast and Lagos, was taken in April 1882. Where the French government was involved in West Africa, after the Egyptian invasion as on the Niger, the policy was to *avoid* antagonism with Britain by finding an alternative route from the upper Niger to the sea that would not affect British interests. The French government, Hopkins argued, was eager to conciliate Britain in the autumn of 1882.[31] However, this view is not universally accepted. Bernard Porter demonstrated that French anger led them to challenge the British claim to the Sudan in 1896.[32] In addition, Professor Stengers believed that the French backed the explorer Savorgnan de Brazza's highly dubious treaties with the Congo chiefs, laying the foundation of a French Empire in the Congo as compensation for the loss of prestige they felt.

However, the Scramble for Africa did not just involve France and Britain, and a 'chain reaction' may not be a wholly satisfactory explanation for the interest of Leopold of Belgium and Bismarck of Germany who were equally involved. Indeed, an over-reliance on Egypt as the 'trigger' factor (ignoring the French annexation of Tunisia, or the extension of British rule in southern Africa with annexations in the period 1877–9), distorts the perspective of what was happening in Africa and the other motives in the partition. G. N Sanderson and Thomas Pakenham point to the fact that the partition of Africa began long before the occupation of Egypt, suggesting that the 1880s was merely an acceleration.[33] For example, the Ashanti struggled with Britain in 1873 to secure control of the lower Niger valley. Further back, in another manifestation of the 'Forward Policy', Britain had established control of Natal in 1843. Robinson acknowledged this himself, and, in refining his original thesis, he described the scramble not as a 'periphery theory', with Europeans acting or reacting on the periphery, but as 'excentric', where Europeans and Africans *interacted* on the periphery: 'there was the Eurocentric circle of expanding economy and power strategy making various intersections with circles centred in the implacable continuities of pre-colonial African and Asian history. Imperialism, especially in its time scale, was not precisely a true function of either circle. It was in many ways excentric to both.'[34]

Fieldhouse wrote that territorial expansion in West Africa 'derived from practical and humdrum problems of existing British and French colonies rather than from mercantile or official imperialism: the need for more customs duties, problems of jurisdiction and the need for security against African states.' He explained that both the British government and the traders favoured an international agreement to preserve their commercial interests, but this did not include annexation. The ideal solution would have been an agreement that recognised the neutrality of African territories. However, the partitions, sanctioned by the Berlin Conference (1884–5), were the consequence of both Britain and Germany losing faith in the idea that neutrality could be preserved. This was due to two factors: (1) Belgian and French annexations in the Congo; and (2) the attempts by British and French private firms to establish monopolies on the West African coast. The result was reluctant British participation in the partition.[35]

Fieldhouse also advanced a political explanation of the New Imperialism. He saw the imposition of formal rule not as the result of economic activity (although this could create instability on the periphery), but because of the greater willingness of European statesmen to protect economic and political interests in this way. This mentality was the natural result of the fact that since 1871 Europe had become an armed camp, with the balance so delicately adjusted that no one dared to risk changes in Europe itself. He concluded: 'Imperialism may best be seen as the extension into the periphery of the political struggle in Europe.'[36]

To a considerable degree, the partition of Africa and Asia was as much driven by European rivalry as any desire to acquire territory for economic value. Ultimately, Africa was poor and there-

fore unattractive to business. Its people had been the only mag-
netic commodity, until the abolition of slavery had ended even
this attraction. Some areas were of almost no economic value,
which supports the 'diplomatic rivalry' in Fieldhouse's argument. This was even a contemporary view. Lord Salisbury had
mocked the French achievement in annexing much of Saharan
West Africa by congratulating the French on acquiring so much
'light land' (punning on 'sand'). Nevertheless, the impact of the
search for profits or raw materials could destabilise regions of
Africa and Asia sufficiently to compel the Europeans to act. Even
the proximity of the imperial economic system, such as mining
in South Africa, or the circulation of trade in South-East Asia,
could disrupt and dislocate the local economy of the indigenous
population. The search for higher paid jobs caused migrations in
the labour force, and even alterations in the social structure.[37]
These are the effects that have interested those historians investi-
gating the origins of globalisation.[38]

In another sense, the attention placed on the partition of
Africa, despite its high drama, is misleading. South-East Asia was
also partitioned in the 1880s, along with the Pacific Islands,
largely due to diplomatic rivalry and strategic anxieties, but also
because they had some economic potential as a tropical cornu-
copia. Taking a more global view, the western states of the
United States, Central Asia, southern Argentina and Australasia
underwent considerable colonisation by European settlers,
a process aided as much by military forces, and epidemics among
the native populations, as by the economic processes of capitalism. In South Africa, the traditional agrarian 'land hunger', the
demand for grazing land, was just as significant as the quest for
mineral deposits pursued by Cecil Rhodes or the mining magnates of the Rand. In other words, the dynamic of capitalism and
the search for resources, the expectation of new markets (which
might reach maturity in the long term) and the staking out of
future claims were only one part of a greater and more complex
process of European expansion and imperialism. Robinson and
Gallagher opened up a debate that continues to resonate: What
importance should be attached to Informal Empire, and therefore to the British Empire as an agent of globalisation?

The extent of Informal Empire is also very difficult to measure in economic terms. It isn't clear what statistics should be

included, or even whether it was by its nature more economic than political or diplomatic. The most reliable measurements might not always be found in the metropolis. For example, although the importance of Latin American states to the British economy was negligible, the local impact could be large. These effects are thought to be typical of globalisation.[39] In this sense, globalisation is more than the establishment of linkages in a global economy; it is also influence, exploitation and domination by economic means. Imperialism was the handmaiden of powerful and exploitative multinationals which are thought to have widened the poverty gap between rich and poor nations. However, Informal Empire was less pervasive than originally thought. British penetration of markets in South America was in fact limited. The linkages of a global economy were mutually permeable and interdependent. Britain was only a part, although a leading element for a short period, in the development of a global economy which can be traced back beyond European imperialism.

British commerce was an important aspect of British imperialism in the eighteenth and nineteenth centuries, but it was particularly significant once Britain was an industrialised power. Patrick O'Brien concluded that the British Empire was an unprofitable enterprise, but 'it seemed inordinately difficult for contemporaries to separate military expenditures . . . from revenues required simply to maintain the framework of imperial rule.'[40] The attempts by governments to limit expenditure were jeopardised by the need to protect British commerce from the threats posed by other powers and the agents of imperialism on the ground. A maturing financial sector attracted the attention of Hobson because it seemed to offer an explanation for the world's inequalities of wealth. More recent analysis has exposed the deficiencies of the older economic explanations.

Recent debates on economics and imperialism

In 1987, dissatisfied with the emphasis on 'area studies' of the periphery, P. J. Cain and A. G. Hopkins sought to refocus on the metropolis and to link together explanations of the more metropolitan or 'core' motors of imperialism with the social structure of Britain itself. They did this by arguing that the financiers of the City of London and the political elites of Westminster were either the same men or had closely connected interests. Cain and Hopkins called the values of a commercial elite, who emulated the aristocracy (which merged with the old landed gentry and their value system of respectability and class), 'Gentlemanly Capitalism'. However, the manufacturers of the north and centre of Britain were 'largely outside of the circle of gentlemanly culture and did not speak the same language as the aristo-financial elite'.[41]

Cain and Hopkins believed the financial and political elites sought to protect their common interests. These included the protection of their investments overseas, as well as their political hegemony at home. This meant that British imperial policy focused primarily on areas of greatest economic concern in the formal empire, such as Egypt or South Africa, and, by virtue of its size, India. Their financial interest also extended beyond the formal empire to Latin America and China (Table 1). Cain and Hopkins rejected the Hobsonian idea that the government was 'in the pockets of the bondholders', but instead argued that the government and financial elites shared a common interest.[42]

Cain and Hopkins presented four new approaches to the historiography of British imperialism:

1. They stressed the long, established role of the financial sector in the nineteenth-century British economy as opposed to the general tendency to emphasise the manufacturing industry.
2. They offered a new definition of the 'official mind'.
3. They claimed that the decisive stage of expansion had been misdated by previous historians.
4. They emphasised that the true metropolitan causes of imperialism had been overlooked.

Cain and Hopkins argued that the industrial revolution as a factor in British imperial expansion had been greatly exaggerated. Part of the problem lay in the timing. Vincent Harlow felt that the relationship between free trade, industrialisation and the acquisition of empire had reached its decisive phase after 1763, even though Britain already had extensive possessions long

Table 1   British overseas investment in 1914 (millions of £)[43]

Within the Empire	
Canada and Newfoundland	514.9
Australia and New Zealand	416.4
South Africa	370.2
West Africa	37.3
India and Ceylon	378.8
Straits Settlements	27.3
British N. Borneo	5.8
Hong Kong	3.1
Other Colonies	26.2
Total	1780.0
Outside the Empire	
United States	754.6
Latin America	756.6
Europe	218.6
Egypt	44.9
Turkey	24.0
China	43.9
Japan	62.8
Rest of the world	77.9
Total	1983.3

before the last vestiges of protectionism were abolished in the nineteenth century. Cain and Hopkins argued that the timing of the industrial revolution, if this were the motor of expansion, would shift the date closer to 1800 or even later. To account for the decisive changes in mercantilism, industrialisation, free trade and imperial expansion, Cain and Hopkins suggest one must acknowledge the 'financial revolution', the development in Britain's banking, insurance and financial services sector.[44]

Revision of the Cain and Hopkins thesis

Cain and Hopkins's views have been challenged by a number of historians. The first criticism was of the emphasis placed on the

English elites in south-eastern England, and their role in the expansion of the Empire.[45] Andrew Porter has shown that strong connections were developed with the Empire, not just by the 'gentleman-capitalists' of southern England, but by Lancashire manufacturers and by those of West and Central Scotland too.[46] To this one might add the large number of aristocratic and middle-class families from rural England or Ireland, who filled the ranks of the military and naval officer corps and imperial administration. David Cannadine has highlighted the connection of interests between industry and government, but also how the financial sector was itself often divided.[47] Martin Daunton argued that the concept of 'Gentlemanly Capitalism' does not adequately explain the nature of the economy in the nineteenth century, and that there was greater synergy of interests between industrialists and financiers than Cain and Hopkins had claimed.[48]

David Fieldhouse also questioned the concept of a 'gentlemanly capitalist class' and illustrated its many social divisions, but he pointed out another, more important imbalance in Cain and Hopkins's theory. He claimed there was too much emphasis for the motivation of Empire on the metropolitan core. Instead, he maintained that there was considerable economic activity occurring at the periphery, which accounted for the British involvement in Africa and Asia in the late nineteenth century.[49] Robinson and Gallagher had argued that the scramble for Africa was initiated and sustained by events on the periphery, namely the financial crisis between 1875 and 1882 in Egypt, and in *Africa and the Victorians*, they also indicated that strategic factors had had a part to play. In 1990, Andrew Porter took up this theme and developed it. He challenged what he saw as economic determinism in Cain and Hopkins's approach, arguing that economic factors alone did not explain the British policy in Egypt or South Africa.

Criticisms of Cain and Hopkins have also led to questions of the relative importance of gentlemanly elites and investment as the driving force of imperialism. Despite the vast sums invested overseas, 68 per cent of British investment went to traditional areas such as the United States, Canada, Argentina, Australia and South Africa. In comparison, little was invested in the newly annexed regions. David Fieldhouse noted: 'The places now to be taken over had hitherto attracted little capital, and did not attract it in any quantity subsequently.[50] The British government could not induce capitalists to sink much money in their new colonies. Only a quarter of British investible funds went into the empire, and only a fifth of private investors assets.[51] The British East Africa Company virtually went bankrupt in the early 1890s, mainly because it could not raise the finance necessary for developments like the Uganda railway, which might have made the colony a commercial proposition.[52] As Muriel Chamberlain put it: 'Far from capital fighting to get out to the colonies in this period it seems to have been very difficult to get it to go.'[53]

In 1997, John Darwin returned to 'historical forces' and the 'role of individuals' to offer a solution to the inconsistent explanations within Cain and Hopkins's theory.[54] He suggested that there had been 'bridgeheads' or footholds from earlier periods established on the coasts of Africa and Asia, and that the success or failure of their personnel dictated whether expansion into the interior took place. He argued that formal annexation was not a last resort, but followed successful lobbying by leaders or groups at the periphery or in London. This could include, but was not exclusively, financiers of the City of London and their political allies. Governments of the period had been weak and inconsistent in their approach, resulting in a variety of different forms of control. The limits to expansion were also accounted for in the same vein: dependence on the British government (for economic support or security), or strong indigenous polities that tended to curtail expansion.

In a similar manner, Fieldhouse stated that the way to understand the economic motives of imperialism was not to create an overarching theory, such as 'Gentlemanly Capitalism', but to examine each region and the forces that produced formal rule, spheres of influence or limits to British power. In effect, Fieldhouse was calling for historians to examine each colonial encounter in some detail, and this has produced some of the best work on British imperialism.[55]

Cain and Hopkins have made a valuable contribution to the explanation of imperialism in a wide-ranging analysis. The increasing importance, from the late nineteenth century, of investment, loans, banking and insurance services and the invisible earnings from these services is highlighted. The close ties between the Bank of England and the Treasury are evident in issues concerning the national debt and interest rates. In particular they emphasise the importance of governmental thrift or 'Gladstonian fiscal doctrine' to decision-making. This theme can be detected in countless examples of British imperialism and reinforces the idea that Britain aimed to influence the world, defend its interests and maintain an empire with the minimum of expense. The desire for sound public finances and balanced budgets was, after all, the principle of good business management: to cut costs and maximise returns.

However, the monolithic nature of 'Gentlemanly Capitalism' has now been successfully challenged. Ewan Green argued that there was a significant difference between industrialists and agricultural interests on the one hand, and the merchant bankers of the City of London on the other, particularly over the issue of bimetallism at the turn of the century.[56] The industrial–agricultural interests hoped that the inflationary effect of coming off the gold standard would counteract the falling prices of the period, but this conflicted with the City's desire to continue with free trade lest it affect their interest rates. Whilst this appeared to endorse Cain and Hopkins's views, Green argued that there was still a discernable difference between *influence* and *direction* by these elites.

Maria Misra also detected greater differences on the periphery. In India, British businessmen (either bankers, investors or overseas merchants) did not share the same values, club affiliations, ideologies or political aims as the government of India, or of the British government. Indeed, it would be unsurprising to find companies and financial houses in competition with each other. Where there was a combination, it was perhaps more likely to have been a *convergence* of particular interests rather than a close co-operation or alliance as Cain and Hopkins implied.

Raymond Dummett has suggested that insufficient attention had been given to the 'irrational' motive of imperialism in Cain and Hopkins's argument.[57] The powerful influences of prestige, war, jingoism and religious faith all had a part to play. In addition, there was a great deal of 'ungentlemanly capitalism', manifest as fraud, 'land grab', hubris and nonchalance towards violence against 'subject' peoples. Nevertheless, Cain and Hopkins attempted to draw together the broad strands of economic imperialism and locate the driving forces within the metropolis. They can hardly be criticised for failing to cover so many other aspects of imperialism when their objective was to focus on one key area. Consequently, despite the criticisms, their work is likely to remain a landmark for many years.

5 What were the motives and effects of colonisation and migration?

Colonies of settlement: Australia, New Zealand, Canada and South Africa

The British Empire emerged over a period of several hundred years and its administration was frequently adapted to suit local circumstances. This resulted in a great variety in the patterns of British rule. India was ruled as a military despotism and commercial enterprise, tempered by philanthropic ideas developed and adapted from English liberalism and radicalism. African and Chinese coastal stations were little more than commercial entrepôts, or bases for the Royal Navy. However, the colonies of white settlement enjoyed a special status. They were regarded as part of a 'greater Britain', and settlers were the agents of British civilisation who took with them British tastes and values. Marc Ferro wrote: 'colonization was the 'power' of a people to "reproduce" itself in different spaces'.[1] It was the emphasis on being able to dominate, and to retain a distinct identity that made colonisation distinct from immigration.

The exploration of new lands was an enterprise full of danger. Commodore Byron and Samuel Wallis, who led the first British voyages into the Pacific, were both shipwrecked before reaching home.[2] The natives of Hawaii killed Captain Cook on his third voyage. Establishing a colony was also attended by great hardship, as the American colonists had found in the seventeenth century. The rivalry of other European powers was another problem. The efforts to colonise South-East Asia were checked by the return of the East Indies to the Dutch after the Napoleonic Wars, and the British bases there, called the Straits Settlements, were confined to the islands of the Malay Peninsula. Climatic conditions, hostile native populations and lack of resources also limited colonisation.

Colonisation was driven by several factors. Initially, colonists were regarded as the suppliers of primary products. In British North America, timber and furs were exported in return for manufactured goods. John Stuart Mill regarded the opening up of new territories as a means to provide Britain with cheaper sources of food.[3] The establishment of outposts in the hinterlands accompanied the search for raw materials and minerals. Hostile natives or foreign rivals often meant that fortifications were required too. These provided security and therefore new settlements grew up around them, as in the case of Jamestown and Fort William (Calcutta). There was also a belief that colonisation was a vital outlet for 'surplus population'. Emigration would avoid social conflict caused by unemployment and the distress of poverty.[4]

From 1783, it was thought that failure to accommodate the aspirations of colonists would lead to a repeat of the American Revolution, so Britain's dealings with its white settlers were designed to retain their loyalty and an imperial association. In part, this could be achieved through the prosperity of the colonies, and notions of imperial federation reappeared throughout the history of the Empire as a means to secure both allegiance and economic viability. Yet the liberal and democratic traditions in Britain meant that similar institutions would be established in the colonies of settlement as part of 'Greater Britain'.

The first imperial federation was established in 1643 amongst the American colonies to resist the French and Native American Indians; this was perhaps the origin of American confederation. But it was the imperial federation idea in the Durham Report of 1839 which, although less significant at the time than it is commonly thought, was to have important consequences on the issue of self-government. Following the conquest of the French province of New France (Quebec) in 1759–60 (and ceded in 1763) and the migration of loyalists after the American War of Independence, British North America was divided into Upper and Lower Canada. By the 1820s, the French-speaking province was seething against British rule and the elected assembly refused to co-operate with the appointed governor, the English dominated executive council or legislative council, which together constituted the government in Canada. In 1837, a rebellion broke out, and a smaller disturbance affected Upper

Canada where a similar dispute had developed between the elected assembly and the nominated governor.[5]

Lord Durham, who served only briefly as Governor-General and High Commissioner before resigning over the refusal of the British government to allow political prisoners to be released, wrote a report that explained the source of conflict in Canada. He argued that it was not a dispute between the elected assemblies and the appointed governors at all, which had been the cause of the rebellion in America, but a clash of the French and English. The solution, he believed, lay in the union of the two Canadas – to swamp the French minority – and the establishment of responsible, local government. Whilst matters of imperial concern such as commerce and defence would remain with Britain, all other affairs would be the responsibility of the elected assemblies and executive councillors (who would also be answerable to the assemblies). This was designed to reconcile the needs of the Empire with the aspirations of the colonists. In the nineteenth century, this was regarded as the model of good government which differentiated the British Empire from other European and ancient concepts. It suggested that once colonies reached a degree of political maturity, power could be transferred to them without jeopardising the coherence of the Empire.[6]

However, Ged Martin refutes the idea that Canada or the Empire developed along the lines of Durham's plan.[7] The Upper Canada Assembly had suggested a united legislature as early as 1822, and its implementation was largely due to Lord Russell at the Colonial Office in 1841, rather than Durham's report. Indeed, a debate on responsible government in 1848 did not conclude with the idea, as Durham had done, that the French should be outnumbered and therefore subsumed, but that there should be an attempt at partnership.[8] This was, in fact, achieved in the first ministry of that year and Lord Elgin approved a further concession (demanded by the new assembly), that of compensation for losses incurred during the 1837 rebellion. John Manning Ward believes that the change in Canada's government was the result of initiatives from Britain in the wake of constitutional reforms such as the Great Reform Act of 1832.[9] Simon C. Smith points out that Earl Grey, the Colonial Secretary of 1846, also saw the need to grant concessions lest the Canadians look to the United States for support against Britain.[10] D. W. Brogan saw the Canadian self-government case as a failure to consolidate power but 'the real claim to political wisdom of the rulers of England is that when they failed they noticed the fact and retraced their steps.'[11]

The early nineteenth century also witnessed the transformation of Australia and New Zealand. The first legislative council was established in 1823, but even when the convict system came under attack (largely because of its inefficiency and devaluing of labour), society in Australia remained divided between 'exclusives' (better-off settlers) and 'emancipists' (former convicts). The imperial authorities soon came under pressure to open the interior, beyond the designated 'Nineteen Counties', for sheep farming. By 1850, colonists had established a separate province of Victoria, and a further subdivision created Queensland in 1859. Despite the creation of South Australia by Parliament in 1834 and the Australian Colonies Act in 1850, which recognised the need for self-government, the identities of the separate provinces remained and were sometimes more clearly defined by the emigration of other Europeans, such as German Lutherans. In New Zealand, a federal constitution and a general assembly were established in 1852 and local self-government followed in 1856, along with Australia. Nevertheless, New Zealand did not become a single state until 1876 and Australia was unified only in 1901.

Despite the apparent apathy of British governments between the 1820s and 1860s towards imperialism, there was no lull in the colonisation of the settler states. In fact, the promotion of devolution was a necessary step to imperial consolidation: self-government did not mean separation.[12] The American and Canadian experience had proven the need to find 'the best means of reconciling this necessary division of powers with the need for a central directing control'. Whilst Britain 'withdrew the legions' (removing its garrisons in the self-governing colonies in 1870 to cut costs), it did not intend to abandon the settler states, even if other colonies might be described as 'millstones around our necks'. In 1865, a parliamentary committee recommended that: 'The object of our policy should be to encourage in the natives the exercise of those qualities which may render it possible for us more and more to transfer to them the administration of all the

Governments [of West Africa], with a view to our ultimate withdrawal from all'.[13] In the colonies of settlement, the process was quite different: a strengthening of the cultural and economic links that bound 'Greater Britain' together.

Motives for migration

Large numbers of people left the United Kingdom between 1815 and 1914 to settle in the colonies and in America. Marjory Harper has estimated that the figure was 22.6 million, but, of all the emigrants from England and Wales between 1861 and 1900, about half returned to Britain.[14] Of these migrants, 62 per cent travelled to the United States, compared with 19 per cent to Canada, 10.5 per cent to Australia and New Zealand, and 3.5 per cent to South Africa. Dispersed throughout the colonies, the numbers who stayed appeared to be quite small. In New Zealand, between 1860 and 1960, the emigrant population was no more than 650,000. Ged Martin and Benjamin E. Kline concluded: 'the mountains of British emigration had produced a range of distant colonial molehills' (see Table 2).[15]

The statistics of emigration raise important questions about the motives of the colonists: Did they give up their life in the United Kingdom because of hardships at home, or because of the attraction of the colonies? Why did so many return home? Journeys to the colonies took many weeks and were not without considerable risk. In 1770, a voyage to Calcutta from England could take up to nine months, depending on the

Table 2 Emigration from Great Britain by destination, 1853–1920 (selected years by 000s)[16]

	USA	Canada	Australia	South Africa	Other	Total
1861–70	441.8	90.2	184.4	12.1	24.9	753.4
1881–90	1087.4	257.4	317.3	76.1	86.0	1824.2
1901–10	837.5	793.2	218.9	269.8	213.8	2333.2
1911–20	379.3	822.0	352.6	94.1	180.8	1828.8
1853–1920	4333.4	2350.1	1704.0	671.5	674.1	9733.1

weather, and tickets could cost £580. British Columbia was five months' sailing time from Great Britain. However, steam power and screw propellers reduced journey times. The opening of the Suez Canal reduced the India voyage from 3 months to 17 days (and second-class tickets fell to £50). The steam packet service run by Cunard from Liverpool to Boston took 14 days in 1840.

Once at the destination, colonists were entering an alien world, often without any guarantees of livelihood or security. However, the 'push' factors were certainly strong enough to induce some to leave their homeland. These included industrialisation (which caused the decline of old trades and crafts, low wages and unemployment), the effects of famine in Ireland, long-term rural poverty across the United Kingdom and an expanding population. Greater distress or economic hardship in the United Kingdom created peaks of emigration during the nineteenth century. The 'pull' factors included the prospect of job opportunities, higher wages, land ownership, better standards of living and freedom from the squire.[17]

The majority of emigrants were poor or working class, and many were unskilled. Some artisans or members of the middle class emigrated, particularly where this was officially encouraged in the early colonisation of New Zealand. Most emigrants were single men or young families, which may account for the large numbers who flocked back to the United Kingdom. The costs of travel had to be found from the colonists own funds, a fact which explains the greater number of settlers going to America (which had the cheapest fares, greater chances of gaining some form of employment and higher wages), but private associations, land owners and colonial employers made contributions. In the case of Australasia, land revenues and agencies that promoted colonisation subsidised the greater cost of the passage. The government intervened only to protect passenger safety on board and to prevent fraud by establishing agencies in Britain's major ports.

The 'push' factors have encouraged some of the most persistent myths about the Empire's colonists. It was alleged that the Scottish settlers were all victims of the Highland Clearances, where unscrupulous lairds drove the peasants from the land to make way for profitable sheep farming, even though contemporaries described the enthusiasm of the colonists as a 'mania' or 'craze'.[18] Neither were the Irish colonists all starving peasants driven out by the famine. Paternalist landlords, rather than the ogres of popular myth, paid fares for the poorer peasants to offer them a fresh start, whilst serving their own interests by removing a financial burden to themselves or the rest of the rural community.[19] Government agencies paid fares too, for the same reasons. The Irish who paid their own fares were often from the middle ranks of the farmers, whilst the poorest, who could only afford the cheaper fare across the Irish Sea, travelled to Britain for work and populated London, Liverpool, Manchester and Glasgow. David Fitzpatrick, whilst illustrating the hardships faced by Irish immigrants to Australia, shows that the exodus was not always induced by the famine, but by more general hardship and a sense of opportunity.[20]

Australians were quick to distant themselves from the convict origins of their colony. They explained the convicts away as political prisoners or the victims of petty and harsh laws. Yet, whilst this did apply to a few, there were many, perhaps for understandable reasons, who had been persistent urban criminals. The reputation of a penal colony, and the expense of the passage south, certainly deterred new colonists. In 1810, there were only 1000 free settlers. To encourage land ownership, the cost of emigration was offset by the sale of Crown lands and the free passage of selected single women in 1831. Eventually, calls for the cessation of dumping convicts were acknowledged (no more were sent to New South Wales after 1840 or Van Dieman's Land/Tasmania after 1852), but Western Australia, established as a new colony in 1829, called for convicts because of labour shortages in 1850 and it continued to be sent convicted men until 1868.

Colonisation was only loosely controlled by the British government. In 1820, the numbers of settlers in Australia had increased to 30,000, divided between New South Wales and Van Dieman's Land. This created a problem because some free settlers began to occupy land as 'squatters' with no payment or legal claim. After the Napoleonic Wars, the approach to the settlement of the colonies was rather negative. The mass of demobilised servicemen, the unemployed created by the agricultural depression, and the surplus population caused by a high birth rate and falling death rate, led to a Malthusian solution:

the resettlement of unwanted people. Intervention was, however, limited. The government's indifference or indecision gave philanthropists, missionaries and speculators an opportunity to assert their own control. Edward Gibbon Wakefield opposed the policy of 'shovelling the paupers' and set up the National Colonisation Society in 1830. From 1831, the sale of lands in Australia and New Zealand was used to pay for fresh waves of settlement. The numbers leaving Britain for Australia and New Zealand rose from 68,000 between 1830 and 1840 to 378,000 in the 1880s.[21] By 1865, there were four self-governing states in Australia with a fifth under British government control, making a total of one million inhabitants. Sydney had grown to 100,000 residents and Melbourne to 200,000, and both were university cities. Part of the expansion was due to the availability of land and the profits of sheep farming, but the discovery of gold, first at Ballarat in 1851, also stimulated colonisation and migration from Melbourne and Van Dieman's Land into South Australia.

The presence of hostile natives did not arrest the migration of settlers to New Zealand. The country's early settlements were based on trade and whaling, but contact with the Maoris was also based on the traffic in liquor and firearms. However, the impact of Western diseases and 'vices' prompted missionaries to call for an end to all colonisation of the islands. Sir James Stephen at the Colonial Office (a member of the Church Missionary Society) supported this line and delayed British possession of New Zealand until 1840. Indeed, it was the prospect of French annexation (and use of the islands as another penal colony) that prompted the Colonial Office to despatch Captain William Hobson to annex the islands once an agreement had been reached with the Maoris. The Treaty of Waitangi (1840) was a landmark. Britain received the islands in return for a guarantee that the Maoris would keep possession of their lands. As protection against land speculators, the government laid down that Maoris could only sell their lands through its own agency. Colonisation followed under the control of Wakefield's selection programme. However, small-scale gold discoveries and a 'land hunger' for the fertile valleys and plains were equally important. Captain George Grey, the governor (1845–68), secured a tenuous peace by restraining the settlers and offering continued support to the Maoris. His departure, and the withdrawal of expensive British garrison troops, led to a war between colonists and Maoris that lasted (despite Grey's return) until 1872.[22]

Government support for emigration to Canada was restricted to the decade after 1815, when free passage was granted to 6640 settlers from England, Scotland and Ireland. Private enterprises, such as Highland landlords, and commercial companies, then took over.[23] Marjory Harper points out that Scottish emigration increased during the famine of the 1840s, with 10,000 arriving in Quebec between 1846 and 1856, which suggests that 'push' factors were still the most important. Canadian settlement increased from 500,000 in 1815 to three million in 1867, and grew from the eastern seaboard westwards. There was pessimism in the British government because it was felt that Canada would eventually go the same way as America and break free of the mother country. In 1837, the rebellions in French-speaking Lower Canada under Louis Papineau and Upper Canada under W. L. MacKenzie seemed to herald the beginning of the end of British rule. As in the Thirteen Colonies of the United States, the agitation began in the elected assemblies. However, the anger of the Quebecois was only directed against the English domination of the Upper House, which was appointed by the governor.

The Upper Canada dispute was similarly only directed against the Church and the oligarchy of wealthy settlers, the 'Family Compact' that owned most of the land, and not British rule. Peace was secured by making concessions. The reforms, such as the Reunion Act (1840) bringing the two colonies together, the granting of self-government (1848) and the Confederation of Canada (1867) became the model for other colonies of settlement.

The abundance of land in Canada also provided a safety valve to the land ownership disputes that had been behind the disturbances of the 1830s, but the vast distances involved created their own difficulties. Delays in exploiting the interior were similar to those in Australia. Without the communications to bring produce out to the coast, the hinterland was difficult to access, and therefore not profitable. The development of railways, however, changed the situation dramatically. British Columbia was joined to eastern Canada in 1885, and it received substantial financial support from the Canadian government for land purchase and bridge construction, but the Canadian Pacific Railway Company was also directly funded to keep it from bankruptcy in 1884, 1885 and 1897.

The development of the colonies after c.1850

Australia experienced rapid development in the nineteenth century. Wool and wheat were two of its largest exports, despite droughts and falling prices in the 1890s. Meat was exported with the development of refrigeration in 1879 and gold mining continued to attract investment. Yet, Australia itself was divided. Each state had its own tariff regulations and, with the exception of the Northern Territory, was self-governing. However, German annexations in the Pacific (Samoa and New Guinea) in 1899 and greater Japanese immigration led to talks on union. In 1900, the Commonwealth of Australia Act established a federated nation whereby each state retained a parliament, but all acknowledged that Canberra's Assembly was the primary decision-making body for national issues or foreign policy.

Political institutions were only one aspect in the formation of an Australian identity. White settlers tended to define themselves as different from other racial groups, a fact which may also explain why Australians also clung to their 'British' identity for so long. Aborigines were regarded as primitives, objects of ridicule or subjects for protection. They had no understanding of European notions of land ownership, and they were poorly armed, so their clearance from coastal areas and the gold fields was relatively easy.[24] There are only estimates of the effect European diseases had on the Aborigine population. It is thought there may have been 750,000 in 1788, but by the 1920s this figure had fallen to c.75,000. In addition, there was contempt for the Chinese labourers who flocked to the gold mines for work (and who made up 15 per cent of the workforce there). Hostility to Asians, which led to rioting in the 1880s, was institutionalised in 1905 as the 'White Australia' policy. This restricted the numbers of Asian (mainly Japanese) immigrants entering the country, but the influx of British (and other Europeans) continued, so that by 1914 there were five million 'Australians'.

Meanwhile, communications across the country continued to improve. In 1917, a railway finally connected Western Australia with the other states and a submarine cable in 1872 gave Australia faster communications with Britain. A call from London for colonial troops in 1885 and in 1899, using telegraph, demonstrated that close military ties could be maintained, and radio communications in the twentieth century seemed to reinforce rather than diminish the imperial bond. There were also the continuing ties with family and friends still in the United Kingdom. One striking feature of the national identity that did emerge was optimism about the future and a strong sense of modernity, which contrasted with the traditionalism of British institutions.

The bitter legacy of the New Zealand Wars (1846–7, 1857–69) was the expropriation of land from the Maoris by white settlers and a decline in the Maori population. From 100,000 in 1769, it fell to 42,000 in 1896. However, from 1900 the Maori population recovered. Moreover land disputes were largely settled, due in part to the fact that Maoris were given full and equal rights as early as 1867. Yet settlers had only countenanced this degree of magnanimity when they had defeated the threat the Maoris had clearly posed to them or their land interests. Such a situation never arose in South Africa, and fears of greater non-British immigration in Canada and Australia meant that racial antagonisms continued.

Economically, New Zealand's meat and butter exports were considerable, dwarfing its gold and mineral reserves. However, the country was more remarkable in the Empire for its degree of state ownership. From the outset, the colony had been reliant on central direction rather than private enterprise for its railways, banks, schools and telegraph networks. By 1900, the state was responsible for the construction of hospitals and the management of loans to build workers' houses. New Zealand's government also implemented old-age pensions, labour exchanges and compensation for employees' injuries in the workplace. In addition, this state direction was accountable to the settler population. All men were given the vote in 1889 and all women in 1893. These reforms were several decades ahead of Britain.

Canada's history in the nineteenth century was one of gradual consolidation. Four provinces had united under the British North America Act in 1867, and in 1870 the Hudson's Bay Company territories joined, from which Manitoba was created.

In 1871, British Columbia agreed to join if a railway was constructed to link it to the east coast. The extensive Canadian Pacific Railway made it possible to exploit the prairies. By 1914, the wheat crop had increased 20 times. Progress into the Canadian hinterland had been slow due to the vast distances involved. It was also because of hostile natives, but military operations, which had culminated in the suppression of the Louis Riel rebellion in 1885, meant that colonisation could proceed. As a result, the population rapidly increased. Alberta and Saskatchewan were created in 1905, although Newfoundland, the oldest colony, refused to join the rest of Canada until 1949. Indeed, despite the development of communication links, each state retained an attitude of 'frontier independence'.

Emigration from Britain continued throughout the period too. The native population of British North America from the beginning of European contact was c.350,000, but disease decimated their numbers. Once again, their thinly dispersed settlements were easily pushed aside. It was curious that institutions had emerged to cater for the separate English and French-speaking populations, but the natives had no representation. Equally, Chinese labourers, brought in to work the gold mines or to assist with railway construction, were subjected to criticism because their numbers appeared threatening and their acceptance of low wages undermined the Canadian workers. In 1911, there were 27,000 Chinese in Canada. Most were men, leading to fears of immoral behaviour and predatory advances towards white women. In 1923, lasting until 1947, all Chinese immigration was halted, whilst Japanese men were deported in 1942 during the war. In 1914, 376 Indian immigrants were prevented from disembarkation by a local campaign in Vancouver for a period of two months. The argument put forward was that even a small influx of Indians would soon swamp the 450,000 'Anglo-Saxon' British Columbians. Although a small number of Indians did settle in Canada, the case reminded Indian nationalists that membership of the British Empire did not imply free movement of labour or equality of opportunity.

Canada's decisions over immigration were one facet of her emerging separate identity, but there were other economic and political dimensions too. In Britain, there was considerable criticism of Sir John Macdonald's government when it introduced protectionism in 1878. The Canadians were uninterested in the Colonial Secretary Joseph Chamberlain's ideas of imperial preference, and had been unenthusiastic about closer imperial union. Indeed, Canada remained a federal state despite unification and so any expectations of acquiescence in centralised authority several thousand miles away in London was perhaps unrealistic.

In South Africa, British settlers were following in the footsteps of a much older and well-established Dutch migration. In the Cape, the Dutch-Afrikaner population outnumbered the British and the overall majority was of black Africans.[25] The greater numbers and density of Africans encouraged them to resist white settler encroachments on their land in a series of Cape Frontier Wars. From 1820, when British settlers arrived in larger numbers and missionaries' influence increased, slavery in the Cape was gradually eroded in favour of the wage–labour exchange. This process was not entirely humanitarian, since the Khoikhoi people had been dispossessed of their land and thus took up the employment offered for survival. However, the abolition of slavery in the colonies (1833) announced a greater liberalisation of relations between whites and blacks in the Cape, a fact which prompted 15,000 Afrikaner *Voortrekkers* to embark on the Great Trek into the interior, away from British rule (1834–40). There, white Afrikaners employed black Africans in the Boer Republics in an unequal relationship lasting until the end of the South African War in 1902. One Boer woman wrote that to place 'Hottentots and Kaffirs' on 'an equal footing with Christians was contrary to the laws of God and the natural distinction of race and religion'.[26]

Relations between the British and Boers of the interior were rarely cordial. Although the British recognised the sovereignty of the two republics, the Boers still viewed the British with suspicion. In particular, the Boers grew uneasy about British expansion. In Natal, a British colony established in 1843, white settlers were able to take advantage of land emptied by the Zulu expansion, the *Mfecane*. The gradual return of Africans, and an influx of Indian labour, threatened white control of the region. As a result, reserved areas were established for non-whites, whilst any threats, such as the Zulu kingdom to the north, were crushed ruthlessly in colonial wars.

Development and prosperity in the Cape made it the most powerful of all the states in southern Africa. New railways linked the interior to the coast, but its greatest resource was the diamond mining of Kimberley. The gems were first discovered in 1867 and Britain acquired the land (Griqualand West) to forestall any Boer claim; 25,000 immigrants came to work the mines, black migrants poured in too, and local agriculture was stimulated by the increased demand. The economic growth was matched by new political aspirations. In 1854, in Cape Colony the franchise was based on property qualifications, not race. In 1877, there was discussion of how all of South Africa might be brought together in a confederation which mirrored the Canadian model. However, despite a brief British takeover of the Transvaal between 1877 and 1881, the Boers rebelled and defeated British forces in a short, but humiliating campaign. Transvaal was guaranteed its sovereignty, including its own jurisdiction over native affairs, subject to a vague 'British suzerainty'. The discovery of gold on the Witwatersrand in 1886 then changed everything. By 1898, the Transvaal had become the largest single producer of gold in the world, and the massive influx of migrant workers, or *Uitlanders*, threatened to outnumber the Boers. As a result, foreign workers were denied political rights in the republic. Cecil Rhodes, the diamond and gold magnate, and Alfred Milner, the British High Commissioner, used this as a lever against the Transvaal government and hoped to gain control of the republics and, as a result, of the whole subcontinent.

After the South African War (1899–1902) and the defeat of the Boers, Milner believed that the region would not be safely 'British' until the English-speaking whites outnumbered the Afrikaners. He hoped that rapid economic reconstruction and an English education system, under the direction of his young, mainly Oxford graduate 'Kindergarten', would turn South Africa into a thoroughly British colony. However, Milner's attempts to settle soldiers on the land, and attract new immigrants, failed. Better opportunities simply existed elsewhere.[27] In addition, a cut in black workers' wages by the mine owners after the war (a decision that stemmed from a concern that after the war profits would remain depressed) deterred African workers from returning.[28] The resulting chronic shortage of labour prompted an influx of Chinese workers on short-term contracts. The move was partly designed to encourage the return of black labourers, but it caused so much fear amongst the white workers, especially the poorer *bywoners*, that colour bars were erected for certain jobs.

However, the greatest disappointment to blacks was the Native Affairs Commission of 1905. Expecting the extension of the franchise, blacks found that this would be at the discretion of the self-governing ex-republics. Land was not redistributed, but returned to the Boer owners (where they had survived). Wages too remained low.[29] Moreover, blacks were increasingly segregated from white populations, including the settlements of the Cape from 1901. The British plan was to accommodate the Boers, reconstruct the country economically and forge the unity between Boers and British they had envisaged as early as 1877. When the draft Bill of Union was proposed, a delegation led by former Cape Premier W. P. Schreiner opposed it, but was unable to avert the march towards unification which had cost the British so much.

In Natal, a colony whose settler population was acutely conscious that it was outnumbered by non-white peoples, laws restricted blacks and Indian migrants. The laws for Indians were designed to suppress their competition and encourage their departure, which enraged the young Gandhi who worked in Natal as a lawyer. The Zulu Bambata disturbances in 1905–6 elicited a harsh response from the Natal authorities, but the British protest (led by Lord Elgin) was regarded as 'interference'. The Natal government resigned and ripples of disquiet spread to the other colonies of settlement. When the Natal government arrested Dinuzulu, the leader of the Zulus, W. P. Schreiner defended him at his trial.[30] Schreiner lost, and the British considered reasserting direct control to replace the authorities of Natal, but it was clear that this would not be accepted.

The Union of South Africa offered another solution. The moderating influence of the Cape, it was thought, and the findings of the Native Affairs Commission would temper Natal's position. But the Union of South Africa threatened to overwhelm Natal with an Afrikaner-dominated assembly, a fact which prompted Natalians to seek a degree of autonomy. In 1910, they signed a covenant against incorporation which predated the Ulster protest against incorporation into a devolved Ireland by two years. They also protested at proposals to create a South African flag in 1926, and maintained a distinct identity within the Union of South Africa throughout the period, even though their laws of racial segregation were adopted throughout the country. The reaction of settlers in Natal to British ideas of how natives should be treated highlighted the problems of central control and self-government. A similar situation arose in East Africa where, once again, the settlers felt outnumbered by black Africans but claimed to own the land. Colonel James Sadler, the British Governor of Kenya, who protested at the harsh treatment of natives was mobbed by angry settlers in 1908.[31]

Migrant labour within the Empire

In 1815, West Indies plantations were still worked by slaves, even though the trade had been abolished in 1807. Natural increase meant that fresh imports were not required in Jamaica and Barbados, whilst Mauritius in the Indian Ocean, which was acquired during the Napoleonic Wars, provided a labour force of slaves that had previously served the French. The abolition of all slavery in the colonies in 1833 and then the introduction of apprenticeship converted former slaves into wage labourers, but the lack of available land in the smaller islands or of alternative employment meant that they continued to work on the planta-tions. On the larger islands, Jamaica, Trinidad and mainland British Guiana, former slaves took up land as small peasant farm-ers and the dwindling plantation workforce was able to demand higher wages. Sierra Leone, the colony for former slaves either rescued by the Royal Navy or freed after the American War of Independence, was also a recruiting ground for free Africans, but only 36,000 were attracted to work in the West Indies in the 20 years after abolition.

The solution to the labour shortages of the plantations was sought in indentured labourers from India. Rural migrants, who had left the land in search of work or to escape from famine, were contracted to work beyond the *kalsa pani* (the Indian Ocean), despite the fact that this placed their caste in jeopardy. Since the labourer was unable to pay for the passage, contractors or the government of India obtained a guarantee that the contract would last for five years. In return, the labourer would be paid and his passage, work and return would be supervised by the government. Indentured workers had the option of remaining in the place of work once the contract had expired. Mauritius recruited indentured Indians from 1834, British Guiana from 1838, Trinidad and Jamaica from 1845. Natal received workers in 1861, Fiji in 1879 and in 1896. Indians were sent to work on the East African railways. Life was tough and the work was of a hard physical nature. There were complaints that some indentured workers had been fooled into thinking their lot would be better, but some profited from their five-year terms. Thousands settled in the new lands and thriving Asian communities emerged in Natal, the West Indies, East Africa and Malaya.

Not all labour was indentured. 'Free' Indians offered their labour or their trades in short-term contracts: tea plantations in Ceylon provided seasonal work, Burmese rice mills and Malayan rubber plantations employed unskilled labourers, and the South-East Asian cities offered enormous potential for skilful merchants. Although the majority of Indian migrants returned to India, some stayed, so that the Indian population of Malaya numbered 630,000 in 1930. Alongside the Indian migrants were some 2.8 million Chinese, the result of a much longer period of immigration that was not directed by the British. Waves of Chinese had arrived, 'pushed' by civil war and poverty in China or 'pulled' by the prospects of work and profit in South-East Asia. Singapore was a particular magnet: over 500,000 arrived between 1900 and 1911. Those who were specifically employed by the British were recruited in the British entrepôts on the Chinese coast. However, despite the vast numbers who migrated into the Empire, the usual pattern was for male Chinese to work for relatively short periods and then return to China.

Apart from the postings of colonial officials and soldiers, there were other white settlers caught up in the mass movement of populations. Children were targets of the philanthropists who favoured emigration for its moral benefits. In an age where urban life was associated with physical and moral illness, the rural life of the colonies was regarded as a restorative for British orphans. It was hoped they would become: 'The bricks with which the Empire would be built'.[32] Thomas Barnado's organisation sent 31,031 children overseas between 1870 and 1914 (the majority to Canada). Many became agricultural workers and domestic servants.

Undoubtedly, individual experiences of migration were often harsh. Encouraged if not actually driven from their homelands, the settlers frequently found the colonies dangerous, unhealthy and remote. Yet, for the indigenous populations the experience could be even worse. Disease, war against technologically superior forces or the loss of lands could be catastrophic to rural communities. Survival sometimes became dependent on finding employment within the settlers' industries. However, the colonies of settlement benefited considerably from British support. Investment flowed in (66 per cent of total investment was British between c.1870 and 1914), loans could be raised at advantageous rates of interest in the City of London, the government offered bonds to investors, subsidised shipping and telegraph rates and paid for the colonies' defence. They were also granted self-government. Nevertheless, non-white migrants were unequal partners in the colonies, even suffering the indignities of exclusion and regulation. This stemmed from both an economic fear that whites might be undermined by cheap 'native' labour, but also from concerns to preserve and reinforce their separate identity.

In the long term, the legacy of colonisation has not been entirely negative. Mixed societies based on the ethics of Christianity, the rule of law and free enterprise have flourished. The legacy of British education, science and technology are evident. The former colonies of settlement model their political systems on British democratic institutions, with free elections, universal suffrage, secret ballots and freedom of assembly and expression. The British conception of property and its protection has been transferred even to the descendants of indigenous populations who claim 'ownership' of the land. The close connection between the former colonies and Britain continues, even with the United States through a poorly defined, but identifiable 'special relationship'. In this sense, the advocates of colonisation achieved their aim of spreading the British people and their values overseas – or perhaps it is simply that one can identify an independent, but parallel trajectory with Britain's own.

6

Collaboration and resistance: was the Empire held by coercion or co-operation?

Imperialism and coercion

In 1876, Lord Salisbury remarked 'it is the nakedness of the sword on which we really rely'.[1] One recurrent question about the British Empire is whether it was acquired or held by force, or whether it was built and sustained through the collaboration of indigenous peoples and by diplomatic accommodation with existing native elites. There can be little doubt that an important element of British imperialism, both in the expansion of the Empire and in its consolidation, was the part played by 'the sword'. The deployment of troops in 1854 indicates this: of the 40,043-strong British Army, there were 39,754 in the colonies and 29,208 in India. Nevertheless, the garrisons were relatively small. To cover the vast stretches of territory of the Empire, there was, in fact, only one regular soldier for every 53 square miles. There were several reasons for this spartan coverage. First, the cost of large garrisons would negate the value of the colony in question. Second, the British often possessed a marked advantage in weaponry, transport and medicine, which enabled them to make rapid and effective movements against native forces. A decisive engagement was the preferred policy, to leave a 'lasting impression' and to prevent desultory guerrilla resistance.

An example of this can be found in Kenya in 1905. Anger against the introduction of taxation and the prospect of being confined to a 450,000-acre reservation sparked a revolt amongst the nomadic Nandi.[2] This led to a 'pacification' or punitive expedition under Sir James Sadler. A small field force, armed with ten Maxim machine guns, set out against the 25,000 strong Nandi and inflicted heavy casualties; 1117 were killed, including the *Laibon* (spiritual leader). In addition, 4956 huts and stores were destroyed, 16,000 cattle and 36,000 sheep and goats were confiscated. A second expedition was then mounted against the Embu, and 407 were killed for the loss of two. Finally, the Kisii were pacified, but the loss of life was small because the presence of the Maxim guns deterred further resistance.

However, the forces at the disposal of an imperial governor were always the smallest that could still offer an impression of security. It was the prestige and presence of imperial forces which were as important as actual coercion. Ronald Robinson noted that: 'Reinforcement was usually sent with reluctance, the need for it regarded as a sign of administrative incompetence. Coercion was expensive and counter-productive except in an emergency, and everyone knew that no amount of force could hold down indigenous politics for long.'[3]

More typically, the British preferred to use the minimum of force to maintain order. In 1939, Raymond Vernede as the District Magistrate of Benares was sent with a detachment of troops to quell rioting and looting that had broken out. A vast crowd of Muslims was engaged in the destruction of the houses of Hindu weavers, but one shot dispersed the assembly, and on a subsequent occasion, the death of one of the rioters pacified the entire city.[4] The authority of whites was such that even the presence of a 'sahib' could deter or prevent violence. F. C. Hart, who served with the Special Branch, used to dump Congress activists, who were trying to get a gaol sentence as a mark of prestige, naked by the roadside rather than resort to violence. Humiliation was a potent weapon against women demonstrators too. Unable to manhandle women who had blocked a road, fire hoses drenched them and turned their saris see-through. In another example, Charles Wright, an NCO in the Black Watch, recorded: 'When the crowd were getting very angry and very unruly and pressing up against us, we would ease them back by gently dropping the butts of our rifles on their toes.'[5] Ronald Hyam believed that British authority was the key factor: 'Force was the acknowledged basis of British rule; but it was a force tempered with an ideal of justice and mitigated by the propagation of the idea that all were enfolded in the beneficent arms of the Great White Queen. . . .'[6] Stephen Bentley of the Seaforth Highlanders felt that British rule was tolerated in India simply because the army was segregated, confined to barracks and almost 'invisible'.[7]

There were isolated acts of violence, the most notorious being the beating, and subsequent death of an Indian cook by a group of the 9th Lancers in 1902, which earned the censure of the Viceroy, Lord Curzon.[8] Curzon felt that 'racial pride and the undisciplined passions of the inferior class of Englishmen' were a danger to the survival of British rule in India.[9] Lord Cromer felt that 'uncontrolled militarism and commercial egoism' were the two main enemies of imperial rule.[10] In the twentieth century, George Orwell said that soldiers and police, like he, did what the 'natives' expected of them; 'He wears a mask, and his face grows to fit it . . . A sahib has got to act like a sahib . . . you could not hold down a subject empire with troops infected with notions of class solidarity.'[11] Nevertheless, there was a degree of empathy between British soldiers and the lower castes, and particularly (but for quite different reasons) with Gurkhas.[12]

When internal security operations were conducted, more often than not locally recruited forces led by British officers carried them out.[13] They were usually small in number: the Nigeria Regiment of the West Africa Frontier Force was 5000 strong in peacetime; the King's African Rifles in East Africa numbered just 3000 in 1930. The only exception to this was the Indian Army, which stood at 133,663 in 1895 and which grew to one million during the Great War.[14] Lord Salisbury once described India as: 'An English barrack in the Oriental seas' and British politicians generally looked upon India, according to David French, as 'an almost inexhaustible imperial reserve, largely because its numbers were not voted by Parliament, [and] because its cost, and the cost of British troops stationed in India, were met by Indian tax-payers.'[15]

The relatively small number of forces and their infrequent deployment suggest that force was only one dimension of imperial rule. Indeed, the British success in recruiting local soldiers points towards the idea that participation in the Empire carried some benefit and it was not maintained by oppression. Recruitment for the imperial armies was certainly regarded as vital to the future of British rule.[16] Colonial troops were not only less expensive than British soldiers, but they were often more suited to service in the tropics.

The British offered a range of inducements to the potential recruit: pay was obviously an attractive feature, but population growth, which put pressure on the availability of land (leading to rural poverty), might also drive young men to military service. In India, certain castes believed it was a clan duty to serve as soldiers, and having never experienced a national, central or sovereign authority, service to a foreign ruler or as a mercenary was not considered unusual. Amongst the Nepalese, for example, even changing sides had been widespread.[17] David Omissi points out that generally in peacetime, enlistment had little to do with loyalty to the Raj.[18] However, in times of crisis, such as the war scare with Russia in 1885 and at the outbreak of war in 1914, volunteers came forward in much greater numbers than before.[19] Sometimes, the best recruiters were recently enlisted young soldiers who returned to their villages better fed, fitter through more exercise and brimming with improved self-esteem. Others felt that there was an obligation to serve the 'Sircar' because they had all 'taken his salt' or lived under his protection.[20] Thus, for many, military service was a result of tradition and mutual respect.

Collaboration or 'sub-imperialism'?

Ronald Robinson argued that imperialism could only really be explained through collaboration. Indeed, he believed it was a function of the politics of the non-European world.[21] In other words, some states were more prone to a European takeover, or collaboration with Europeans, because of their internal weaknesses. The less 'European' their economy, the more likely it was that there would be some European intervention. Robinson stated that imperialism and collaboration were not the result of European powers being imperialistic at all times, but being so in some places and in different periods. These periodic interventions were themselves dependent on the internal political or socio-economic condition of the satellite state.[22]

This theory is one based on the relative strengths between Europeans and the non-Europeans. It is convincing if applied in general terms to the gradual British expansion in India in the eighteenth century, or to African states in the late nineteenth. However, it does perhaps draw too great a distinction between the coloniser and the colonised. Armies, administration, commerce and consumerism were all vital components of imperialism, and there is ample evidence of mutual support. Responses to the British were rarely clear-cut: some were willing collaborators, some mercenaries, and others merely preserved the Empire by not actually resisting it. However, in so far as Robinson's theory emphasises the interconnected and interdependent nature of the Empire, it does have considerable value.

Collaboration, without its pejorative connotations, was the most typical aspect of British imperialism. Trading and consumerism are the obvious examples. Of course, it might be said that consumerism was part of the development of world capitalism rather than British imperialism. Nevertheless, whatever the cause, Toyin Falola notes that in South Africa there were benefits for some consumers in the colonial economy. Larger political units, caused by the creation of colonial borders, increased the volume of trade. Large farms and those oriented for export certainly prospered. Africa, like India, became less reliant on imported textiles as machinery (often bought from Britain) made it possible to produce its own. Other imports increased as elites, and those others who could afford it, developed a taste for British goods. Many Africans made use of British transport systems, wore European style clothes and adopted British customs, manners and language.[23]

However, Falola argues that this consumerism was not all positive. Since taxation had to be paid in money, African farmers were forced to grow and sell. Cash cropping could earn greater profit, so old diversified structures atrophied and, in some areas, food production was abandoned altogether. As old land tenure systems were disrupted, farmers were compelled to sell up and seek new employment. Whilst many historians have asserted that British imperialism was undoubtedly to blame, P. J. Marshall points out that the picture is unclear. He wrote: 'Economic change, like the evolution of cultures, involves a process of interaction.'[24] Some colonies had abundant resources, land and manpower, others did not. The British introduced commercial crops – sisal, jute, tea, coffee, cocoa and cotton – purely for the export market. These were a catalyst to modernisation, which brought both costs and benefits to imperial subjects.

Acquiescence in colonial rule may have been the only rational response to the overwhelming power of the West. Collaboration was the result of opportunism, and the chance for political prestige or material gain could be an irresistible attraction. This could conveniently coincide with imperial needs. When the numbers of British administrators available was small, existing elites were retained, and if none were available, then new ones could be created and employed under a policy of 'Trusteeship'. Frederick Lugard exercised authority over Nigerians using local chiefs. Similarly, the sultans of the Malay States, the Fulani emirs and the Indian princes retained their powers subject to British supervision. On the North-West Frontier of India, the Afridi tribesmen who lived astride the strategic Khyber Pass had a system of democratic village councils or *Jirgas*, which did not fit the hierarchical requirements of the British. The solution was to despatch 'Politicals', British officers of the Political Department, who would work alongside, protect, issue subsidies to and represent the interests of the tribesmen.[25] Elsewhere, *Arbabs*, middle-men, were often appointed. In southern Nigeria, as with the Kikuyu of East Africa, the British promoted individuals as intermediaries to make the administration work.

The British also had their preferences. In Nigeria, the Hausa people were preferred to the more Westernised and settled coastal inhabitants. The Malay natives were favoured over the immigrant Chinese Malays. There was a general preference for the peasant over the urban inhabitant, the educated clerk or even the prince. Nomads were regarded as more romantic than the wage labourers, and warriors and hill men were felt to be the closest in spirit to the British themselves.

British attempts to recruit collaborators were limited by the peoples of the Empire, even when economic conditions seemed to favour participation. When 1000 Punjabis were recruited in 1863 to form a pioneer unit of 'Sappers and Miners' and were shipped to Ceylon, they found that they were, in fact, being employed as labourers and made to break stones for road building rather than doing military work. The men refused to do the work and were eventually all sent back to the Punjab. Similarly, in 1901, an attempt to raise a regiment of Coorgs from south

India failed, even though they faced economic hardship and were descended from a 'warrior tradition'. Their desire to remain close to their homelands, their wish to remain in agriculture, and their patrilineal joint-family structure (which kept land holdings together) proved too strong to overcome.[26]

Much has been written on the sense of superiority that the British had over the Africans and Asians in the Empire, and explanations have focused on a general, if understated acceptance of Social Darwinism and racial eugenics. Curiously, the British themselves stressed that they were performing a service to the people they were responsible for. This expressed paternalism was apparently 'imposed' by the British on the peoples of the colonies. Individual British officials were given wide responsibilities and were inculcated with a feeling that they were superior because they had inherited custody of an Empire of enormous scale and age.

However, these practices were sometimes accepted by non-Europeans because they fitted local norms of authority and government. For example, in India there were older traditions stretching back to the days of the Mughals, where it was considered a right to petition the local official to redress grievances. The *Ma-Bap* principle, an expectation that those in authority should behave as the mother and father of the people, according to Charles Allen, 'drew its authority from an Indian initiative, [but] it was reinforced by the public school mentality which required the school prefect to look after those under him'.[27] The obsession with fulfilling one's duty ran throughout the civil authorities across the Empire. Knowledge of local practices and protocol was crucial during negotiations or in the administration of justice, and mastery of language was an important part of gaining trust. An acceptance of *Dastur*, or custom, was not a decision made by the British, but rather it was the acceptance of a *fait accompli*. It was this ability to compromise, perhaps, which accounts for the longevity of the Empire.

Paternalism in colonial forces like the Indian Army was also a mark of respect. Claude Auchinleck noted: 'There was no question of ordering them about. They were Yeomen really and that made all the difference.'[28] There were frequent references to the pride British officers had in their men and they described the soldiers as 'the best in the world', 'physically as fine a race of men as the world can produce', with 'wonderful spirit'. Loyalty to the regiment was reinforced through uniform and symbolism, and devotion to commanders was personalised, even when after the Mutiny regiments were made up of companies from different religions.[29]

Indian troops, like many others across the Empire, were categorised on the basis of physique, courage and loyalty. The explanation for this endless categorisation has often been seen as a desire to 'divide and rule', or a plan to pacify by inculcating a sense of inferiority. However, the evidence for an imperial plan is based on a selective interpretation of imperial epistemology and it seems that the British responses were, in fact, eminently practical. For example, Indian rulers or landowners who subjected their peasants to tyranny were removed. This was partly because the British thought of themselves as protectors, favouring the underdog, but also because a failure to do anything about it would foment unrest. The Western-educated imperial subject was a threat since they were more likely to challenge British authoritarianism and point out the contrast to their own democratic institutions at home. The British administrators embraced the paternalism of imperial rule because it gave them freedom from the red tape of modern states. Urban and modern life was associated with degeneracy in the late nineteenth century, or with bureaucracy and state intervention in the twentieth. The peasant, the hillman and the warrior represented a natural, raw, elemental community. They were thought to be unsullied by the luxuries of modernity, stoic, obedient and brave. A direct, personalised rule fit more neatly with the chivalric, paternal model to which the British aspired.

Tapan Raychaudhuri argued that 'the forces of law and order were almost invariably deployed in favour of the oppressor' in India, but cites only police abuses and the expense of the legal system as evidence, without asking who the forces of 'oppression' were.[30] However, he acknowledges that some did benefit from the Raj: the princes and big landlords were 'secure in their possessions and privileges' as were professional classes who had enjoyed a Western education. The peasant, though, was 'enmeshed in ruinous law suits', became indebted to moneylenders and was condemned to poverty. In fact, some access to resources and power was necessary to ensure stable government and the welfare of Indians was important where it did not conflict with British interests, but Raychaudhuri maintains, somewhat vaguely, that the Muslim–Hindu rivalry was a 'perception' that was important in the allocation of resources. By contrast, A. J. Stockwell notes that the creation of greater regional polities was to overcome fragmented societies that 'are almost impossible to govern'.[31] Consolidation, therefore, rather than division was designed to 'improve administrative efficiency, economic development and security'.

However, these apparently contradictory interpretations could be resolved if one considers that the aims of the coloniser and colonised coincided. For example, Sikhs and Punjabi Muslims were recruited as policemen for service in Hong Kong, Perak and the Straits Settlements, in Nyasaland, Kenya, Uganda, East Africa and Somaliland. The motive for the men to enlist was partly financial, but it was also based on the prospect of improved social status. The British needed cheap labour, and felt that Sikhs and Muslim Punjabis were loyal and trustworthy. It was these groups that had assisted the British during the Indian Mutiny, and were therefore employed as subordinate partners in imperial rule. The use of Indians across the Empire was itself a symbol of Britain's 'success': the Empire appeared to function like a great machine across the entire globe. The collaborating forces of law and order would have no compunction about firing on rebels from the indigenous population, and they were therefore part of the worldwide imperial fabric.

Ronald Robinson concluded that the idea that the British had sought to 'divide and rule' was misleading because it took no account of how the British involved a number of social groups: 'The secret of a successful system, from a European standpoint, lay in this variety of choice and combination. It is often said that this was a policy of divide and rule. More truly, rule was possible because its subjects were socially divided and could not unite.'[32]

Resistance

Overawed by British power, traditional and pre-colonial symbols seemed to take on a new potency. Despite the decay and collapse of the Mughal dynasty in India in the eighteenth century, the

Mutineers of 1857, drawing on religious principles, flocked to the ancient capital Delhi and proclaimed the ageing last dynast, Bahadur Shah, their leader. Similarly, the Ndebele were inspired by a revival of the oracular cult of Mlimo (or Mwari) in 1896, which promised that the white man's bullets would turn to water. A religious zeal characterised the massacre of all 200 white men, women and children in the outlying areas of Matabeleland.[33] Captive wounded were mutilated as a purging act of revenge. Within weeks the rising was crushed, but then the Shona rose up, similarly inspired by spirit mediums promising immunity from bullets. As in the Indian Mutiny, the attack on women and children and the mutilation of the dead produced totally unrestrained reprisals. When the warriors turned to flee from engagements, they were shot down in large numbers. Prisoners were often executed summarily.

In the nineteenth century, the British believed that resistance to the Empire was not nationalist and sustained, but tribal and sporadic. Nationalist movements, where they did exist, were often seen as small, unrepresentative minorities with no connection to the traditional authorities that were direct descendants of the pre-colonial order. The groups that resisted the imposition of British rule were considered 'savages' standing in the way of progress, commerce and civilisation. Opposition to established rule was regarded as rebellion, mutiny or banditry. Despite the differences in nomenclature and style of resistance, there were often similarities in the causes. In New Zealand from the 1840s, the loss of land to settlers prompted armed retaliation by the Maoris. In southern Africa, frequent clashes with the Xhosa, then with the Zulus, Mashona and Matabele also accompanied the conquest of land. Threats to traditional ways of life or to religion also contributed to the resistance of the Pathans of the North-West Frontier of India, the Sudanese and the Burmese. For example, in 1890 the Wazirs of the Zhob Valley attacked road builders and their escorts since they felt a new road would threaten the security of their mountain communities. The Sudanese believed that the war against the British in 1896–98 was a *jihad* (holy war).[34] In Burma, the deposing of King Thebaw of the Konbaung dynasty in 1885 was thought to have ended a Buddhist world epoch, so *Pongyi* (Buddhist monks) were instrumental in fostering rural rebellion for five years.

Resistance could be provoked by a great variety of factors. The invasion of the lands of a warrior society like the Zulus in 1879 quite naturally produced a military response.[35] Natural disasters, such as famine through crop failure or the ravages of locusts in 1890–5 and rinderpest in 1896–98 in Rhodesia could also provoke rioting and unrest.[36] New sources of dispute stemming from taxes (such as the hut tax on the Matabele) or industrialised working patterns converted these grievances into violence. In southern Africa, unionisation of Africans was banned and workplace discipline tended to reinforce obedience. However, after the South African War, withdrawal of labour by Africans was more effective than striking or violence as a form of protest. Wages were gradually increased to return to pre-war levels to attract labourers back to the mines of the Rand.[37]

The inherent consciousness of 'alien rule' meant that passive forms of resistance were often understated but typical. For Indian men, the preservation of culture within their home life and the seclusion in *purdah* of their womenfolk were symbolic of an India beyond the reach of the British. Passive resistance, often with female motifs, was increasingly popular in India after the First World War. Religions or religious practices within Christianity were also forms of more passive resistance. When Bishop Samuel Ajayi Crowther was removed from the episcopate of the Niger Delta in 1891 for his sympathy with greater Africanisation of the leadership of the Church Missionary Society missions, James 'Holy' Johnson led a movement of protest.[38] There had already been a move towards a more 'Ethiopian' style of charismatic worship. The Niger Delta was then further divided by the breaking away of the Bethel African Church in 1901, whilst a number of radical branches of Christianity and syncretistic Independent churches emerged – usually based on a charismatic leader – in central and southern Africa in the twentieth century. These churches could be the springboards for political action. In 1915, John Chilebwe, who had built up a church following in Nyasaland, launched a rebellion against the British. In India, Hindu revivalists such as Raja Rammohun Roy sought to restore confidence in Indian society through organisations like Brahmo Samaj (1856).[39] Muslims scholars challenged the Protestant missionaries with critical Catholic texts from the West, and promoted the cause of political reform at the same time.

In the twentieth century, there was some continuity with the movements of resistance of the nineteenth century. Land ownership continued to be a source of friction in African colonies, particularly as populations grew.[40] In Burma, the economic depression of the 1930s prompted the protests of Saya San, a Buddhist monk who preached a revival of the monarchical order and provoked a rebellion in the Irradwaddy delta. The 'Mad' Mullah of Powindah who led the Mahsuds from 1898–1913 (and whom Kitchener labelled the 'Pestilential priest') and the Fakir of Ipi who roused the Waziris to rebellion in 1936 and 1938–9 (and continued to be a thorn in the side of the Punjab authorities until his death in 1960) also represented continuity in Islamic resistance.[41]

Intellectuals resisted the Empire in their writings, and often by their actions too. Bhikhaiji Rustom Cama, a Parsi from Bombay, was a reformer like her husband. At the international socialist conference of 1907, she announced that the aspiration of the Hindus of India was *swaraj*, self-government. During the Bengal partition controversy, reformers urged all Indians to boycott British goods and services, in favour of *swadeshi* (home produced) materials: a policy later adopted by Gandhi.[42] Boycotting had already been a feature of the Irish nationalist struggles for self-government and land ownership, and there were similarities between Irish and Indian nationalism. The Irish nationalists had even greater sympathy for Afrikanerdom. Irish volunteers fought for the Boers in the South African War, maintaining an older mercenary tradition, and they took up their cause in Westminster. James Connolly proposed the seizure of Dublin Castle during the war and some of the 1916 Easter rebels were veterans of the fighting in the Transvaal. The guerrilla warfare of the South African War was perhaps the harbinger of resistance operations in the twentieth century.

Terence Ranger argued that the nineteenth-century resistance groups were directly related to the modern nationalist movements of the mid-twentieth century – undergoing several stages of development, but still recognisably traditional in nature. However, this view has been challenged. Ronald Robinson argued that it was not the modern nationalist movements that were seen as a threat, but their potential effect on the broader masses of the population: 'In the Sudan, as in India and elsewhere in black Africa, it was not the radical modern elite as such that the colonial rulers feared. It was rather the combination of these urban malcontents with populist movements among rural peasantry and tribes through an alliance between modern urban, and rural traditional elites.'[43] Moreover, these Western educated nationalists owed little to traditional forms of resistance. Their aim was simply to prise the old elites and their supporters away from collaboration. Their success was their ability to damage the old forms of collaboration. Robinson noted: 'Necessarily in pre-industrial societies, [collaborators] were preponderantly neotraditionalist religious, social and ethnic units . . . all the national movements that won independence were more or less functions of neotraditional politics organised in the form of modern political parties. Each party was essentially a confederation of neotraditional local ethnic, religious and status interests, managed by a small modern elite.'[44] Unfortunately, many of these coalitions fell apart as soon as the imperial authority passed away. Yet the irony remains. Many of the nationalists were educated through collaboration with a Western system, and some even studied in Britain. The adoption of Western forms of protest and opposition provided them with the means to rid themselves of colonial rule.

Collaboration and resistance: conclusions

Overall, many non-European peoples chose to resist imperialism, despite the odds against them. Time and again challenges to traditional ways of life characterised their motives. However, resistance to the British was frequently made more difficult by divisions within pre-colonial societies. In addition, as Jeremy Black points out, since the British defined resistance in European terms, their struggle was regarded as 'rebellion' and was 'suppressed' rather than following the patterns of conventional warfare, where terms might be offered to the defeated side.[45] Resistance was offered at various points of European contact, sometimes initially as the British took over, and sometimes when the enormity of British influence began to make itself apparent. This would account for the lull between, for example, the Chinese Wars (1839–42, 1858–60) which were directed by the

Chinese governments, and the so-called Boxer Rebellion (1900) which enjoyed much more support from the lower classes.

However, resistance, in all its forms, was only part of the response to British imperialism. Consumerism, the co-operation of political elites, the enlistment of soldiers and policemen, and the acceptance of wage labour, all contributed to the survival, indeed the flourishing, of the British Empire. This collaboration created winners and losers, but the beneficiaries were not exclusively British. Whilst there was a disparity of benefits and losses, it is clear that some took advantage of the presence of Europeans to pursue their own agendas of sub-imperialism, or alternative methods of resistance.

7 Colonial discourse: was there an ideology of imperialism?

The language of power

Dissatisfied with the standard approaches to the history of the British Empire, a number of academics have attempted to uncover the reality of imperialism through its texts or 'discourse'. The foundation of the new approach was an attack on the premise that, using the exercise of reason, one might discover universal truths about the human condition.[1] Instead, it was proposed that *all* knowledge is relative, and that there is no objective truth.[2] Indeed, there was a feeling that what was portrayed as 'truth' was often little more than a European interpretation of the world, which was made convincing by a series of 'constructions' (such as literary devices, language or vocabulary). Moreover, there was, it seemed, a hidden agenda: the inventions of these truths was motivated by a desire to construct power positions over other peoples.

When Europeans spoke of 'natives', it conjured up a range of other terms associated with that word: savage, tribal, mob behaviour, ill-educated, irrational, child-like, criminal, excessively sexual, filthy, amoral and irreligious.[3] The whole European discourse about the rest of the world seemed to be demeaning and critical. Non-Europeans were 'problematised', their views were relegated or ignored. In some cases, they even lost their identity, being referred to by names the Europeans had themselves invented.

Eric Hobsbawm and Terence Ranger argued that many institutions and protocols had been invented in Europe and were transferred to the colonies. The new approach suggested that as a result, natives were stripped of the capacity for reform, benevolence or progress.[4] Moreover, according to Michel Foucault, Western academic writing on imperialism tended to seal off its views from criticism.[5] Its authorisation, through bibliographies, footnotes and vocabulary, tended to be self-referential. Those who examined 'colonial discourse' revealed a language of power that served imperialism. Subject races were categorised and subcategorised, and their past was written for them by the Europeans.

A particularly significant development occurred with the publication of Edward Said's path-breaking *Orientalism* (1978).[6] Said brought together existing ideas on colonial discourse, with work on literary theory and the arguments of Foucault, to accuse Western liberal historians of perpetuating the imperialist paradigm. Using Jacques Derrida's technique of the 'deconstruction' of texts, Said showed that the European portrayal of Islam and the 'Orient' was an invention which bore no resemblance to the real Middle East.[7] Most startling was Said's accusation that the Enlightenment's methodology of reason occurred at precisely the moment of imperial expansion and served the imperialist idea: the Enlightenment was, essentially, the vehicle for oppression. Said argued that, throughout Western history, Europe had portrayed the Oriental as the 'Other', the very antithesis of the virtues of the West. Moreover, the Western model of development and modernisation was assumed to be the only path of progress, which led to assumptions that the Orient was 'backward'. The West, in fact, defined itself by reference to others as inferior.

Post-colonial theory

Said's work spawned a host of followers who sought to extend his ideas into more detailed aspects of imperialism. Conscious of the need to reject the existing vocabulary, loaded as it was with 'imperialist' connotations, a new language was borrowed from literary critical circles. Hence, the imperialist discourse became a 'paradigm' (and individual words were 'signifiers' or 'signs'), all 'knowledge' was a relative 'construction', all aspects of non-European culture were 'essentialised' (an attempt to explain with reference only to a Western notion), and 'texts' (which could refer to written documents, architecture and art) required a special post-modernist reading. Throughout the work, there was a desire to seek out the methods of imperialist power through the colonial language. For example, masculine criteria were identified as defining colonisers and colonised: Englishmen were manly, strong, resourceful and brave; natives were weak, cowardly and even effeminate. It was argued that so powerful was 'colonial discourse', it had altered not only the way of thinking of the colonisers, but also of the colonised. They were indoctrinated with a sense of inferiority. This, it was felt, had important implications for the post-colonial nation states that had emerged.

Post-colonial writers rejected traditional history and identified groups that had been marginalised and ignored in the history of the Empire and the non-Western world: women, working classes, blacks and coloureds, and homosexuals. Anne McClintock was struck by the fundamental role of imperialism in Britain itself, arguing that: 'imperialism and invention of race were fundamental aspects of Western, industrialised modernity, [which] became central not only to the self-definition of the middle class but also to the policing of the "dangerous classes": the working class, the Irish, Jews, prostitutes, feminists, gays and lesbians, criminals, the militant crowd and so on.'[8] Ranajit Guha tried to redress the balance with 'Subaltern Studies', a collection of works focused on a 'history from below'.[9]

The biggest problem was the lack of sources from these 'hidden' groups, since most of the documentary material that had survived was written by the elites. However, by specific 'rereading' with an awareness of the language of oppression and supremacy used by the elites, the subtext could be glimpsed. By the late 1980s, the Subaltern Studies group were rejecting historical narratives altogether, along with notions of 'class' or 'individualism' as Western designs unsuited to a truthful analysis of the local society. With these boundaries 'deconstructed', the way was open to embrace fragments, without typicality, order or reliability. Myth and fact were subsumed and given equal validity. It was also maintained that all authors had to lay out their agendas, to acknowledge as Foucault did that all written work is fiction. Moreover, 'Subalterns' (those who had lived under the rule of the British) could only really write 'Subaltern' history since they were free of the 'constructions' of Western epistemology.[10]

Subsequent developments in the writing of post-colonial studies have laid stress on the interconnectivity of imperialism with other 'hidden' histories, although Leela Gandhi has pointed out the limits of post-colonial theory, its politics and its divisions.[11] McClintock argued that: 'race, gender and class are not distinct realms of experience, existing in splendid isolation from each other; nor can they be simply yoked together retrospectively like armatures of Lego. Rather they come into existence in and through relation to each other – if in contradictory and conflictual ways.'[12] Mrinalini Sinha also stressed the importance of seeing the relationship between coloniser and colonised as a dynamic and continually changing one, which requires an understanding that 'Orientalist discourse was neither monolithic not unidirectional'.[13] Clare Midgley recently called for more research into the 'construction of both British imperialism and anti-colonial nationalisms as essentially masculine projects' and a 'fuller debate on the relationship between post-colonial theory and new histories of imperialism'.[14]

The criticisms of post-colonial theorists forced historians of imperialism to respond. Since post-colonial theorists had challenged the very basis of historical method, there was bound to be a counter-challenge. Indeed, it quickly emerged that rather than one imperial discourse emanating from Europe, there was, in fact, a variety of responses and not all of them were in any way sympathetic to imperialism.[15] The rational assumptions of the Enlightenment and the Age of Reason were challenged from within Europe by the Romantic Movement in the early nineteenth century. Post-colonial scholars tend to draw no distinction between imperial discourse of the 1790s and the 1890s, even though there were huge differences in attitude towards race, reform and colonisation.[16]

The post-colonial insistence that Orientalism was constructed, designed and intended for Europeans, leaving Orientals inert and marginalised, meant the periphery studies of the British Empire (those which concentrate on the indigenous peoples or events in the colonies) have had to acknowledge the interaction of local people. But, historians of empire invariably would prefer to focus on the local people anyway, not the discourse itself, just as they were already doing before the advent of post-colonial ideas.[17] Although post-colonial theorists insisted that Europeans had invented concepts, such as tribe and caste, research revealed that these terms had been in use before the arrival of Europeans. Whilst they translated words, the *meaning* of the term was not always an 'invention'.[18]

Perhaps the fundamental weakness of the post-colonial approach is the assumption that Western 'knowledge' was the vehicle of oppression that pervaded all aspects of society. In India, as Sheldon Pollock pointed out, local elites shared the 'same ideological base', which was 'one contributing factor to the effectiveness with which England consolidated and maintained its rule'.[19] Collaboration was, in fact, a factor on which the British Empire relied and whilst contact with the British could alter social and political structures, it did not invent them. This adoption of local structures helps to explain why the Empire was so diverse in its political systems, from self-governing dominions, such as Australia, through to 'benign despotism' in the Pacific Islands. John Mackenzie wrote: 'The modern critique of Orientalism has generally committed that most fundamental of historical sins, the reading back of contemporary attitudes and prejudices into historical periods.'[20] He was disappointed by its 'disturbingly ahistorical forms', its 'moral condemnation befogging intellectual clarity', and its slavish need to pander to political correctness.[21] He concluded a study of European Orientalism in literature and the arts, where the British had adopted Eastern styles into their own fashions, as follows: 'By creating a monolithic and binary vision of the past they [post-colonial theorists] have too often damaged those intercultural relations which they seek to place on a more sympathetic basis for the future. In reality, Orientalism was endlessly protean, as often consumed by admiration and reverence as by denigration and depreciation.'[22]

Washbrook points out that there is a contradiction in the post-colonial theorists use of Romanticism, which they see as a movement that championed the 'traditional' against the West's 'modernity'. The post-colonial approach tends to see, in the Romantic philosophy, a means of resistance to the West. Yet, the Romantics were not liberators at all. They sought to conserve old elites and forms of authority in order to legitimise the new Western rule. Attempts to show that Western culture was a monolithic episteme are also flawed. European culture was itself the product of influences from other parts of the world over many centuries. Languages, alphabets, concepts, academic disciplines and technologies have all been imported as well as being inherently European. Kenan Malik has noted that post-colonial use of the term 'culture' to mark out the West has taken on the same connotations that Europeans used to ascribe to race at the end of the nineteenth century.[23]

Washbrook believed that post-colonial theory does not so much seek to 'displace' Enlightenment science as to 'replace' it with its own hierarchy where 'European and white' are moved from the top to the bottom. This very charge has been made of Said's work where, using the same tools of the Enlightenment he criticises, he essentialises and dehistoricises the history of the West according to his own new criteria. Indeed, an insistence that 'any and all representations are embedded . . . in the language, and then in the culture, institutions and political ambience of the representer' means that Said's own work is guilty of that charge.[24] Washbrook concludes: 'In practice, discourse theory – like the romanticism which gave rise to it – appears inextricably bound to the Enlightenment which it cannot entirely "reject" without silencing itself.'[25]

Gyatri Chakravorty Spivak defends post-colonial theory on the grounds that it can refer to its own 'essentialist' forms of representation, which continue to empower those groups that have been marginalised by the methods of the Enlightenment. This means that post-colonial theorists resort to 'counter-constructions', using techniques which are made without reference to evidence as it is understood by historians. Wrapped in the impenetrable jargon of post-modernism, defences are made on the grounds of 'conceptualisation, transformatory encounters, or redefined objectivity as an interactive relationship between inquiring subject and external object'. These studies, which reject historical knowledge as flawed, resort to throwing out evidence altogether in favour of novel-like suggestions.

Marxist historians have criticised the Subaltern Studies group for abandoning the terminology of 'class' and 'capital', and for the reduced interest in the urban and rural masses in preference for the 'angst of the Calcutta intelligentsia'. There is a sense in which new elites' interests are being served by post-colonial discourse, in that the advocates of the post-colonial approach are themselves drawn from middle-class or privileged sections of the former colonial societies, or from the American universities that have embraced them in their departments.[26] Washbrook argues that post-colonial theory fits the modern rhetoric of racial and ethnic 'victimisation', and it appeals to a multi-culturalism, which, in turn, gives power to those who seek to reassert affinities with (and claims to authority over) the societies they left behind. It also gives a loud voice, and an epistemology that cannot be challenged, to a group making claim to a 'history of their own', and thus serves as a modern mechanism of imperialism.

Defenders of post-colonial theory now point to the more flexible term 'dialogues' rather than the more rigid 'discourse'. The emphasis is less on European imposition, than on the cultural mixing and interplay of language, forms and societies. This has meant more interest in creole, hybrid or mixed culture. A reexamination of what constitutes 'European' concurs with what critics of post-colonialism had pointed out: European culture itself was a hybrid and changed through time.

Despite the criticism, Clare Midgley feels that two insights of post-colonial theory have not been diminished.[27] The first is that dominant forms of knowledge provided the basis for the exercise of imperial power, and that colonial discourse was, and still is, the platform for imperial history. Drawing on what Gyan Prakash called the traditionalists' 'leaden understanding of colonialism as History', Midgley also believes that historians of the British Empire persist in representing the Empire as modernising, and a force for civilisation that contrasts with the passive, 'savage' societies. Leela Gandhi argued that Western epistemology now regards post-colonialism as 'Other'.[28] Post-colonial theorists are, in fact, divided over who the 'worst victims of colonial oppression' were and who should 'represent' the Subaltern class.[29]

The second dispute itself is interesting: post-colonial theorists aim to represent a particular group whereas the historian attempts to observe and report without being partisan. Post-colonialism, like post-modernism, is concerned with the location of power and is intensely ideological. In addition, there is disagreement about the use of Marxist or post-structuralist terminology. The aim, though, is to interrogate the colonial past and to disinter the 'painful and humiliating memory of the history of race and racism' in order to uncover the overwhelming and lasting violence of colonisation.[30]

Dane Kennedy believes that post-colonial theory is a positive influence on imperial history as it 'raises provocative and fundamental questions about the epistemological structures of power and the cultural foundations of resistance'.[31] More than this, it helps us to understand the impact of imperialism, how imperial rule was maintained, how race and tribe became more important in the identification of groups, the interconnections of the periphery and the metropolis, and the way that language and ideas shaped British colonial policies. Nevertheless, she acknowledges that 'there is a great deal wrong with post-colonial theory.'[32]

C. A. Bayly points out that much post-colonial theory exhibits 'faddishness' and is 'retrogressive' because it overlooks the great body of British intellectual history on Orientalism and imperial ideas.[33] Post-colonial theorists were so intent to prove their own theory that they only looked for episodes where the British had created the 'Other', rather than at the debates on commerce, politics and virtue that took place. Worse still, Asians, Africans and Polynesians were denied 'agency' (the ability to act and decide) in their own history 'more thoroughly than had the nineteenth-century Imperial writers', such was the eagerness to show the pervasiveness and oppression of the dominant European culture.[34] More recently, historians have sought to place the constructions of ideas about indigenous peoples into their proper historical context. Eugene F. Irschick has shown how the British created and used their stereotypes of people in South India.[35] Some of the discourse had little to do with domination and reflected intellectual traditions that changed through time. In other cases, the changes in British views of the Empire and relationships with subject peoples is also now acknowledged as less fixed and less ideological. The British were essentially practical in their application of government, always tailoring their designs to meet changing circumstances.[36] In Canada, for example, local representative institutions were created to head off the sort of conflict between governors and local assemblies that had sparked the American Revolution. In the 1860s, this apparent 'model' was used to justify attempts to unify the territories of South Africa, but when South Africa was eventually unified in 1910, entirely new political arrangements were necessary, especially to secure the loyalty of both Natal and the former Boer republics.

Post-colonial theory continues to be focused on nationalist movements, the achievement of independence and a range of contemporary imperial legacies. Neil Lazarus noted that African post-colonial writers: 'tended to overvalue the emancipatory significance of their independence. One consequence was that, as their hopes were punctured in the years following decolonisation (as they invariably were), a rhetoric of disillusion began to replace the earlier Utopian rhetoric in their work: it emerged as fatalism or despair or anger or the accusation that postcolonial leaders had betrayed the "African Revolution".'[37] However, the transfer of blame to the former imperial powers tempered these failures by nationalist leaders. This camouflaged the fact that the adoption of socialist economic policies, intended as an alternative to capitalist 'imperialism', often condemned the new states to stagnation and poverty.

Missionaries: ideologues of imperialism?

A common African verdict on British and European imperialism ran: 'When the whites first came, they had the Bible and we had the land. After a while we found that things changed around. Now they have the land and we have the Bible.'[38] However, the relationship was never as simple as this statement implied. In some cases, missionaries welcomed the arrival of formal imperial control as a means to break down the anti-Christian forces and hierarchies that stood in the way of conversion. Yet radical Christians could oppose imperialism with equal vigour, deploring the effects of colonisation and working to halt imperial expansion. Andrew Porter noted: 'religion and Empire frequently mingled, but were as likely to undermine each other as they were to provide mutual support.'[39] Is it possible, then, to discern the impact of 'discourse' or 'dialogues' through a study of missionaries?

Religious groups had a dichotomous relationship with the British Empire. Whilst missionaries might enjoy the Empire's protection and share in its march towards progress and civilisation, they did not always share its values and methods. Many religious Dissenters had populated the early settlements of America, and Nonconformists criticised the Anglican ascendancy down to the nineteenth century. Political radicalism was often intertwined with religious dissent, and Nonconformists used their political platforms to advocate both religious and secular reforms. On the other side, the Anglican Church, which promoted the mutual obligations of monarchy and subjects and the values of faith, duty and social order, was regarded as an anchor for the colonies. The Canada Act of 1791, which apportioned land and revenues to the Church and encouraged education, was just one example of 'the indispensable adjuncts to the civil authorities'.[40] Bishoprics were also established in Jamaica, Calcutta and New South Wales in the early nineteenth century to underpin imperial rule. Yet the Anglican Church lacked any missionary enterprise until the late eighteenth century as its overseas work was designed entirely for the service of British personnel abroad.

The historian E. Ayandele described missionaries as the 'pathfinders of British influence' in West Africa because they provided the British government with so much local information.[41] Missions did extend British influence in so far as they were the conduits for the English language and for the values that were the basis of a legal system. Harry Johnston wrote that missions: 'strengthen our hold over the country, spread the use of the English language, they induct the natives into the best kind of civilisation and in fact each mission is an essay in colonisation'.[42] Missionaries therefore have been blamed, despite their small numbers of converts, for the undermining of self-confidence, the erosion of respect for traditional beliefs, and the creation of social and political conflict across Africa and Asia.[43]

However, it would be misleading to make direct connections between missionaries and imperialism, as their agendas were quite distinct. Although critical of non-Christian beliefs, the missionaries were egalitarian: all men, regardless of race were equal in the eyes of God and in need of salvation. Co-operation between missions of different European origin was contrasted with the competitiveness of secular forces. There was open criticism of national chauvinism, commercial rapacity and the

expropriation of land. Nevertheless, there were limits to this separateness. Missions on the Niger clashed with private traders,
particularly over the sale of alcohol, but were to some extent
dependent on the Royal Niger Company.

The missionary societies, such as the Baptists' (BMS,
1792), the London (LMS, 1795), and the Anglican (CMS,
1799) emerged at the end of the eighteenth century and were
in the forefront of anti-slavery activity. Despite the pressure of
these societies, the political elites calculated that the abolition
of the trade in slaves could be sustained without damaging the
wealth of the West Indies plantations. Indeed, the natural
increase of black people already in the West Indies was
expected to offset the loss of supply. However, competition
from European slave plantations and a fall in world sugar
prices caused a decline in the West Indies' profits, and the
missionary societies kept up the pressure. By 1823, the
Methodists had 50 missionaries in the Caribbean, but there
was growing tension with the authorities that were suspicious
of any encouragement to slave revolt. The outbreak of the
Jamaica Rebellion in 1831, which led to the intimidation of
missionaries, merely fuelled the anti-slavery campaigns in
Britain, culminating in the abolition of slavery in 1833. There
was a great deal of respect for those who had suffered at the
hands of the plantation owners and this merged with a profound sympathy for missions that were established elsewhere.
This belief coincided with considerable optimism about the
future since Britain's mid-century dominance seemed to point
to a unique spiritual destiny: the conversion of the pagans
across the world. Moreover, the CMS and the Methodists of
West Africa were convinced their work was recompense for the
wrongs inflicted by Britain during the years of slavery.

Not all of the promotion of Christianity came from missionaries, for a strong religious faith also characterised many of the
administrators and soldiers too. Herbert Edwardes, a soldier-
administrator of the Punjab, regarded himself as a 'pioneer of
Christian civilisation'. Neville Chamberlain, another frontier soldier of the 1850s, wrote: 'A horse and a sword were all that were
needful and no one ever gave a thought as to danger. Not that
there was any levity in facing death; it was simply that one
was possessed of a light heart to meet anything that came. There

was nothing but God above and duty below.'[44] Asians and Africans were not inert to this ideological onslaught. The migration of former slaves from Sierra Leone carried Christianity into the interior, and there were demands for more missions from African rulers. On the other hand, missionaries were sometimes martyred for their beliefs. James Chalmers, for example, was killed and eaten in 1902 on Goarbari Island. Above all, the reaction to missionaries was selective. They were welcomed for their medicine, education and for the consolations of the Christian message, but they were opposed if they threatened local beliefs and social conventions.

In fact, the effect of missionary work was mixed. By 1840, after 20 years of missionary activity in New Zealand, almost half of the Maoris of the Bay of Islands were converts to Christianity. Edward Gibbon Wakefield, a spokesman in favour of British migration, advocated massive European colonisation, but British missionaries were alarmed that Maoris would lose their lands. When Wakefield formed the New Zealand Company, and began preparations to acquire territory in 1839, lobbyists prompted the British government to step in. William Hobson was despatched as Governor-General and concluded the Treaty of Waitangi with 50 Maori chiefs in 1840, guaranteeing the protection of their lands from settlers. None the less, the colonists discarded the treaty terms and the Maoris clashed with the British in the 1860s. However, as Tom Gibson remarks, diseases eventually did more damage than the *Pakeha* (white men). From a population of *c.*120,000 Maoris in 1840, only 46,000 were recorded in 1870.[45] It was not surprising that many turned away from the mission stations and rejected European education, religion and agriculture.

The missionaries were more successful in preserving the rights of the 'Hottentots' (Khoi) in South Africa, persuading Sir George Murray, the Secretary of State for the Colonies, to grant them legal equality under the Cape government in 1828. Thomas Fowell Buxton, who had been instrumental in the campaign, was less successful in combining trade and Christianity in the Niger expedition of 1841. Decimated by disease, the expedition was abandoned and further missionary work was greatly deterred by Africa's reputation as the 'white man's graveyard'.

The resistance of the churches was most clearly highlighted in the West Indies. In Jamaica, the poverty of the ex-slaves and the denial of civil and political rights led to an explosion of anger at Morant Bay in 1865.[46] Looting, arson and murder were dealt with in a sweeping reign of terror led by the governor, Edward John Eyre. Fearful of wholesale black revolution that would engulf the small white community, and backed by troops who had seen atrocities inflicted on white women and children in the Indian Mutiny, the reprisals were severe. Eyre mistakenly had a leading member of the Jamaica House of Assembly, a Baptist minister named G. W. Gordon, hanged for inciting the revolt. The deaths of 439 blacks, many by hanging, caused anger and consternation in Britain. Frederic Harrison, a member of the Committee that tried Eyre for murder, typified fears that such brutality in the colonies might merely provoke further unrest.[47] Gad Heuman noted that the local Baptist churches provided a focus around which resistance had developed.[48] In Britain, Christian sensibilities were severely disturbed. Denis Judd concluded: 'The question was whether the British dependencies, and eventually perhaps, Great Britain itself, were to be under the government of law or of military license.'[49] The question was answered: the British government moved to abolish the old colonial order, and imposed direct control.

Muriel Chamberlain wrote: 'Many motives drove men into Africa during the great age of exploration, a hope of gain, a love of adventure and just plain curiosity . . . The interior of Africa held the most tantalising mysteries left in the world after the exploration of the Americas, Australia and much of Asia. The public at home shared the thrill of discovery of the man on the spot.'[50] A pantheon of intrepid individuals set out to find the sources of the great rivers in the mid-nineteenth century. Following the travels of Mungo Park, Hugh Clapperton followed the Niger in the 1820s, Richard Burton and John Hanning Speke sought the headwaters of the Nile, and Henry Morton Stanley crossed central Africa, earning his reputation for determination amongst Africans as the 'breaker of stones'.[51] To the increasingly literate public, Africa was exotic and intriguing. Yet few caught the public imagination more than David Livingstone, who had established mission stations beyond the Cape from 1841 and who had turned his attention to traversing and mapping the interior along the Zambesi. His calls for the destruction of African slavery, his 'rediscovery' by Stanley and his death among the Africans inspired generations of Christians in Britain, but also gave an impetus to the idea that 'Christianity, civilisation and commerce' would together be the basis of progress in Africa.

However, there was a great deal of pessimism about the capacity for reform and improvement of Africans and Asians in the late nineteenth century. Explorers like Richard Burton referred to East Africans as children, prone to stupidity after puberty.[52] There were plenty of theories, from Darwinian cat-egorisation of Africans as an inferior part of the natural world (which apparently fitted them to the role of servants and labour-ers), to the 'Hamitic Theory' which posited that all progress for Africans was the result of impositions from outside (meaning Europe), including the civilisation of the ancient Egyptians. Even Livingstone, who was keen to see 'improvement' for Africans, was a complex man who also doubted the benefits of progress.[53] There were still many who wanted to see 'improve-ments' in the way that Britain was doing at home, but there were plenty of objections on the grounds of cost.[54] Ronald Robinson and John Gallagher concluded:

> Although the public opinion might be stirred by a Burton or a Livingstone, with their pleas for spreading Christianity and commerce, no serious national interest in the east African interior existed. Decades of failure had dimmed Buxtonian hopes. The country lacked anything which the world wanted to buy (except slaves), and so the lawful trade never became more than an appendage to philanthropy. The humanitarians put forward plan after plan for the development of the interior; but humanitarianism was not enough.[55]

Nevertheless, Andrew Porter notes that the missionaries did not share the pessimism about the races. In the years before 1914, there was already a determination to incorporate local culture into the teaching of Christianity so that missionaries began to influence the training programmes on the basis of their experi-ences. Moreover, they maintained their distance from the Empire and sympathised with their converts, criticising taxation, labour policies and settlers in the process.

The missionary impulse was one aspect of Britain's new worldview in the nineteenth century. When slavery was abolished, missionaries – who were a rather exceptional and highly motivated minority – turned their attention to the salvation of souls in the wider world. Their religious convictions sustained them on the periphery in spite of considerable hardships. It also enabled them to see their work as a benign enterprise, to rescue, to heal and to prevent abuses. Missionaries were supported by large congregations at home, and their reports were followed with interest, projecting information about Africa and Asia back into Britain. Missionaries were therefore part of the colonial British identity and cannot be separated entirely from the Empire, but in their aims and methods they were quite distinct. Missionaries were ready to criticise the Empire, even when at other times they welcomed its security and commercial support. Indeed, in each case, the missionaries pursued their own agenda and supported imperialism only where they saw some advantage to themselves and their missions.

Ideologies and identities

Post-colonial theory still fails to fully acknowledge that imperialism was more than political subjugation, economic plunder or cultural vandalism. In many cases, as the *Oxford History of the British Empire* shows, British imperialism replaced existing empires or their decaying remains, such as the Mughals of Persian descent in India or the Ottomans of Turkish and Arab origin in Egypt and Palestine. It is also clear that the British were not following some grand design, and often responded to local administrative arrangements or threats from other powers. In India, for example, rivalry with France and the Indian states and then with Russia drew the British into occupation, despite frequent attempts to reduce the expense and scale of administration. The restructuring of society was designed to accommodate British rule, but also to meet manpower demands for industry, local administration and the armed forces. Yet the negative legacies of imperialism, and the lack of partnership and fundamental inequality of treatment of non-whites within the Empire, still seems to demand moral judgement. This cannot be entirely separated from history.

However, the criteria which post-colonial theorists use seem so loaded with their own ideology that they are in danger of excluding or denying any other form of enquiry. The approach is self-limiting and threatens to damage the empirical study of British imperialism. There is a chance post-colonial studies will reorient themselves towards enquiries about race and national consciousness, thus making a contribution to our historical understanding of culture and identity. The alternative is that it will remain confined by its own self-referring vocabulary and endless re-examination of language and texts.

The intellectual history and ideology of British imperialism need not be restricted to the field of post-colonial studies. The transfer of British values and ideas was a cultural diffusion that was not entirely negative nor was it solely concerned with power as the missionaries illustrate. The outflow of Western influence was accompanied by a taste for new cultural artefacts and consumables from around the world, such as Chinese porcelain, South Asia tea, fruit from the West Indies, rugs from the Middle East, and African tribal art. It is true that colonials and expatriates generally resisted the notion of adopting indigenous cultures, disparagingly called 'going native', and there was indifference to what was seen as 'primitive', but there was genuine fascination in the arts, literature, ethnography, history and archaeology of Asia and Africa. In this sense, the modernisation that accompanied imperialism was looked upon with mixed feelings.

8 Was the British Empire racialist or racist?

Stereotyping the coloniser and colonised

To many, any distinction between racist and racialist may be a little academic. However, the differences are important. Race is used to denote any group of people, united by common descent and identified by skin colour and physiognomy. Common bonds are also usually expressed in terms of shared language, history, culture or outlook. In the nineteenth century, race became a social scientific tool to explain not only diverse characteristics and types, but also levels of development. It became a universal tool of categorisation, but also the key to understanding customs and behaviour.[1] Racialism was thus a term used to describe differences between races.[2] Racism, by contrast, is a belief that some races are inherently superior, and that others are inferior and those races therefore require different treatment. Stereotyping of temperamental qualities, intelligence, capacity for work and the ability to create a valuable culture typically follow. Explanations for racism vary: from economic needs to find and harness an underclass of slave labourers, to Satre's explanation that racism was sexually motivated by a fear that another race would take its women.[3]

The most blatant announcements were made by relatively few imperialists and not until the end of the nineteenth century. In the late eighteenth century, expressions of British superiority were based on morality, law, religion and political institutions and there was a belief that certain factors made non-Europeans different: the debilitating effects of a hot climate, the effects of living under unenlightened 'oriental despots', and the necessity for each society to pass through the same stages of development. There was an optimistic view that humans were the same across the world, that all would eventually come to realise that barbaric and inhuman practices could be eradicated, that all could eventually become Christian and that everyone was capable of reform. The British aimed to liberate non-Europeans from both political and social tyranny to enable them to live a free and independent existence. The continued rapid development of Britain in the nineteenth century and the relatively slow progress of change in the Empire meant that the optimism gave way to criticism. The emancipation of slaves and the abolition of slavery in West Africa did not give rise to the anticipated renaissance in Africa or the Caribbean. Experiments in reform in India also failed to produce the great advance anticipated. Instead, there was a rejection of British influence with the Indian Mutiny/Rebellion in 1857 and the Jamaica rebellion of 1865. This merely confirmed suspicions that 'natives' were unable to grasp the significance of the improvements they were being offered. It was assumed they were incapable of governing themselves.

The colonial stereotype of Africans helped to justify the partition of the late nineteenth century. The Africans were regarded as people without history or culture, 'indulging in abhorrent practices such as human sacrifice and cannibalism . . . politically decentralised, living in small villages, often naked, dominated by witchcraft, living in terror of their neighbours'.[4] There was little recognition that, for example, the Fulani of West Africa could trace a continuous heritage stretching back 1000 years, and all technological innovations were thought to have been introduced from outside, that is, from the west. The Senufo farmers of the Kerhogo region had adopted the plough from earliest times and planted yams in the ridges between the furrows. However, even though this saved on labour, the Senufo realised that by returning to the use of the hoe (heaping the soil up around each plant by hand) they could grow thicker tubers. The plough was therefore abandoned, but to Europeans this seemed backward.[5]

A more scientific examination of the 'problem' of races was perhaps inevitable. As certain native populations such as Maoris and Aborigines went into decline, anthropologists sought to discover what it was that enabled some races to flourish and others to become extinct. Charles Darwin's *The Origin of Species* (1859), which emphasised evolutionary change through natural selection, seemed to confirm that humans might follow the same pattern as animals. He confirmed this point in *The Descent of*

Man (1871), pointing out that 'hybridism' was often 'sterile'. Darwinism provided an answer to the question of unequal development across the world. Science, and the analysis of eugenics, seemed to offer an irrefutable explanation of hierarchy between the races. Consequently, racialist ideas that humans were different, which had existed before Darwin, were confirmed and, in turn, intellectual justifications slid towards racism. Physical segregation increased and 'colour' was added to the class barriers that were erected. In 1883, the Ilbert Bill, which proposed giving Indian judges powers over white defendants, caused a storm of protest in the subcontinent. The Anglo-Indians' charge was that: 'What would please our Indian fellow subjects more than to bully and disgrace a wretched Englishwoman? The higher the husband's station and the greater his respectability, the greater the delight of her torturer.'[6] What lay behind this was the fear that the Indians would use the law to attack both British prestige and the basis of British rule in India.

By the late nineteenth century, biological evidence became inseparable from the relativist judgements that Europeans were superior. Europeans, and Aryans in particular, were associated with exemplary standards of beauty, intelligence, physical strength, moral integrity and courage. The savage was the antithesis of this civilisation, the result of stagnation in culture and development. Black skin was 'evidence' of being a 'human fossil' or 'infantile'. The absence of literature or technology was seen as evidence of ignorance. Rebellion or resistance to white rule, and therefore to civilisation, was used as proof of underdevelopment, impulsiveness and immaturity.[7]

Sir Harry Johnston, explorer and administrator in Africa from 1876, expressed doubt whether the 'Negroes would ever advance much above the status of savagery in which they exist in those parts of Africa where neither European nor Arab civilisation has yet reached them'.[8] However, he also praised the Africans ability to adopt new skills as 'an excellent short hand clerk, telegraph operator, skilled photographer, a steamer-engineer . . . or an irreproachable butler' with 'extraordinary readiness'. He felt the 'Negro is more likeable, and more akin to us of the white race in disposition' and that eventually blacks would only differ from whites in life in Africa 'in the colour of their skins'. Johnston's view is thus more complex than simple racism.

There is little doubt that his views were prejudiced and Africans appeared to fit only servile roles in his philosophy, but he was optimistic about the future. This contrasts with Sir Alfred Milner, the High Commissioner for Cape Colony on the eve of the South African War, who noted in his papers that: 'My patriotism knows no geographical but only racial limits. I am an Imperialist and not a little Englander, because I am a British race patriot'.[9] Milner made it his aim to ensure that the colonies of settlement became more closely bonded to the Empire, a view shared by the Colonial Secretary Joseph Chamberlain. Imperial consolidation was to be extended to non-white states, but the hierarchy was strictly racial and class based.

The bombast of Cecil Rhodes, the diamond and gold mining tycoon of South Africa, is even more notorious: '[The English are the] chosen instrument in carrying out the divine idea over the whole planet . . . we are the finest race in the world and the more of the world we inhabit the better it is for the human race.'[10] In *Greater Britain* (1869), Charles Dilke had argued that if white English-speaking people worked in unison, they could 'inherit the earth'. This view was sometimes extended beyond the British Empire to include the United States and even the 'Saxon race' of Germany. Yet for all the apparent optimism about the future, there was, in fact, a deep pessimism. Those who worked in the colonies were conscious of being on the edge of their civilisation and felt they could so easily slip into barbarism or despotism. It was the barriers they erected that 'preserved' them from becoming a part of the jungle, the bush or the wilderness that surrounded them. The abandonment of British rule also carried the fear that there would be a general collapse. Sir John Strachey stated: 'We cannot foresee a time in which the cessation of our rule would not be the signal for universal anarchy and ruin.'[11] The British regarded themselves as the 'guardians', who, through thankless duty, brought civilisation to the non-Western world.

Nevertheless, not all advocates of empire were racist. David Livingstone hoped that European intervention in central Africa would bring an end to the Arab and African slave trade there. He wrote: 'In this light, a European colony would be considered by the natives as an inestimable boon to inter-tropical Africa. Thousands of industrious natives would gladly settle around it, and engage in the peaceful pursuit of agriculture and trade of which they are so fond, and undistracted by the wars and rumours of wars, might listen to the purifying and ennobling truths of the gospel of Jesus Christ.'[12] Courtenay Ilbert, the author of the Jurisdiction Bill of 1883, deplored the racial animosities that were fanned by the opposition to the legislation and which, he suspected, were a ruse to discredit the Liberal government. His Viceroy, Lord Ripon, was eager to extend the basis of support in India beyond the narrow confines of the Indian princes and junior Indian officials. Eventually, Ripon wanted to see the extension of local government that Britain enjoyed in the 1880s. Earlier, in the atmosphere of revenge generated by the Indian Mutiny/Rebellion, Lord Canning had refused to accept the demands for reprisals and condemned 'the less violent, but not one bit less offensive course of refusing trust and countenance and favour and honour to any man because he is of a class and creed.'[13] Mary Kingsley, the traveller and popular writer on Africa in the 1890s, deplored the attitudes of the: '"stay-at-home" statesman [who] thinks that Africans are awful savages or silly children, people who can only be dealt with on a reformatory or penitentiary line'. The MP Henry Labouchere criticised imperial expansion and felt that British officials were inclined to mistreat natives because they succumbed to 'greed and love of domination'.[14] However, he was unable to find a solution to slave trafficking outside of British colonies without intervention and never advocated the dismantling of the empire because he did not know how to provide an adequate and humane hand-over of power if the British left.

After the First World War, the idea that races were incapable of change began to break down. There was an understanding that people could be 'less' or 'more' advanced, and gradually the idea of permanent 'trusteeship' gave way to the prospect of 'partnership'. There were important exceptions and delays. In 1923, the settlers that had lived under the British South Africa Company in Southern Rhodesia were offered the choice between incorporation into South Africa or self-government with a franchise that excluded virtually all non-whites. In Kenya, white settlers hankered after self-government and Indian settlers demanded improved civil rights, whilst the indigenous Masai were eager to recover lands lost to the whites.[15] In Jamaica, despite government loans to develop shipping lines and banana plantations, the depression of the 1930s (which caused a decline in sugar prices) brought grievances over low wages and poverty to a head. In India too, the British felt the people were not yet ready for self-government, which stemmed in part from a lack of trust in their abilities (particularly care of the peasantry) or their motives (for they suspected Congress of greedy political ambition).[16]

Segregation, class and identity

An underlying lack of trust encouraged the British to set up segregated areas for whites in towns and cities across the Empire, often called cantonments or lines (a military expression referring to the horse lines, the tethering place). An early example was the construction from 1802 of Calcutta's spacious colonial district. In coastal areas, colonial towns grew rapidly, partly as a result of their function as trading centres or docks for shipping, and partly because they attracted local labour and traders. Hong Kong, for example, began as a village in a sheltered natural harbour. Similarly, Singapore developed because of its port facilities even though it was previously uninhabited and it grew rapidly because it attracted labour from outside the indigenous peoples. The greatest influx was of Chinese traders, merchants and workers, 650,000 into the Malay Peninsula between 1901 and 1904, and the population of the city had reached 400,000 by the 1920s. Cape Town was also a magnet to a variety of racial groups such as Malays and freed slaves, as well as whites and the indigenous Khoikhoi, but typically, separate wards developed which led to the creation of 'plural societies'. In Kingston, Jamaica, there was also a mixed population of whites, blacks and interracials; the latter a product of the interaction between races on the island over several generations.

Segregation became far more formalised in the nineteenth century for a variety of reasons. In India, there was concern that the local population might transmit diseases to the colonisers. This was an ironic anxiety since white populations had often brought diseases from Europe that had devastated groups like the Maoris and Aborigines, although this was not the case in

India. Indeed, the proximity to the old cities, the shared water and food supply and daily interaction with staff, workers and servants meant that disease could travel into the white cantonments quite easily. Security was another cause of segregation. When new towns sprang up in Natal, there were widespread anxieties about the local Zulus, who flocked into them for work, because of their fierce reputation. In 1906, a Zulu revolt seemed to confirm that a threat existed. Africans were kept out of city centres because of a fear of disturbances and housed in 'locations'. Passes were required if they wished to travel into the town. Similar systems were adopted against the warrior tribes of Rhodesia and Kenya.

In Canada, New Zealand and Australia, where there was no threat from the local peoples, towns were not divided in the same way, but suburbs with avenues of trees and a parkland layout reminiscent of country estates in Britain became common. In India, Simla became a genteel version of a British town. Like the other settlements modelled faithfully on Britain, it provided a means to escape the local environment. Surrounded by other British people, it allowed hard-working personnel to forget that they were in a foreign land, a long way from home. They provided a sense of community to Britons leading otherwise isolated lives as planters or administrators. On a smaller scale, the 'club' was an important focal point for reinforcing identity. This identity could have specific regional aspects, including Orange Lodges for Ulstermen, and Hibernian lodges for the southern Irish.

Colonists themselves maintained that clubs were not designed to be racist; they were an opportunity to be 'amongst your own kind'. One expatriate who spent 42 years in Africa, which he loved, still felt it necessary to escape the African people: 'where I was not on parade, or on show, where I could tell a joke and not have to explain it or give unwitting offence'. He related that there were areas where he would not be welcome amongst Africans for the same reason.[17] Colonists could demonstrate unswerving loyalty to 'their' servants and retainers, even when involvement in criminal activity was beyond doubt too. British army officers maintained this exclusion against their own 'Other Ranks', but were just as capable of defending their soldiers, white or non-white. Whilst British soldiers could be uncharitable, abusive and even violent towards 'blacks', there were other occasions where soldiers would support local people. For example, during the Second World War, one Military Police corporal went out of his way to represent a young Egyptian boy who he felt had been wrongly accused of theft by the Egyptians.[18] However, most working-class soldiers were indifferent to the Empire, which hardly touched their lives. Apathy was widespread, and many soldiers on duty a long way from home were simply not interested in the local people or their lands. It was this dislike, bred of ignorance and homesickness, and inflamed by alcohol or misunderstanding, which produced outbursts of anger. But this attitude should also be placed in context. Indifference and hostility to British Other Ranks by their own kind merely fostered a mutual contempt for civilians, regardless of nationality.[19]

There may have been an extent to which segregation was desirable to both whites and non-whites. In Fiji, the British enjoyed a relationship of mutual respect, based on a policy of non-interference. However, in 1933 the local population requested separation from the immigrant Indian workers and their families who had arrived in large numbers and whose population was growing more quickly than the indigenous one. Thus, outside of the administered villages, populated by approximately 60,000 Indians, the 150,000 Fijians lived under their own chiefs, their way of life protected by the British. In many ways, the protection came too late, as diseases swept away large numbers of the population, and the islanders' potential as a labour supply was threatened.[20]

Racial mixing, miscegenation, was gradually regarded as ill-advised once the 'scientific' approach to race developed in the second half of the nineteenth century. Before then, given the scarcity of white partners, many British men had taken local women as wives or mistresses. In India, it was an accepted norm, but the British aroused indignation in Afghanistan during their occupation of 1839–42 for beginning liaisons with Afghan women.[21] Whilst this became less common in India by the 1890s, in East Africa the practice of having a mistress continued. Racial mixing was frowned upon in the same way that sexual contact between classes aroused suspicion and condemnation in Britain. Discreet prostitution and contact with lower classes was tolerated, but respectable behaviour was expected in the public domain.[22] Whilst European women were permitted to act as prostitutes in Singapore, any *British* prostitutes were deported back to the United Kingdom.

Racial contact was also maintained through institutions like the Indian Army, and through sport such as cricket matches. Masonic Lodges accepted members equally, regardless of race, as did the churches in their congregations and their ministries. Chambers of commerce, and the very process of trade, could create strong working relationships between races. In many of these situations, class distinctions were waived as other loyalties took precedence: Regimental *esprit de corps* in certain Indian Army regiments, for example, team loyalty in cricket teams and shared values in commerce.

The local people were vital to the imperial community as a labour supply and distinctions were, again, often class based and not necessarily racial. Other Ranks in the British Army usually got on better with non-Europeans than their middle-class officers, although there was often a different kind of rapport between the ranks which developed out of mutual respect. The social ordering of labour did, nevertheless, reflect a combination of class distinction and racial differences. In the colonies of settlement, whites took up skilled jobs and held positions of leadership, or were engaged in work regarded as 'respectable'.[23] For men, this might include skilled mine workers in South Africa or farmers in Australia, whilst women might become governesses or nursemaids. Unskilled work was given to the non-white locals. This division was by no means absolute, for white prostitution was common in Australian and South African mining towns. In India, local people provided a whole range of services and wherever possible preserved their own strict hierarchy.

The British tried, wherever they could, to work with existing social structures, but they made decisions about what constituted the local elite on their own terms, often based on notions of class. David Cannadine believes this sense of social hierarchy was far more important in the practical business of running the empire (with its need for rewards and inducements as well as exclusions) than the racial hierarchy of the social Darwinists.[24] In India, the princes of the older Mughal order were preserved within a formalised, but British-invented hierarchy demarcated by decorations, protocols on precedence, and even the firing of gun salutes. According to Charles Allen, the Indian princes were 'above the usual conventions – and more than equals'.[25] On the North-West Frontier of India, the tribal council, or *Jirga*, was the clan's decision-making body whose actions could be swayed by devout Muslim clerics or influential speakers. The British therefore preferred either to encourage *maliks* (local headmen) or use charismatic British political officers like Sir Robert Warburton (himself half-Afghan) to influence the tribes. In Singapore, local elites were encouraged to ensure peace between the *dals*, the multi-caste factions. In many ways this was a practical response to huge migrations and social mixing, especially in towns that had developed as a result of British imperialism. Tensions between ethnic groups and religious communities needed to be defused through some administration and, lacking detailed knowledge of these communities, the British sought intermediaries.

Some of the middle classes and aristocracy were frequently disdainful of the vulgarity of 'new money' in Britain. Those that tried to ape their superiors were ridiculed. The same was true for Africans and Indians such as the Bengali *Babu*. Jokes were made at their expense because of confusions over the English language. Bengalis were regarded as 'litigious, and very fond of an argument', according to H. T. Wickham, a police commandant.[26] Mrinalini Sinha argued that the educated and politically self-conscious Hindus were categorised by the British as the odious 'effeminate babu', the gendering of the target being a specific way of denigrating and humiliating their opponent.[27] Expressing fears of a different kind, John X. Merriman, reflected a concern that there was a threat to the Empire from 'the cosmopolitan breed of financiers and the awful power they have created in the stock exchange'. He argued that 'Our struggle [in South Africa] is to retain a virile European population on the soil that can form an aristocracy, under whose care the natives may advance in civilisation.'[28]

The British, especially missionaries, were adept at influencing local populations to adopt Western values, dress and behaviour as the outward signs of 'civilisation'. Baptists set up villages among the plantation workers of Jamaica and instilled Western modes of etiquette in all social intercourse, from meals to language. The adoption of British values was sometimes pervasive. Colonel Kenneth Mason recalled how an Indian, who asked to become a member of a mixed club, cleared his throat and spat on the floor during dinner prior to his acceptance. During the subsequent voting, it was the other Indian members who denied the new-comer a place, not the British, illustrating the degree to which the Indians had adopted what they thought were British manners.[29] British schools were an important aspect of the missionary experience and imparted 'Britishness', but the most popular venues were the hospitals. Dr Theodore Pennell opened a mission station and hospital at Bannu on the North-West Frontier of India. He won several converts, but was constantly struggling to preserve the Christian faith amongst a people who favoured blood feuding, and always carried firearms.[30]

Africans and Asians sometimes adopted Western religion, education or forms of behaviour if they felt it had something to offer them. They were not necessarily 'indoctrinated', but were capable of opportunism. Yet the adoption could bring only limited advantage. Indian civil servants, or lawyers, for example, never rose to high rank. In a twist of irony, it was the fact that the British succeeded in ruling India as one state, where previously it had been so divided, that encouraged the Indian nationalists to consider independence for a united India. Denied a share of the most senior positions in government (beyond a handful of posts, including a seat on the Viceroy's council) and subject to the inequality of the legal system, Indian nationalists were struck by the fact that democratic participation and selection on merit were the essential features of government in Britain and increasingly so in the 'white' dominions.[31]

Segregation was also part of the way of preserving, even fostering a colonial identity in the settler states that became new nationalities in Canada, Australia, New Zealand and South Africa. Many colonists thought of themselves as British for generations and this, along with loyalty to the monarch and the Empire, may help to explain the enthusiastic response to conflicts such as the South African War and the First World War. Nevertheless, New Zealanders actually managed to incorporate Maoris into the new dispensation, extending the franchise to them in 1867. In the Cape, the franchise was based on property ownership, not colour, from 1854 until it was abolished by the Afrikaners 100 years later. However, despite the Cape's association with liberalism, the Native Affairs Commission of 1905 endorsed racial segregation throughout South Africa for security – and to provide pools of cheap labour. Thus in South Africa, Afrikaners were also incorporated in a British dominated South Africa following the defeat of the Boer forces in the South African War. However, the price of their loyalty was full autonomy and that effectively handed power over to the Afrikaans-speaking population in the establishment of self-government in the two ex-Boer republics in 1907–8. In Natal, blacks were always effectively excluded from the franchise. Therefore, the inequality of representation in the Empire could also have colour implications.

The denial of rights to non-whites in South Africa and India, and to a large extent in Australia, was part of a general phenomenon in the European colonial empires with settler populations. This was due in part to the sizes of the populations. Outnumbered by non-whites in South Africa and India, the granting of representational rights would, it was thought, threaten British rule altogether and encourage 'irresponsible' behaviour. Nor was this threat limited to indigenous populations. In Australia, South Africa, and to a lesser extent in Canada, Chinese labourers were regarded as a multitudinous 'yellow peril'. The Chinese provided an inexpensive workforce in mines and in railway construction and, although colonial authorities were happy to make use of this labour supply, the Chinese became objects of suspicion because they threatened to outnumber the whites. Whilst numbers of immigrant Chinese women were restricted, the men who had no partners were viewed as sexual predators. However, in the 'Chinese Slavery' affair of 1904–7, where 54,000 Chinese labourers were brought in to reconstruct and operate mines after the South African War and were crammed into barrack blocks, they were regarded as men likely to become homosexuals. Humanitarians objected to their conditions, and some mine owners were concerned about the competition with existing black workers.

Nevertheless, Chinese and Indian labour was preferred in Natal because, unlike the local Africans, they could not return home when the hardship of the work didn't suit them. Short contracts of three years were designed to prevent the Chinese and Indians from becoming immigrants. However, many of the

Indians remained, and from the 1880s, they were engaged in commerce in the towns of Natal as well as on the land. When Natal received self-government in 1893 and tried to restrict the movement, the trade and the franchise of the Indian population, Mohandas Gandhi organised local opposition. In Australia, fear of the overwhelming influx of Asians led to a 'White Australia' policy, banning the immigration of Chinese in 1888.

The most notorious government endorsements of racial prejudice in the twentieth century, other than Japan and Nazi Germany in the 1940s, were those of South Africa after 1948. The antecedents of apartheid can be traced to British rule in South Africa, through the Native Affairs Commission and the exclusions of blacks in Natal mentioned above. However, Dr Malan's policy statement in 1948 reflected anger with British legislation that had tempered the racism of Afrikaners from the 1830s. It was not until Malan's government that the edifices of apartheid were erected. In 1949, mixed marriages were banned; racial segregation and categorisation were rigidly enforced throughout public places, sports, transport and universities. Civil disobedience campaigns met with sharp reprisals. Mark Ferro believed that the violence of apartheid was a result, not of nineteenth-century Afrikaner prejudice, but the British industrialisation of South Africa.[32] Paternalism had once 'tempered' the oppression of 'fisticuffs, whip lashings and fire-arms'. It was, he argued, a monetary economy that destroyed the need for paternalism. However, Ferro fails to mention the violence of the Battle of Blood River (1838) where Afrikaners slaughtered a Zulu army in the process of seizing African land, or the British efforts to legislate against racial prejudice, and he equates the economic development of wage labouring with the political provisions of apartheid. Moreover, he does not acknowledge Malan's desire to unite Afrikaners against British influence (a process that had begun as early as 1934) and to bring about greater control of African labour.[33]

Race and Empire: conclusions

The racial dimension of British imperialism was to leave important legacies for the post-colonial world. The parallel existence of self-governing dominions and 'enlightened despotisms' was a cause of bitter resentment across the Empire. In more recent times, allegations that 'institutionalised racism' still exists in Britain, whether acknowledged or not, has been blamed on the British imperial legacy. Nevertheless, there are other legacies that are worthy of consideration. Wm Roger Louis believes that the British tried to establish 'orderly and efficient government, as well as rule under law, the establishment of the courts, and the development of constitutions' and therefore he includes the anti-imperialist nationalist movements as part of the achievement of the Empire because they were based on English political values.[34] Terence Ranger felt that Africans had sometimes made use of European 'traditions', but had also retained and developed their own nationalist identities from pre-colonial occupation that found expression in nationalist movements.[35]

In addition, racial competition and conflict in former colonies, like that between the Sinhalese and Tamils of Ceylon, could be seen as a product of imperialism, but equally it might be regarded as a manifestation of South Asian racism. Indians, who were themselves settlers, were expelled from Uganda as a result of Idi Amin's xenophobic and racist policies. Mark Ferro notes that Arab racism was particularly marked during their nineteenth-century slavery period.[36] Chinese racial chauvinism blinded its military leaders to the threat the British really posed to their country. Unable to see the Europeans as anything other than 'barbarians', and conscious of the need to remind their subjects that the Middle Kingdom was the centre of the civilised world, the Chinese commander I-Ching prepared for battle in 1841 by holding tea parties, poetry readings and a competition for the best written proclamation of victory.[37] Although British control of China was limited, the 'loss of face' was not eradicated until the return of the island of Hong Kong in 1997.

P. J. Marshall argued that the British, like other Europeans with colonial empires, believed in racial hierarchies and enforced rigid racist policies.[38] Colonies of settlement were, at times, hostile to non-white immigrants and towns had clearly demarcated racial boundaries. Mixed race marriages, and miscegenation were frowned upon and people of mixed descent were often despised. David Fieldhouse pointed out that the Empire was racist in its distribution of business opportunities, although this was probably a less clear-cut case since trading was always a two-way process and a system of exchange. The inequality was much clearer in the labour legislation of South Africa at the end of the nineteenth century.

The British Empire consisted of those who held racist beliefs, but it was also made up of many who deplored antagonism between races and wanted to avoid any interference with existing social structures. There were those who felt the Empire was genuinely doing good in its capacity as a civilising mission. There were others who thought the whole Empire was an expression of Anglo-Saxon supremacy and that whites had a right to rule. The British West Indies had thrived on slave labour in the late eighteenth century, but the Royal Navy was tireless in stamping out the trade wherever it could be found in the nineteenth. Some apparently racist activities resulted more from accident than design, but the worst brutalities, such as the Amritsar massacre (1919), were condemned by the British themselves.

On balance, it would be fair to say the British Empire produced both prejudice and sympathy, genuine philanthropy and indifference, a strong sense of duty and self-interest. These combinations would be true of all empires, but the nature of an imperialist system was such that the British ruled over other peoples, and outside of the colonies of settlement, without consent. Without doubt, the worst aspect of British imperialism was its association with racial division, and the greatest error the British made was to pursue partnership in such a half-hearted manner until the advent of the Commonwealth. When they no longer ruled, but shared and eventually surrendered their power, they were clearly less liable to the charge of racism.

9 What was the significance of gender to British imperialism?

'No place for a woman'?

It wasn't until the 1970s that gender was regarded as a distinct aspect of the history of the British Empire, but in recent years gender historians have explored the role that sexual identity played in the ideology of imperial rule. To some extent, this development was due to the interest in the construction of power by Michel Foucault and Antonio Gramsci, and the work on the powerful role of knowledge by Edward Said. Gender has become, like many areas of imperial history, a battleground of ideas.

One provocative myth, which seems to encapsulate the debate on gender as a whole, suggested that women were responsible for the destruction of the rapport developed by colonising men with the colonised.[1] In India, it was suggested women had put an end to the chances of racial integration by recreating 'little Britains' in the stations.[2] Ronald Hyam rejected this idea, emphasising that women tended to integrate themselves into the accepted hierarchies.[3] Others wrote about the way that British women engaged themselves in positive welfare work, which, although beneficial, did nevertheless perpetuate the Empire and collaboration with it.[4] To the post-modernists (a term used here to embrace post-colonialists and post-structuralists), this would mean that British women were subjugated just as much as the colonised. Nevertheless, it was generally agreed that native women were at the bottom of the social hierarchy.

Indigenous women, initially seen as victims of the colonial order, were, in fact, already reduced to a low status in many regions prior to the arrival of the British.[5] Indeed, according to feminist historians, Indian men tried to preserve the *purdah* (concealment and absence from public life) of Indian women from the British as a symbol of their preservation of India from the foreigners. In this way, they succeeded in maintaining a patriarchy. It follows, in this argument, that Indian women were repressed both before, and as a consequence of, British rule.

Yet it is noticeable that no historians defend the practices inflicted on women which were outlawed by the British. The ritual of *suttee* (*sati*), the sacrificial burning of widows on their husband's funeral pyres, was regarded as barbaric. The British banned it in 1829, although it continued to take place in territories outside British jurisdiction. In the Punjab, four wives of Ranjit Singh were burned in 1839 and 310 mistresses of the *zenana* were killed on the pyre of Raja Suchet Singh. As a result of this and other incidents, the British banned *suttee* in the Punjab when they annexed it in 1848.

The justification given for *suttee* was that it symbolised an unbreakable matrimonial bond, it removed women whose remarriage was impossible and therefore freed a section of society from the burden of supporting an unproductive female. Yet, *suttee* was not common amongst the lower castes who saw the advantage of using female labour. Moreover, those in the higher castes who advocated it were actually in a financial position to support widows. For nationalist and feminist historians and post-colonial theorists, it was important to show the Empire as paternalistic and patriarchal in order to demonstrate the enlightened nature of their own ideas. *suttee* thus presented a real problem. Gayatri Spivak claimed that women had been denied a history of their own, their voice was unheard, and this fact revealed the Empire at work: 'there is no space from where the subaltern (sexed) can speak.'[6] However, the silencing of 'third world women', as Chandra Talpade Mohanty put it, could not negate the fact that lives were saved because *suttee* was banned.[7] Whatever the verdict on it, *suttee* remained a source of conflict during British rule. On 2 September 1932, for example, a high caste Brahmin man died at Fathpur Sikri near Agra. His young widow was dissuaded from committing *suttee*, but a crowd gathered and demanded she die. The police locked her in her house to protect her, but the mob burst in and dragged her to the pyre. Shooting broke out in which three died, but the police rescued the girl.

Similarly on humanitarian grounds, the British curbed other Indian rituals. Female infanticide was widely practised in India before the arrival of the British, usually as a means of escaping ruinous dowries. Lord Wellesley banned infant sacrifices to the Ganges, Lord Hardinge outlawed female infanticide, and Major General Sleeman in Oudh and Colonel Walker in Kathiawar raised money themselves to pay for dowries and avoid the deaths.[8] Between 1847 and 1854, Sir John Campbell prevented the Khond people of Orissa from executing men and women as human sacrifices to their fields. Moreover, in 1843 the British freed millions of female slaves by abolishing the practice throughout India.

The abolition of tribal practices against women was not limited to India. Female circumcision, a Kikuyu practice in East Africa, was also banned. Few would defend this mutilation directly, even if it can be explained with reference to 'culture'. Throughout the colonies millions of women, although hardly liberated by the British Empire, at least enjoyed for the first time some protection against these practices from the law.

The identities that were associated with gender have aroused a lot of interest, particularly since the mid-1990s. There has been an assumption that racism and sexual identity were somehow linked, although class identity has largely escaped this association.[9] Mrinalini Sinha argued that colonised men in Bengal were regarded as timid and 'effeminate', particularly if they seemed to favour intellectual interests and careers. The British men, the colonisers, associated themselves with manly, warrior pastimes that tested their courage and endurance, such as hunting.[10] Diana Wylie contends that 'Imperialism was so powerful that it could make some men feel as if colonised men had lost their gender.'[11]

It has been alleged that sexual jealousy between white and brown men transformed British class snobbery into racism.[12] Ronald Hyam suggested: 'the maximisation of sexual opportunity overseas was probably an essential part of the dynamics of empire, crucial to the way the whole imperial and expansionist enterprise worked.'[13] He argued that sexual relationships 'soldered together the invisible bonds of Victorian empire', but that sex had been a motive for expansion because 'nearly everyone [was] looking out for sexual gratification'.[14] However, it could be argued that as with some biographies, the subliminal and intimate is exaggerated to account for the great events of history. Did it matter, for example, when considering the causes of the South African War that Alfred Lord Milner had a number of secret liaisons before finally getting married at the age of 67?

In the Indian Army certain castes and races were considered 'manly' and 'martial', especially those from the Punjab or the mountain states on the fringes of India. The Madras soldiery from the southern plains were, by contrast, seen as 'effeminate' because they had not been engaged in frequent wars and had become 'soft' because of pastoralism and the tropical climate.[15] For some, these categories merely reflected the impact of ideas on the colonised. In other words, Madrassi troops were less effective because they were made to feel inferior compared with Sikhs who were constantly praised for their courage. However, this kind of measurement of an army's courageousness and effectiveness was very crude. Morale, leadership, willingness to take casualties and the cause for which troops were fighting may also have had a part to play. The Gurkhas were regarded as brave soldiers before the arrival of the British, and they maintained their reputation for fighting prowess. Their military qualities stemmed from a whole range of factors, but the British preference for them was probably because they reflected the values the British themselves admired: endurance, ruthlessness without barbarity, cheerfulness in spite of all conditions and gallantry. Tony Gould noted that regimental pride was also important: 'an impersonal pride that is the opposite of vanity – was still an evident characteristic of Gurkha soldiers and their better officers. This counted for something, however much it might be undervalued in the contemporary world.'[16]

Women and post-colonial theory

Imperial literature is a favourite target of post-modernists and a rich ground for the exploration of the connections between class, gender and race. Anne McClintock rejected the traditional debates about imperialism – the self–other of orientalism, or the metropolis–periphery of economic imperialism – to ask: what were the origins of people's feelings about gender, class and race?[17] The 'shifting relationships' she discovered may throw some light on policies and institutions, but it is such an opaque view, which leaves out so many of the real forces behind the British Empire, as to leave its significance in doubt. Indeed, this is a criticism that could be levelled at all gender studies of the Empire. In seeking to shine new light into the recesses of the imperial experience, the most significant or important areas are left out. John MacKenzie may be right when he points out that much of the language of the Empire was gendered – hunting and war were associated with men, and grades of responses to that manliness were used to reinforce categories of 'Other', northern from southern European, white from black, and mountain dwellers from plains dwellers. But does it amount to any more than that?[18] Language was the response, not the cause, which shaped the forms that later developed.

Clare Midgley complained that there had been a lack of attention to: 'the gender metaphors which are so central to imperial discourse: to the descriptions of colonial exploration and conquest as the penetration of virgin lands, and to the feminised representations of colonised men'.[19] Yet once again, Midgley seems to be unable to answer the key problem of whether language was a motive force of imperialism. It was not as important as the more practical and fundamental business of making money, reaching new converts or protecting trade with military force. All these factors also had their limits, and so it must also be true of language and gender.

'Discourse', nevertheless, continues to make a universalist claim over Imperial History. Midgley supports the attack on colonial history and its 'discourse'. The radical and feminist basis of the gender approach to imperial history, which she favours, was a reaction to the idea that imperial history was rooted in the nineteenth century, where it had been used to justify the Empire. However, this reveals another erroneous assumption, that there is no difference between mainstream Imperial History of the nineteenth century and the writing of the present. For example, Midgley attacks Peter Marshall's *Cambridge Illustrated History of the British Empire* (1996), claiming that it attempted to 'diffuse radical challenges to its legitimacy' by inclusion of a minority of alternative views which were 'relegated' to the 'dominant, apologetic tone' of the book. She also claims that: 'Imperial History provides the last place within the various sub-disciplines of history where the Whig approach [which stresses that Britain brought less developed countries forward and left a legacy of enlightened government] continues to thrive. The reason for this, I would argue, is ideological: it provides a means of justifying British imperialism.'[20] Can it really be said that authors of British history, or indeed any history, are in the business of justifying something? Where does this leave female historians who are trying to write a history of women in the Empire?

Dane Kennedy criticised the feminist and alternative approaches because they tended to slide into hostility towards writing history at all and claimed that writing a history of those who had left few sources, such as illiterate women in the colonies, was almost impossible.[21] Indeed, even Midgley admitted that unless these critics moved beyond writing about culture, they would be in danger of not being taken seriously at all. The problem which arises is that in trying to write in a role for women, there is a risk of exaggerating their importance. This might result in a history that suits modern sensibilities, but not one that is really a typical or representative account of the past.

Nevertheless, there is a history of women in the Empire to be written that is not loaded by another agenda. Jenny Sharpe has examined the complex position of white women as both members of a dominant race and the subordinate gender, highlighting the ambiguity of 'position' for women, poor whites and other marginalised groups in the Empire.[22] Antoinette Burton and Benita Perry have carried out investigations of women in India and found them conservative and integrated.[23] Margaret Strobel argued that the picture in Africa is a complex one of complicity *and* resistance.[24] Rosalind O'Hanlon has shown how female labour was a significant factor in the machinery of Empire.[25] Changing labour relationships, such as the influx of single women into the jute mills of India or the Copper Belt camps of Zambia, could have a major social impact on indigenous societies. O'Hanlon also shows how customary laws emerged – adaptations of local customs combined with British laws – to alter the status of women. For example, the Shona of southern Rhodesia were liable to punishment for adultery, even though sexual relations were not 'private' in the European sense. To bring the Shona women, liberated by equality before the law by the British, back under the control of the family unit, new laws were passed to make men and women equally liable for adultery in 1916.

Women as symbols

Women also became the icons of idealised notions of the state, for both colonisers and colonised: Gandhi saw the suffering and self-sacrifice of women as a distinctive form of spirituality, which eschewed violence for selflessness, endurance and compassion. Women have also become political icons for nationalists, for instance Sarojini Naidu, who was the first woman to become the elected President of the Indian National Congress in 1925.[26] To colonisers, British women were expected to pursue the ideals of motherhood, a particularly vital concern when social-Darwinist fears about racial degeneration were becoming more widespread from the 1880s. For the young there was the Boy Scout Movement to promote manliness and the Girl Guides for feminine preparations for later life.

The Indian Mutiny illustrated the status and vulnerability of women and girls in a dramatic way. The massacre of 200 women and children at Cawnpore left an indelible mark on Anglo–Indian relations for the remainder of British rule in India. At Delhi too, 49 women perished, and across all the stations of the province of Oudh there were tales of women having been tortured, sexually assaulted and murdered.[27] Atrocities against women led to later scares about the 'black peril' in other parts of the Empire, particularly a fear of rape in Africa and South-East Asia.[28]

The imposition of Western forms of behaviour between sexes coincided with larger numbers of British women emigrating, in some cases to further their careers as missionaries, and in others simply to accompany husbands. This gave rise to a belief that the arrival of British women, with their tastes for 'civilised standards', drove down the numbers of native mistresses and widened the gulf between the rulers and the ruled. There was even a fear with the advent of the militant Suffragettes in the Edwardian period, that the 'female howling Dervishes', as Curzon called them, would create havoc overseas and perhaps foster colonial revolts.

However, there was a long tradition of contact between Western men and women and colonial women, without there necessarily being any sexual connotations or implications for politics. *Ayahs* were the servants of British families in India and they were divided into hierarchies of their own, but they enjoyed an intimacy with British children and their parents which, along with the contact with other servants, bearers and *syces* (grooms), refutes the idea of total segregation. Men in the Indian Army and political service were discouraged from early marriage either by financial constraints or by their careers, and as a result their native servants remained in service for many years and developed strong bonds of loyalty. For many young women, India, like colonies in Africa, was terrifying: diseases, insects and wild animals didn't appeal to all.[29] The 'intrusion' of having servants was also a shock, and having to manage a household in an unfamiliar culture tended to encourage British women to recreate as much of their original homes as possible. They were unable to alter traditions, or *Dastur*, such as bowing, in the cooking of meals and the codes of behaviour, even when they tried. More often than not the local language was used, not English. Nevertheless, the relationship was feudal: protection and wages were given in return for service.

Officially, British soldiers were dissuaded from mixing closely with the local women, but brothels were unofficially tolerated and some soldiers married Eurasian girls in India because British women were scarce.[30] Even for married personnel, separation was common. Children over five were often sent back to Britain for their education. Husbands, particularly those in the army, could spend months in other parts of the country. In one case, perhaps not an untypical one, a wife spent only three years of 13 years of married life with her husband.[31] Some women did try to break down the exclusion of women in India by holding 'purdah-parties', but they had a limited impact, partly because of the vast cultural differences between them (they were still regarded as part of the colonial order), and also because there were so few British women. In India in 1900, the proportion of women to men was 38 to 100. In Rhodesia, there were twice as many British men as women, and in West Africa women were even scarcer. Most marriages between British colonial men and British women took place in Britain, but there were women who went in search of available and suitable men in the so-called 'fishing fleets'. Once married, the wife accompanied the husband overseas and had to make rapid adjustments in lifestyle.

The stereotype of the British *memsahib* only leading a trivialised life is misleading. Women were often engaged in estate management and farming, and were increasingly occupied by teaching, nursing and philanthropic work. Some women even travelled into the Empire to champion reform, like Mary Carpenter, who aimed to provide education for Indian women in 1866, and Eleanor Rathbone, who wanted to see the franchise extended to women in India in the 1920s. For women in the colonies of settlement, their life was often as hard as the life led by agricultural workers in Britain: the least well off in British society. In Australia and New Zealand, it was hoped that the emigration of women would force the men there to adopt more civilised patterns of behaviour, and improved work routines. Single men were thought to be susceptible to the vices of indolence and drunkenness, but women would act as 'God's Police'. Another reason for the encouragement of female emigration was to increase the size of the population in the colonies, but this was a painfully slow process. In Australia, for example, women did not equal the number of men until after the Second World War. New Zealand's population did not reach a million until 1908 and the entire population of Canada in 1914 did not exceed the population of London.

Women and imperialism: conclusions

British women did have a role in the Empire and it is one worthy of further study. So far, there has been an imbalance in portraying women in terms of 'culture' rather than examining the practical roles they played too. Studies will need to move, as Margaret Strobel's have done, beyond the endless search for victimisation and the relationships and language of power to examine the impact they had in supporting the Empire.[32] Instead of only looking at the impact on women, there is still the need to show what women did and how it was done. To reflect the relative importance of their role, this should be set in the context of the whole history of the empire. The results may reveal that the differences between the genders were not that great. An analogy can be found in imperial literature: women were regarded as stoical, civilising but generally submissive, but then again, the characteristics extolled for men were bravery, endurance, discipline and duty – the similarity of values is striking. When the same formula is applied to women's work on the farms of Australia, the mission stations of Africa and the social systems that accompanied the administration of India, then a more accurate history of women and the Empire can be written.

The impact of British imperialism on non-European women was no less important than the impact on men. New labour opportunities were created, social relations were regulated and British legislation affected their status before the law. The lives of non-European women and the role of women as symbols of the colonised offer considerable opportunities for further research. In particular, there is still scope to incorporate the experiences of the British colonisers such as those recorded by Iris Portal. During her conversations with Indian women while doing child welfare and hospital work, the wife of a *Jemadar* (Indian Officer) asked her if it was true that 'English ladies run about in their underpants'. Iris Portal denied it, but the wife was adamant that her husband had seen women 'running about in pants'. She added: 'I think it's absolutely disgusting'. Portal had to explain that they were: 'just innocent English girls playing tennis in shorts', but the immodesty of dress was incomprehensible to Indian women.[33]

10 The Great War: watershed or continuity?

The First World War was a global conflict because it was a war of empires. It profoundly affected the British Empire and was known to contemporaries as the Great War. Ever since, scholarship of the war has focused primarily on casualty statistics and controversy has arisen over the relationship between leadership and the 'butcher's bill'. Republicans in Australia draw attention to the sacrifice of the 'Diggers' at Gallipoli as evidence of British incompetence, and Canadians at the Western Front memorials in France regard the First World War as the crucible of a fully independent nationhood. There is little doubt that the war dead still evoke strong emotions. In Ireland, nationalists felt compelled to make their own blood sacrifice in 1916 against the background of the war. Indeed, the war encouraged large numbers throughout the Empire to reconsider their position *vis-à-vis* Britain, producing both fierce loyalty and bitter enmity. However, hundreds of thousands of imperial subjects volunteered to serve the Empire, and many of their units sustained high casualties without opposition to British leadership, unlike the mutinies that occurred in France and Russia. India, for example, produced the largest volunteer army in history for the Empire. Those who had eagerly sought imperial consolidation before the war were encouraged that, in the supreme test, there was a strong sense of solidarity. This was due, in part, to the sense that the Empire was on trial.[1] Men, food, raw materials, equipment and money were freely offered and these sustained Britain's imperial war effort. Outside of the European theatre, imperial troops played a significant operational role.

The contribution of India

When the war broke out, George V declared war on behalf of the Empire. This meant that the colonies of Africa and the Imperial Dominion of India automatically joined the war. It was anticipated that due to the needs of internal security, India would only be able to provide two divisions and a cavalry brigade, but such was the widespread support for the war effort that by 1918 India had 573,000 in the field. India despatched two infantry and two cavalry divisions on the outbreak of war as well as four artillery brigades. A total of 23,500 British and 78,000 Indian troops (more than had been planned in 1913) went overseas. By the end of 1914, six Expeditionary Forces were mobilised and more followed in 1915. By 1918, 1.3 million men, 172,000 animals and 3.6 million tonnes of stores had left India for the war.[2] In addition to the regular Indian Army were the Imperial Service troops of the Princely States. Although most of the 100,000 men were retainers, about 21,000 were trained by British officers and armed in the same way as the Indian Army. As well as this manpower, the Princes made other gestures: the Nizam of Hyderabad offered Britain 60 *lakhs* of rupees (£400,000) and the Maharaja of Mysore donated 40 *lakhs*. Major-General Sir Pratab Singh Bahadur, the Regent-Maharaja of Jodhpur, served in the war (even though he was 70) because he believed that if the British were shedding their blood like water, the Rajputs should demonstrate their gratitude and shed their blood too. The Jam Saheb of Nawangar, K. S. Ranjitsinjhi (the Sussex and England batsman), mobilised every horse and motor vehicle for the war effort and also equipped a field hospital.

The Indian Corps landed at Marseilles on 26 September 1914 and took part in the early fighting on the Western Front. However, the haste created by the sudden crisis meant that the Indian troops were poorly equipped for a European climate. Heavy casualties amongst the British officers and an unprecedented number amongst men combined with the cold and unfamiliar weather to cause a decline in morale.[3] It was difficult to replace these men quickly and Indian units' *esprit de corps* relied on a close-knit relationship: British officers of the Indian Army had to speak the language of their soldiers and were expected to fulfil the role not only of leader, but also of father-figure and advisor.[4] They were expected to be conversant with the religious or caste nature of their men. Despite the losses, there were successes. Scores of Indian troops were decorated for gallantry and the Indian Corps scored a notable victory on 10 March 1915 at Neuve Chappelle.[5]

At the end of 1915, two divisions were withdrawn from France to augment the Indian Army Expeditionary Force in Mesopotamia. General Townshend's force of only 13,000, initially successful against the Turks, was besieged at Kut el Amara.[6] Despite attempts to relieve them, the garrison was starved into submission in December 1915, an event regarded as a major blow to prestige. The failure of Indian troops in East Africa, and the collapse of the Gallipoli offensive, produced feelings of disappointment. However, Indian troops continued to serve in France until 1918 and their successes in East Africa and Mesopotamia in 1917 and 1918 did much to restore the reputation of the Indian Army.

In India itself during the war, the population was relatively unaffected by anti-imperialist agencies. The theosophist and socialist Annie Besant (who founded and later became the president of the Indian Home Rule League before leading the Indian National Congress in 1917) launched a propaganda campaign that was ineffectual. Indian Muslims were worried that the war would compel them to fight Muslim Turks, but declarations by the government of India and expressions of support for Britain by Muslim princes calmed sectarian anxieties. German Intelligence tried to support the Muslim Ghadr revolutionary faction by a shipment of arms under the direction of Har Dayal in 1915. The move was detected and the Ghadrites were suppressed. In Bengal, revolutionaries had attempted to assassinate the Viceroy, Lord Hardinge, and his wife in 1912, but their wartime disturbances were limited. In the Punjab, *dacoits* (bandits) were also rounded up, whilst on the volatile North-West Frontier, the Mohmand rising of 1915 was ended by a 'blockade' (embargo). The charismatic Mullah Powindah inspired a rebellion amongst the Mahsuds, but this was ended by a military operation in 1917. Given that British forces in the subcontinent numbered only 15,000 (before the arrival of Territorial Force reinforcements), it is perhaps surprising that there were no serious rebellions. Indeed, given the military setbacks of the war, the absence of a general insurrection points to the widespread acquiescence to British rule and provides an interesting contrast with the atmosphere of the 1920s.

There were only two episodes when the loyalty of Indian troops was in doubt. The first disturbance occurred in Singapore in January 1915 when three Pathan companies of the 130th Baluchis feared they were being sent to fight their Turkish coreligionists. Their protest amounted to a refusal to board a troopship. On 15 February 1915, again at Singapore, the 5th Light Infantry were persuaded by an *imam* to believe that the Germans were Muslims, a notion also encouraged by Ghadr agents in the city. Although the unit was on its way to Hong Kong, the rumour that they were to be sent against fellow Muslims sparked a mutiny. The officers and British sentries were murdered, but the mutineers received no assistance from the German civilian internees they had released. An *ad hoc* collection of Malay States Volunteers, Royal Navy bluejackets, 200 Japanese 'special constables', French and Russian sailors, British, imperial and European civilians, and the troops of the Sultan of Johore were used to capture the mutinous sepoys. Compared with the Mutiny of 1857, and given the nature of the war and its cost, the unrest at Singapore was not serious and German-inspired revolutionary agitation was successfully contained throughout the war.[7]

India's part in the Great War was thus significant and it produced some far-reaching concessions from Britain. In financial terms, India had contributed £160 million to the war effort by 1919, but taking account of all expenditure related to the war the figure was closer to £214 million. The initial wave of loyalty and the popular condemnation of Prussian militarism was sustained, but there was disappointment because of the initial performance of the Indian Army and the experiences of sepoys outside of India, the heavy toll of casualties (Table 3) and unfulfilled expectations that some reward would follow the sacrifice made in a war of freedom against tyranny. In 1917, Lord Chelmsford, the Viceroy, and Edwin Montagu, the Secretary of State for India, calculated that with the war going badly for the Allies, some promise of reform would encourage the educated classes of India to continue to support the war effort.

Table 3   The British Empire's casualties in the First World War[8]

Imperial Forces	Deaths
Great Britain	662,083
Canada	56,119
Australia	58,460
India	47,746
New Zealand	16,132
South Africa	6928
Other Colonies	3649

The famous Montagu-Chelmsford declaration mapped out 'the gradual development of self-governing institutions with a view to the progressive realisation of responsible government in India as an integral part of the British Empire'.[9] The franchise was extended to one-thirtieth of the population (which nevertheless included many who were illiterate), local government Legislative Councils were enlarged and Indian participation in government was to be conceded by instalments. This produced a form of administration named Dyarchy: education, local self-government, public health and excise were handed over to the legislatures, but responsibility for law and order, land revenue and famine relief were retained by a British Governor in Council.[10] The Executive Council was still responsible to London, but a Legislative Assembly was set up with 140 members (105 elected) and a Council of State, or Senate, of 60. Alongside this reform, the Indian Princes were invited to form a Chamber of Princes which would be inaugurated after the war. The Princes were not yet incorporated into British India, but neither were they fully independent as they all had to acknowledge Britain as the 'paramount power'. Thus, India was promised the logical development of rule by a democratic state: the granting of Western-style constitutional government. As George Boyce points out, the reforms were 'unprecedented', because they were based on the principle that parliamentary government was appropriate for India.[11] The war therefore accelerated moves towards 'responsible government'. However, after the war, anxiety about sectarianism made the British cautious, and this, in turn, fuelled the frustrations of India's own elites.

Australia and Gallipoli

Australians see the two world wars as marking greater distinctions between themselves and the motherland, but the degree of severance has been exaggerated in a post-war re-reading of history. Australia demonstrated its loyalty in 1914 by declaring war in support of Britain and by the despatch of the Australian Imperial Force (AIF).[12] All of Australia's troops were volunteers, conscription having been rejected in 1916 and 1917 by referenda. This voluntaryism and the prestige the AIF enjoyed (based on a relaxed view of discipline whilst maintaining a purposeful approach to the war), generated an *esprit de corps* that sustained them in the toughest fighting. Despite the image that they were 'men from the bush', many of the recruits were recently arrived British immigrants or urban men, factors which made the national history-making of republican Australians somewhat ironic.

The greatest controversy surrounding Australian participation in the war concerns the ill-fated Gallipoli campaign.[13] An unsuccessful naval attack on the Dardenelles Straits, part of a plan to capture Constantinople the Turkish capital, prompted an amphibious landing on the Gallipoli peninsula on 25 April 1915. British troops landed under fire at Cape Helles, whilst ANZACs (an acronym for the Australian and New Zealand Army Corps) disembarked at Anzac Cove, but neither force was able to get far inland. Attempts to break out at Suvla Bay and Anzac Cove failed and the whole operation was abandoned in January 1916. Given both the heavy casualties that were sustained and the lack of any lasting success, Gallipoli has come to be associated with the 'futility' and poor leadership of the war. Little praise is offered to Mustapha Kemel and his Turkish troops for their brilliant defence, and Australian tourists are frequently reminded of their national sacrifice on Britain's behalf.[14] However, Australian troops suffered equally heavy casualties on the Western Front. Of the 332,000 troops who served overseas, 212,000 were wounded and 58,460 were killed which represents a casualty rate of 82 per cent: the highest proportion of casualties sustained by any army in the war (see Table 3). At Pozieres on the Somme a simple plaque records that to capture this strategic ridge: 'The Australians fell more thickly than at any place on the Western

Front.' Such an epitaph can only evoke sympathy for those that fell and understanding of the anguish still felt in Australia. Yet, far from feeling that Australia was a mere utensil of the Empire, British contemporaries and British military histories were universal in their praise. One typical view was that of Sir William Birdwood, who regarded his service with the ANZACs as: 'the greatest privilege [of which] I shall be prouder to the end of my days than any honour which can be given me'.[15]

The question of Australian loyalty to Britain during the war was not raised during the conflict – but after. It was only Germans and Turkish troops who did not understand why Australians volunteered to fight 'England's War'. The proportion of Irish Catholics who joined the AIF also indicates that loyalty to the Empire was greater than loyalty to Sinn Fein or the cause of Irish independence. Nevertheless, Australian troops had exasperated Sir Douglas Haig because they regarded themselves as allies, and therefore they could not be directed as if part of the British army.[16] Anzac Day rightly became a point of national pride, and gradually an icon of national identity. Although it was sometimes thought later that the losses at Gallipoli were sustained in the cause of 'another country', at the time Australians thought of themselves as belonging to the British Empire. Memorials referred to 'Independent Australian Britons' without fear of contradiction.[17] Indeed, this was fitting, for the Gallipoli campaign was a *combined* British and ANZAC operation.

Canada and New Zealand

Canada automatically joined the war in 1914. Sir Wilfred Laurier, the Leader of the Opposition in the Canadian House of Commons, declared that Canada was of one mind and one heart: supportive of Britain. However, recruitment amongst the French-Canadians was less enthusiastic than in the English-speaking population. As in Australia, a specially raised force, the Canadian Expeditionary Force (CEF), was sent to Europe. Its first division arrived in February 1915. A total of 418,000 CEF served overseas, but a further 14,500 reservists returned to Britain and 21,000 Canadians served in British units. Conscription was introduced in the winter of 1917–18, but it raised only 86,000; far less than the volunteers. Like Australia, many of these volunteers were recognisably 'British', rather than self-consciously 'Canadian'.[18] Yet, once again, casualties were high: 210,000 (including 56,119 dead) representing 48 per cent of the total overseas force. It was this loss, and the military achievements of Canadian soldiers, that was seen as the common bond of national identity. The Secretary of State, Lawrence MacAulay, referred to this as: 'the very fabric of our nationhood . . . In some senses, we became a nation because of what they accomplished.'[19] From 1832 the small colony of Newfoundland had remained outside British North America, and subsequently, perhaps because of the shared losses of the Great War, it became part of Canada. Although celebrated as a 'Canadian' wartime force today, it was not actually incorporated until 1949. In financial terms, Canada also shouldered a great collective burden. Its national debt rose from £67 million to £317 million. Nevertheless, the French-speaking minority reacted angrily to conscription and riots broke out in Quebec in 1918. The social division of the English- and French-speaking communities was, at least, contained. In the light of this tension, it is understandable that Canadians wanted to see the war as a *common* sacrifice and the crucible of a national identity.

New Zealand's war effort was as impressive as any of the other dominions. Half of the eligible male population served in the armed forces and 58,000 became casualties. About 25 per cent of New Zealanders were British-born, so the enlistment figures truly represent dominion loyalty to Britain. In the South Pacific, the Nive of the Cook Islands, with a population of only 4000, sent £164 to the New Zealand government and an offer of 200 men, describing themselves as: 'a small child that stands up to help the King stand fast'.[20] New Zealand brought in conscription to supplement volunteering in August 1916 and the only opposition to it came from miners, who went on strike in April 1917 until they were exempted. However, the effects of conscription were limited: 92,000 of the 124,000 enlisted were volunteers anyway.

New Zealand's contribution to the Great War has not been criticised to the same degree as in Australia, but Glyn Harper's *The Massacre at Passchendaele: The New Zealand Story* illustrates both the terrible conditions of the Third Battle of Ypres in

1917, and 'faults in the British Imperial command structure'. In one sense though, this work is a typical history of the war: plenty of criticism of the leadership, but no mention that the battles of Messines ridge (7 June) and of Broodseinde Ridge (4 October) were successes planned by the very same 'British Imperial command structure'.[21]

South Africa and the campaigns in Africa

In 1910, South Africa had become a united state, and the election of that year returned to power the South African Party which was based on Louis Botha's Transvaal *Het Volk* Party. Botha, formerly a guerrilla leader against the British, spent the years after the South African War trying to reconcile Boers and Britons. He was ably supported by his defence minister, Jan Smuts, who had also led guerrilla commandoes in the conflict of 1899–1902. However, at the outbreak of the First World War, some of those Boers who still harboured resentment of British rule, including J. M. B. Hertzog, remembered that Germany had, in the past, sympathised with the Transvaal and Orange Free State. Botha agreed with London that South Africans should assume responsibility for the defence of South Africa and they should occupy German South-West Africa. However, a group of leading Boer generals, all veterans of the war of 1899, declared themselves in favour of independence from Britain and launched a rebellion. Botha assumed command of the loyal forces and defeated each of the renegade leaders in turn. By mid-December 1914, the 5700 rebels had been killed or rounded up, but it had been a small, badly co-ordinated effort against Botha's 40,000 strong Afrikaner Defence Force. Sentences were lenient, most prison terms were short and only one was shot (for desertion in the field), which was in strong contrast to British treatment of the Irish rebels in 1916; but, by then, attitudes had hardened because of two years of war. However, Hertzog, who had split from the South Africa Party and formed a new National Party in 1914, on a platform of Afrikaner nationalism, South African self-sufficiency and opposition to participation in the 'European war', raised a challenge to the imperial connection and helped to foster that siege mentality which did so much to distort South African politics in the decades that followed.

The British Imperial Forces were instrumental in helping Britain win the campaigns in Africa. In April 1915, Botha launched three columns of South Africans into German South-West Africa. With overwhelming numerical superiority, he captured Windhoek and received the German surrender on 9 July. In West Africa, the small forces available were scattered across Sierra Leone and Gold Coast in internal security duties, so it was difficult to mount any operation against German Togoland and Cameroon. However, attempts to declare Togoland neutral by the German commander indicated the weakness of the German garrison and it was captured, after skirmishes at Kamina, by the Gold Coast Regiment and Senegalese Tirailleurs. In Cameroon, the Inspector-General of the West-African Frontier Force, under Major-General Charles Dobell, led 4300 British and French African troops to Duala. The Germans, after some resistance, retreated into the interior. Reinforced at Yaunde, it was impossible to move against them until columns were organised from the coast, from the east (a force of Belgians, French, the British West Indian Regiment and 5th Indian Light Infantry), and from the north (4000 British Africans). Despite slow progress, the German troops were compelled to trek into Spanish Guinea where they were interned.

The greatest organisation by General Smuts was essential to defeat German resistance in East Africa. Initially, the Germans were able to attack British East Africa (and its strategic railway to Uganda) at will as the local forces numbered only 15,000 European and 2300 African defenders. Using British, East and West African, South African and Indian troops, Smuts pursued the German forces until the end of the war. Overall, Britain's African Empire had proved its loyalty just like the colonies of settlement, although it was only white South Africans who were employed as fighting troops on the Western Front.

For black troops who had been employed as labourers on the Western Front or in shipping, the war revealed that the British could suffer military setbacks. In addition, black stevedores employed at Liverpool's docks were amazed to find that white men worked alongside them, even though they had been told that whites did not perform manual labour.[22] *The Lagos*

Weekly Record announced in 1917 that allied victory would mean: 'democracy for all peoples, regardless of race, creed or colour', a hope that seemed to be reinforced by the 'Fourteen Points' peace plan offered that year by President Woodrow Wilson. The war was thus a catalyst for new aspirations in Africa as well as in Europe.

Ireland and the Easter Rising

The question of Home Rule for Ireland had provoked a constitutional crisis before the war, and, although it was strictly a question that concerned the United Kingdom, there was a fear in right-wing circles that the 'loss' of Ireland would damage the Empire. John Redmond, the Irish nationalist leader, hoped that the war would give Ireland the status of the other dominions. Irish loyalties were divided by the outbreak of war. The Ulster Volunteers (the paramilitaries formed in 1912 to prevent six, mainly protestant counties being subsumed into a devolved, Catholic state) formed their own Ulster Division (the 36th) as a mark of solidarity with Britain. They fought with distinction throughout the Great War and suffered particularly heavy losses at the battle of the Somme in 1916. The Irish Volunteers, paramilitaries in favour of Home Rule, also joined the British Army. John Redmond told them that they were fighting for Catholics in Belgium, but large numbers were joining up anyway. Some felt that it was their duty since they were still part of the United Kingdom, others looked for adventure.

However, a handful of extremists believed that 'England's difficulty was Ireland's opportunity'. The Irish Volunteers therefore split: a small, hard-line group called the IRB (Irish Republican Brotherhood) divorced themselves from the Volunteers and began to plan a rebellion against British rule. They were led by Padraic Pearse, a utopian schoolteacher, and James Connolly, a socialist and Irish nationalist, and supported by Sir Roger Casement, a disaffected former British consular official. Pearse called for a 'violent gesture', even a sacrifice, without the need for any particular or lasting achievement. This tragic attitude reflected the view of the time; the war was thought to be a 'cleansing' process for old problems and only a great blood sacrifice was appropriate when thousands were dying in the trenches. Connolly was in favour of preparation for a rising, but the training was still inadequate which has lent an air of heroic failure to the myths that came later. Nevertheless, there was an ominous sense that violence for its own sake was the purpose of the rebellion. According to George Boyce, the blood sacrifice of these volunteers persuaded later generations of nationalists to see any compromise as a 'sell out' to the ideals of these men. For loyalists, the heroic sacrifice of Ulstermen on the Somme, dying for their country and their cause, has given a similar sense of commitment for their successors ever since.

There were a number of problems in the preparation and execution of the rising. The IRB Council decided to delay the rising until Easter Monday 1916, but with so few men or resources they would only be able to seize the centre of Dublin. This was supposed to act as a spark to a general uprising by the people. The rising itself began as 1600 IRB volunteers occupied the General Post Office in Dublin as its headquarters. Supported by artillery and the gunboat *Helga*, 12,000 British troops engaged the IRB in street fighting. On Sunday 30 April, Pearse and Connolly surrendered; 450 had died and 2614 were wounded, many of whom were civilians. The British losses were 116 killed and 368 wounded. Far from signalling a general rising, Dubliners were appalled at the damage and regarded the rebellion as a futile gesture.

It was the aftermath of the rising that changed opinion in Ireland. To the British, already under pressure in France, the action of the IRB was nothing short of treachery. General Maxwell, in command at Dublin, was determined to prevent more disturbances. He angered local opinion by arresting 3430 men and 79 women and interrogating them; 1841 were interned in England, but the rest were released. Of the ringleaders, 15 were executed. Connolly, who had been wounded in the fighting, was strapped to a chair and shot. The rising was a squalid episode, but the British response, although legal in wartime, turned the Irish public against them.[23] Redmond's nationalist supporters dwindled to be replaced by the more hard-line Sinn Fein, and De Valera, the future President of the Irish Free State, was released from gaol in July 1917, whereupon he won the East Clare seat as an anti-British candidate.

The British government tried to encourage compromise between the Ulstermen and the southern Irish. In May 1916, Lloyd George tried to bring Sir Edward Carson, the Ulster leader, and Redmond together. He promised Redmond that Ulster's exclusion from a united Ireland would be temporary. To Carson, he suggested that exclusion would be permanent. Clearly, Lloyd George was hoping for a compromise in the short term, and banking on a softening of sectarian antagonism in the longer term. However, the Conservative members of the Cabinet refused to accept that Ulster might be cut off and the talks broke down. In July 1917, the Irish Convention was set up, but Sinn Fein refused to join. Ulstermen argued that they would not, indeed they could not make concessions. The Convention lasted until July 1918, but the prospect of peace between north and south seemed slim at the end of the war.

The Easter Rising was the most serious rebellion Britain faced during the war years. In peacetime, given the strength of the British Army in Ireland, it would not have been attempted. The greatest irony was that it need never have taken place. Irish self-government was already on the statute books awaiting implementation, and even the die-hard opposition to Home Rule, the Ulstermen, sought only to exempt themselves – not the South. Irish nationalists quickly attributed the greatest significance of the rising to the martyrdom of its leaders, but this had not been the initial aim (except, perhaps, for Pearce). From an imperial perspective, the response to the rising demonstrated Britain's continued strength. It was able to suppress a rebellion at a critical stage of a war which had already absorbed much of its military capacity. However, George Boyce, referring to the 'Anglo–Irish War' of 1919–20, concluded: 'The assumption that empire – white empire – was based on consent, on the belief that the mother of parliaments, Britain, did not coerce her children, was now to receive a rude setback'.[24]

Sinn Fein set up an Irish parliament in 1919, but also declared Ireland independent. Responding to this defiance and also to a wave of murders and arson by the IRA (the new title of the old Irish Volunteers), demobilised British soldiers were enrolled to support the police as auxiliaries. The methods of the Black and Tans, the name that reflected their mix of police and military uniforms, were the same as those of the

IRA but with the experience of years of trench warfare. Terror was thus fought with counter-terror. However, the chief difficulty for the British was distinguishing between civilians and the IRA, a problem that was to resurface in many wars of decolonisation. On the other hand, the handling of the war was quite distinct from the anti-guerrilla operations in South Africa between 1900–2. It was regarded as a police operation rather than a war. The British Army was not deployed in a conventional campaign to advance on Dublin. Instead, the conflict, which was regarded as an internal matter for the United Kingdom rather than an 'imperial' issue, was concluded with a political settlement.

The Government of Ireland Act (1920), which granted southern Ireland and Ulster their own Home Rule parliaments with a joint council of Ireland, failed to satisfy Sinn Fein. The pattern of terror and counter-terror continued, but, in mid-1921 General Neville Macready warned Lloyd George that victory would require: 'an operation of war more extensive and more bitter than would be acceptable to the judgement and conscience of the British people'.[25] Lloyd George knew that the British pubic were unlikely to back any campaign that smacked of 'Prussian frightfulness' and he arranged a truce in July 1921. The compromise struck with Michael Collins and Arthur Griffith in December that year was the partition of Ireland, and the recognition of the Irish Free State as a dominion under royal sovereignty. Ireland was also to shoulder part of the national debt and permit the Royal Navy to use three treaty ports. In January 1922 the Irish parliament ratified the treaty, but when power was transferred in March, De Valera led a faction that refused to accept royal sovereignty and a civil war broke out. De Valera's faction was defeated and the treaty was accepted until a new constitution was approved in 1937. This ended Ireland's dominion status, its allegiance to the Crown and cancelled the treaty ports arrangement. The need for a compromise peace in Ireland, as in South Africa in 1902, certainly influenced the British government in its dealings with India in the mid-1920s. However, in the short term, the British were prepared to fight for the maintenance of the Empire, and they dealt firmly with the Irish, as they were also to do with Indian and Egyptian rioters.

War and Empire: conclusions

There can be little doubt that the British Empire was an imperial arsenal and granary. The colonies of settlement provided Britain with a vast amount of *matériel* and foodstuffs: Canada supplied Britain with half of its shrapnel by 1917, 42 per cent of the 4.5-inch shells and 25 per cent of the 6-inch shells; 97 per cent of Australia's meat was consumed in Britain and 35 per cent of Britain's copper requirements was provided from there; New Zealand supplied frozen meat, wool, dairy produce and minerals; India's jute supply was turned into sandbags. O'Brien calculated that 80 per cent of the casualties and 88 per cent of the expenditure incurred by the British Empire to defeat Germany and Turkey came from the United Kingdom's Treasury and from domestic taxpayers. However, the contribution of the colonies was significant and had far reaching consequences.

The administration of the Empire was altered by the war. When the Liberal government was superseded by a coalition in 1915, Alfred Milner and George Curzon were returned to power and they were eager to assert an imperialist agenda. Imperial supplies got preference in British markets and plans for an Imperial Customs Union were again discussed. There was due consideration to joint decision-making, and, following lobbying by the dominion leaders, representatives from the colonies were invited to join an Imperial War Cabinet on 20 March 1917. It met 14 times during the first six weeks of its existence, and greatly improved the co-ordination of the war effort. Nevertheless, some dominion leaders pursued an independent line. William Hughes asserted that he spoke for Australia in his capacity as Prime Minister and Robert Bordon, the Canadian Premier, refused to send troops in 1915 for Britain's use unless he was consulted on their operational deployment.[26]

There was nothing surprising about the desire of the dominion leaders to have more control over the manpower resources of their countrymen, for in the final analysis, the defining feature of the war was the cost in lives. In addition to the great demands for military manpower at the Front, there was also a shortage of labour for all manner of construction tasks and transport duties: many Africans were recruited as porters in the African campaigns, but as many as 100,000 are thought to have died from disease; and 90,000 Chinese labourers supplemented the Indian workforce, many of them ending up digging trenches in France. At the end of the war, the Spanish influenza epidemic travelled with the troops and labourers. Two million died in India, and possibly as much of 2 per cent of the population in Africa, far more than in the fighting of the Great War. The demobilisation of the armies also placed an immediate burden on the post-war economy, as thousands of men returned to the labour market. The dislocating effects of the war, fought as it was on an unprecedented scale, took several decades to be healed.

Despite all the costs of the war, the victorious British Empire was still intact in 1918. Nevertheless, several historians have seen the First World War as a watershed. Max Beloff argued that the Dominions had asserted their own, independent policy lines during the conflict.[27] W. David McIntyre took a similar line, arguing that the war had been an important factor in the growth of national feeling.[28] Ronald Hyam believed that the war had destroyed the old imperial policies and that a new, more efficient and humane approach was taken, despite the excesses of repression in the immediate post-war years.[29] The war did create a desire for change, both in the colonies and in Britain, but the extent of the change in the inter-war years appears to have been uneven. It was perhaps a watershed in aspirations, but not always in reality.

11

How did British imperialism meet the challenges of the inter-war years?

It is difficult to speak of mass support for modern nationalist movements before the First World War, despite the existence of groups that opposed European influence.[1] Whilst protests in the nineteenth century often attempted to resist the modernising tendencies of British imperialism in the hope of preserving a traditional society, many twentieth-century organisations embraced modernity and even defined themselves by European standards. This generalisation cannot be absolute. Mahatma Gandhi rejected 'British civilisation' in the hope of regenerating an older, more spiritual India. In this sense, Gandhi had more in common with some of the nineteenth-century religious leaders who hoped for a purification and restoration of an older, religious order, than with his contemporaries in the Indian National Congress. Some movements combined atavism and modernity, recognising the developments that had accompanied imperialism as permanent but aspiring to reconstruct a lost past, before the imperial epoch. Francis Robinson has identified how Muslims redefined themselves in the face of British expansion, but also how the Muslim world was able to use the Empire to spread Islam.[2]

The problem for historians is to determine the significance and importance of the nationalist movements in this period. Metropolitan approaches might give the impression that nationalists were marginal, particularly as they failed to secure independence in the inter-war years. Nationalist historians, who are eager to trace the origins of the independence that was eventually achieved, set little store by Britain's 'magnanimous gestures'. They challenge the idea that Britain made a voluntary concession of independence and claim that apart from the 'white dominions', it was a myth that Britain was working towards self-government before the Second World War. As George Boyce points out, even though Britain was obliged to change, 'she did so in order to stay the same', retaining her Great Power status with a whole vocabulary of 'adjustment, accommodation and gradualism'.[3]

Conversely, too much emphasis on the 'success' or 'significance' of independence movements risks distorting the past to suit nationalist sensibilities. In this situation, recourse must be made to the events and sources of the period to determine the extent of British sympathy for self-government in the colonies, the support for nationalist movements and the degree of success they achieved, and how they contrasted with the continuing strength and appeal of the British Empire.

The inter-war years were marked by events of great significance. The Middle East created new problems for the British Empire, as Jewish settlers clashed with Arabs and British rule in the Mandated territories looked increasingly like another form of imperialism. Ireland split away from the United Kingdom. The Indian National Congress appealed for self-government and engaged in protracted negotiations amidst episodes of civil unrest. The Amritsar Massacre of 1919 was an infamous event that has been used to define the brutalities of British imperialism. It appeared to typify the violence inflicted on non-Europeans from the beginning of the Empire. Yet it is possible to see Amritsar as a unique event too, one which has been elevated to the 'symbolic' rather than being typical.

The controversy of the Amritsar Massacre

In April 1919, in the city of Amritsar, the arrest of two Indian politicians led to rioting, arson and the murder of four Europeans. Similar disturbances spread to other cities in the Punjab and then to outlying rural areas where telegraph lines were cut and railways damaged. On 13 April, Brigadier-General Dyer, commander of the Julundur Brigade, who had been instructed to go to Amritsar with reinforcements to control the unrest, ordered his men to fire on unarmed civilians at Jalianwala Bagh, an extensive enclosed wasteland near the city centre. Although proclamations forbade any mass meetings, no warning was given before the shooting. The firing had continued for 10 minutes, resulting in casualties estimated to be 372 dead and 1200 wounded. Ever since, controversy has surrounded the incident. In a wider context, the question of typicality has arisen: was the Amritsar Massacre evidence of routine brutality inherent within the Empire, or was it an exceptional event, provoked by the unique circumstances of 1919?

The significance of the event lies also in its causes and its consequences. In the Punjab, there was resentment at the extension of the wartime curtailment of civil liberties into peacetime, known as the Rowlatt Act. The Montagu-Chelmsford Reform of 1919 (named after the Secretary of State for India and the Viceroy) stated that the goal of the government was to introduce self-rule by stages, but the Lieutenant-Governor of the Punjab, Sir Michael O'Dwyer, was unsympathetic to the 'troublesome and insistent minority' of nationalists.[4] There were also many local grievances, namely the exhaustion of the railway system, a failure of the rains, deaths through influenza, food shortages and a delay in demobilisation, all of which was worsened by wildly exaggerated rumours. However, the shootings and the measures that followed the disturbances in the Punjab damaged Britain's reputation as a civilising influence in India.

Essentially, there were two views of the incident: (1) The riots were spontaneous; the shooting was a 'massacre' and Dyer a murderer. (2) The riots were the prelude to further violence and Dyer had saved the region from a worse bloodbath by prompt if severe action. The Hunter Committee was set up in September 1919 to investigate the incident, but the Indian National Congress staged its own unofficial enquiry (known as the Committee of Enquiry). The key evidence in the controversy is the written testimony of Dyer and his oral responses under questioning. However, some attention has also been given to Dyer's explanations of the 'crawling order', where Indians were ordered to crawl at the place where an English missionary woman had been beaten and left for dead. Significantly, it is thought that this incident had influenced his decision to fire on the crowd at the Jalianawala Bagh. The result of the enquiry was that Dyer was censured and relieved of his command. There was a wave of support for him in Britain and from the British community in India, and a sympathetic response from the House of Lords. It was this sympathy that caused the first non-cooperation campaign by Congress in 1920–2.

Dyer admitted he had, in fact, opened fire at once on arrival at the Bagh. He wanted 'to make a wide impression . . . from a military point of view'.[5] This was not about dispersing the crowd, but about creating a 'sufficient moral effect . . . there could be no question of undue severity'. He felt that, as Europeans had been murdered, with the countryside in turmoil and his own force outnumbered, this was necessary. When challenged about the 'crawling order', Dyer said: 'We look upon women as sacred, or ought to . . . I was looking for a suitable punishment to meet this awful case. I felt the street ought to be looked upon as sacred.'[6] Dyer claimed his action was in keeping with Indian practices for holy ground and that he had the perpetrators flogged in the street for the same reason.

Dyer's actions, and the sympathy for them, had not been typical but were the result of unique circumstances. As Lawrence James points out, many felt that the British Empire was threatened: Soldiers were going on strike because of delays in demobilisation, a handful of revolutionaries had taken over in Russia and were propagating a doctrine of 'world revolution' (which was being broadcast from Tashkent into South Asia), there were anti-British riots in Egypt and a terrorist war against British rule in Ireland. It was against this background, and memories of the Mutiny, that Dyer acted with such severity. However, it was damaging nevertheless because it was designed to be 'neither salutary nor surgical; it was . . . vindictive.'[7] Dyer's actions raised questions about the appropriate use of force in upholding the Empire, which echoed British unease over the handling of the Morant Bay rebellion in Jamaica in 1865.[8]

The incident is still one the greatest controversies of the Empire, and interpretations are often partisan.[9] Equally, the initial statements of approval for Dyer's actions from senior officials were overlooked when Dyer was subjected to the enquiry. He may have been a scapegoat for a government embarrassed by the loss of life. Robin Neillands described the incident as 'disgraceful' but argued that it was an exception since the army was not an 'instrument of oppression'.[10] The immediate effect was the withdrawal of the army from the role of 'military aid to the civil power' in the years that followed, but the events at Amritsar have acquired a wider significance. Christopher Blake, a former officer of the Dogra Regiment, felt that Amritsar was subsequently portrayed: 'as if it was an everyday occurrence'. He continued: 'From what has been written by twentieth-century critics, a man from Mars might get the impression that the British Empire was acquired by force and ruled by vain, corrupt autocrats, addicted to alcohol and women.'[11] Sir Charles Gwynn concluded that Dyer had not followed the 'accepted principles' of imperial policing.[12] Nirad C. Chaudhuri, by contrast, described the British in India in the early twentieth century as 'the Nazis of their time'.[13]

Gandhi and the Indian National Congress

Congress before the First World War had been an urban, educated and elitist organisation with little popular support, coherent organisation or ideology. Its strength, however, lay in its modern outlook. It embraced the idea of change and the acquisition of British-style institutions for India, which set it apart from traditionalist and atavistic opposition groups. Nevertheless, its first successful agitation over the proposed partition of Bengal in 1905, which caught the public imagination, was essentially conservative. Administrative efficiency was not as attractive as the notion of an attack on the mother goddess Kali and *Bande Mataram*, 'Hail to the Motherland', became a popular slogan against the partition. Student demonstrations, and the burning of foreign cloth indicated that there were other grievances below the surface: the lack of prospects of advancement for university graduates (particularly after the reduction in numbers of universities in 1904) and the dominance of British textiles.

Other anti-Western movements also sprang up in this period, such as the Arya Samaj, founded in Lahore by Dayanand Sarasvati. They preached a militant Hinduism that rejected the influence of Christianity or Islam, condemned the killing of cows and claimed that the Vedas scriptures had predicted the inventions associated with Europeans such as steam engines, gunpowder and flying ships, thus reclaiming modern technology as Indian. Violence was promoted by Lala Lajpat Rai and he too assisted in the formation of the orthodox Hindu association, the Mahasabha. The Theosophical Society, founded by the American Colonel Olcott and Madame Blavatsky and later led by the socialist Annie Besant, exalted Hinduism and assisted in the religious revival of the period. Of even greater significance was the work of B. G. Tilak who revived interest in the philosophical poem the *Bhagavad Gita* (Celestial Song), which stated that it was legitimate to kill in the line of duty. This point was driven home in his paper the *Kesari*, which urged people to purge the land of *mlecchas* (foreigners). Two young men, inspired by Tilak, murdered two British officers engaged on plague-prevention duty in Poona and he was imprisoned. This was repeated ten years later after Tilak had inspired the bombing of two English women at Muzzaffarpur.

Terrorism became the most common tactic in Bengal. Gangs armed with *lathis* (clubs) began to extract funds by force, and police, government workers and witnesses were murdered. Sponsored by organisations in London and Paris, assassinations were also carried out against British civilians. G. K. Gokhale, a moderate politician, spoke out against the violence, but, on the suggestion of John Morley the Secretary of State for India, concessions were made in the Indian Councils Act of 1909 and this extended responsibility for a number of areas of local government and enlarged the numbers of councillors. At the 1911 Coronation Durbar, further concessions were announced and in 1912 Lord Hardinge (the Viceroy) spoke out against the harsh treatment of Indians in other parts of the Empire, although his words were, in fact, directed against South Africa's racial laws. They seemed to make little difference. Canada refused entry to a ship of Sikh immigrants, and there was an assassination attempt against Hardinge in 1912. For nationalists, direct action had moved the British government to reform.

After the war, Mohandas Ghandi replaced the older moderates. He had trained as a lawyer in Britain and travelled to South Africa where he took up the cause of the Indian community there against the race laws of the state of Natal. He served in the South African War and later the Zulu Revolt as a stretcher-bearer, and he founded an *ashram* (community) although he spent much of his time working in Johannesburg. It was in South Africa that, pondering his readings of Christianity,

Ruskin, and the *Bhagavad Gita*, he advocated *satyagraha* (soul force).[14] The *hartal* had long been a protest against unjust authority, but Gandhi preferred the method by which the person who had been wronged would, according to tradition, sit patiently (the *dharma*) at the door of the wrongdoer and fast until death, whereupon the moral responsibility for the life lost would be on the wrongdoer. Gandhi's legal experience had given him a clear understanding of the basis of British law and the ethos of the British constitutional system. He knew that the British had to be seen to be doing Christian good work in the service of others in order to justify the Empire. He knew that the basis of the system was the law and that the British would apply considerable force to uphold that law against insurrection. This raises important questions about Gandhi's methods: were they typically Indian or drawn from a hybrid of Western and Indian ideas? Were they, in fact, the only methods that Gandhi could use? Until the Amritsar Massacre, Gandhi was a keen supporter of the Empire that had given him advancement and a wider, global view. He believed: 'the British Empire had certain ideals with which I had fallen in love, and one of those ideals is that every subject of the Empire has the freest scope for his energies and honour and whatever he thinks is due to his conscience.'[15]

Yet Gandhi adopted the ascetic life in 1915 on his return to India, rejecting the modernisation associated with British rule. He felt that materialism was the problem: 'India's salvation consists in unlearning what she has learnt in the past fifty years. Railways, telegraphs, hospitals, lawyers, doctors and such like, all have to go, and the so-called upper classes have to learn to live, consciously, religiously and happily the simple peasant life, knowing it to be life-giving true happiness.' Such views placed him at variance with his Congress colleagues. Gandhi advised the acceptance of British concessions in 1919, which were concessions towards a parliamentary and Western system, and therefore illustrate that Gandhi's own aims were sometimes obscure. His 1933 hunger strike was directed against 'nobody in particular but in the cause of truth'.

Gandhi was not a conventional nationalist but a moralist and religious reformer. He celebrated the rural idyll and idealised the life of the peasant, which, ironically, was not uncommon in

Europe in the early twentieth century. In this, Gandhi's view was typical of a widespread desire to reject globalisation, modernisation and, above all, industrialisation. He longed for a spiritual world order. His rejection of British rule was in fact only a part of this greater transformation in his thinking. In 1920 his non-cooperation movement was broadly in favour of *swaraj*, Home Rule, but it was still the spiritual objective that took priority and so informed the methods. His followers had difficulty in following Gandhi's ideal, however. In Bombay in February 1922, there was serious rioting in which 53 died, and 21 policemen were burnt to death at Chauri Chaura.

Sectarian rivalry, heightened by the prospect that British rule was about to pass over to the Indian people, descended into rioting and bloodshed. In Calcutta in 1926 there were 40 riots in which 197 died and 1600 were injured. The Simon Commission, which toured India in 1927, recommended that Indians be placed on an equal footing with Europeans, but at the 1929 opening of the Legislative Assembly, Congress boycotted the proceedings. The two campaigns of civil disobedience between 1930–1 and 1932–4 plunged India into rioting again, although Gandhi scored a moral victory in his 'march to the sea' to retrieve sea salt as a symbolic protest against the salt tax. Gandhi claimed to represent all India and fasted against British measures to control civil disobedience, but also against the separate representation of the 'Depressed classes' (the poor) at the Round Table Conference convened in 1931.

The Government of India Act (1935) was the British compromise. It gave full responsible government in the provinces and set up Dyarchy at the centre. The British saw this as the logical next step in the gradual granting of power, but were still concerned that whilst the educated Indian classes were impatient and eager for power, the masses of illiterate and rural people, and the minorities, might be exploited. The franchise encompassed only 54 per cent of the population, so there was no indication of the feelings of the majority. The reluctance of the princely states to enter into federation, and the opposition from the Congress 'High Command', stalled the implementation of the Act. This had the effect of convincing Congress that the British were insincere. In the 1937 election, Congress won seven of the 11 provinces. In some places, such as Bihar, there was some progress in education reform under the new provincial government. However, in the United Provinces an aggressive Hindu government provoked communal violence between Hindus and Muslims. There were 2000 casualties in just two years, and this confirmed the British fear that too swift an implementation of Indian 'responsible government' would result in anarchy.

Tapan Raychaudhuri argues that most British historians have assumed that Indian nationalism was limited in its support and that the British enjoyed the support of the majority of collaborators or 'sub-imperialists'.[16] He contends that these quantitative analyses pay insufficient attention to the 'non-rational factors, such as frustration, a pervasive feeling of humiliation, and the need for cultural self-assertion'. D. A. Low nevertheless argued that the base of support had been widespread and that Congress had effected real change.[17] Gyanendra Pandey suggested that despite the lack of general support, the loyalty of the Hindus of the United Provinces still achieved much.[18] Sumit Sarkar used a post-structuralist solution, maintaining that the narrow base of support did not affect Congress' claim to be a legitimate 'substitute' for the absence of popular backing.[19]

The British regarded the sectarian division of Hindu and Muslim, and the communal violence that was to reach its nadir in the mid-1940s, as the reason for caution in granting autonomy. B. Chandra has argued that communal division was the result of a deliberate policy of divide and rule, designed to perpetuate the Raj.[20] However, Lawrence James concluded: 'it is difficult to imagine how successive viceroys could have resisted demands for special representation from the spokesmen of nearly a quarter of India's population. To allege that the British could have disregarded or deflected the pressure assumes the Raj was stronger than it was.'[21] Moreover, Chandra fails to acknowledge that any encouragement of religious antipathies would have run counter to the aims of the British. Since Muslims were disproportionately represented in the army and the police, and they had borne the brunt of the casualties of the Great War, the British were eager not to cause any affront to this minority. Their sense of justice would not allow them to abandon any other minority to a 'tyranny of the majority'. Therefore, the preservation of religious peace was not just the justification of power; it was the whole basis of British rule in India.

The dominions

At the peace conferences, the new status of the dominions, as virtual partners of Britain, was illustrated by the fact that their own representatives signed the various treaties and they became members of the League of Nations in their own right. Under the terms of the Versailles and Sèvres settlements, Germany and Turkey lost their colonies to League of Nations' 'Mandates' (the authority to govern as a protectorate in the name of the League). As the leading powers of the League, Britain and France became the actual administrators of former German and Turkish possessions, some of which, like Iraq, came into being for the first time. Palestine and Trans-Jordan also came under the British mandate, whilst Iran was placed under Britain's 'dominant influence'. Much of the latter work was due to the Foreign Secretary, Lord Curzon, who felt that he had finally blocked Russian influence across central Asia, and therefore concluded a struggle for supremacy in Asia known as the 'Great Game'. Mandates were not colonies and were, strictly speaking, subject to the supervision of the League, but the distinction was lost on those that lived there. Australia, New Zealand and South Africa shared in this responsibility for former German colonies in Africa and the Pacific, marking their enhanced status as partners of Britain in the Empire.

Although the dominions had thus acquired a measure of international recognition, their constitutional relationship with Britain remained unaltered. This dichotomy was a source of tension. In 1921, Jan Smuts, now the South African Prime Minister, stated: 'The national temperature of all young countries has been raised by the event of the Great War' and he warned that unless the colonies were incorporated and their aspirations met in good time, then they might go the way of Ireland and break away.[22] However, Lloyd George failed to consult the imperial partners when he threatened Turkey with war in 1922 during the Chanak Crisis. His aim was to bluff the Turks and uphold the Treaty of Sèvres, but the Canadian premier Mackenzie King told his parliament that it was for the Canadian parliament 'to decide whether or not we should participate in wars in different parts of the world'. In 1923, Mackenzie King went further by unilaterally signing a Canadian–United States fisheries agreement, when previously it would have been a matter for the British government. At the 1923 Imperial Conference, Britain recognised the desire of the dominions, particularly Canada, to make their own treaties, but it was still unclear how far Britain was responsible for foreign policy and if its decisions applied to the dominions. In 1924, Canada claimed it was under no obligation to sign the Treaty of Lausanne, which replaced the Treaty of Sèvres, because it had not been represented at the talks. The following year, Britain signed the Locarno Treaty, with no expectation that the dominions would be obliged to support an agreement on European boundaries. A separate government department was created in 1925 to deal with dominion affairs and Britain expected to grant further concessions in the 1926 Imperial Conference.

In South Africa, the nationalist General J. B. M. Hertzog had secured power in 1924 and he was determined to secure recognition of his country's independent status. The Irish Free State, which had become a dominion in 1921, was also keen to clarify its constitutional position. Thus, a committee on inter-imperial relations was established during the 1926 Conference. It consisted of the premiers and principal delegates of the dominions, under the chairmanship of Lord Balfour. The resulting report described the dominions as 'autonomous Communities within the British Empire, equal in status, in no way subordinate one to another in any aspect of their domestic or external affairs, though united by a common allegiance to the Crown, and freely associated as members of the British Commonwealth of Nations'. Five years later, the report was given legal status by the Statute of Westminster.

The extent to which the Statute of Westminster of 1931 weakened the Empire is open to debate. In some ways, the Balfour Report and the Statute appeared to be recognition by Britain of full dominion independence. The reference to their 'free association' with the Commonwealth implied that they could exercise the right to secede. On the other hand, it can be argued that the Balfour Report and the Westminster Statute were attempts to preserve imperial ties. By making timely concessions to the dominions, Britain hoped to prevent separatist tendencies, particularly in South Africa, Canada and the Irish Free State. Australia and New Zealand appeared to have remained loyal to the Empire: there was little demand for change in constitutional arrangements. In 1927, the Dominions Secretary Leo Amery noted: 'If imperial sentiment is strong in Australia, in New Zealand it is a passion, almost a religion.' There, it was a question of keeping faith with the motherland and to the memory of those who had died for the Empire. It is therefore not surprising that Australia and New Zealand did not adopt the Westminster Statute until 1942 and 1947 respectively.

There seems to be little evidence that Britain felt pressured to make concessions to the dominions during the inter-war years by the dominion leaders themselves. This was largely because the crisis of war and the tensions it had created had passed. Britain's recognition of dominion equality was possible because there was a calculation that the dominions themselves would see an advantage in remaining in the imperial 'club'. Britain's armed forces provided protection not only to the dominions' territories, but also their trade routes. Economically, the dominions were closely integrated with Britain and their future prosperity was to some extent dependent on the imperial connection. The only possible exception was Canada which, remote from the international crises of the 1930s, could look to the United States to defend the North American continent. Indeed, the proximity of the United States and Canada gave the Canadians a greater degree of economic flexibility too. In the 1920s, Britain did lose some of its dominion trade, the result of increasingly 'globalised' commerce, but this did not last long. It was the onset of the Depression in 1930 that illustrated economic interdependence. The stagnation of world trade caused industries to cut back on production, whilst currency values fell dramatically, resulting in widespread hardship for industrial workers in the 'staple' sectors of mining, ship building, heavy industry and some textiles.

The Ottawa Imperial Conference of 1932 succeeded in its aim of stimulating trade within the Empire during the Depression. Britain allowed the free entry of primary produce in return for imperial preference for some goods in the dominions. The 1932 Imperial Conference may have helped British manufacturing to some degree, but the new light industries in the United Kingdom were less affected by the Slump than heavy industries. According to P. J. Cain and A. G. Hopkins, the share of British investment in the dominions gradually decreased during the inter-war years, resulting in the development of their own money markets and financial houses.[23] Nevertheless, it was the debts of the dominions that kept them dependent on the financial lifeline of the City of London.

The Middle East

Britain maintained a garrison in Egypt during the First World War which repulsed a Turkish attack on the Suez Canal before going on to fight Turkey in Gallipoli and Mesopotamia. Ultimately, neither of these theatres provided the military solution required and the setback to Russian forces in Armenia in 1915 meant that it was even more important to protect the canal and the oil fields of the Persian Gulf with actions in the Middle East.[24] According to Robert Holland, this became a 'Suez fixation' in the years to come.[25] Initially, progress was slow but by supporting an Arab revolt, British and Imperial Forces eventually made their way northwards through Palestine to Jerusalem and Damascus. The Sharif of Mecca, Ibn 'Ali Hussein, had agreed to raise a revolt against the Turks with the British High Commissioner of Egypt, Sir Henry MacMahon, and Hussein understood the reward for this alliance would be the granting of Arab independence after the war.

However, Britain had several concerns. The Young Turk revolt of 1908, and the reorientation of the old Ottoman Empire towards Germany, had demonstrated the need for British intervention in the Middle East if it was to preserve the security of the region. The vital strategic and commercial artery of the Suez Canal and the proximity of the Persian Gulf to India placed the Middle East high on the diplomatic agenda. In addition, France was interested in sharing the spoils of victory, especially where it involved the security of the Mediterranean. It was imperative to preserve French co-operation in wartime, so the secret Sykes-Picot agreement enabled the French to re-establish a historic link with Syria in any post-war partition of the Ottoman Empire.[26] Balfour's declaration in 1917 announcing the creation of a Jewish homeland in Palestine further complicated the situation. Although it was designed to win over Jews to the war effort, it was clear Zionists would demand that the promise be honoured after the war.

Therefore, after the war Britain did not forget the vulnerability of its arterial route to and from the East, and despite promises of full Arab independence, Britain sought to retain its influence over the region.[27] The need to grant Jews a homeland also cut across Arab aspirations for the Middle East.

British involvement in the Middle East in the inter-war years therefore appears inconsistent if not perfidious. It was clearly difficult to balance the aspirations of Arabs and Jews. Yet, despite trying to satisfy implacable foes, the priority was still one of self-interest. Britain tried to fulfil its obligations through a League of Nations mandate and preserve its own strategic and commercial interests at the same time. In occupying the region, Britain found itself responsible for a conflict that did not serve its interests at all. However, in the short term the chief threat was still from Turkey. The armistice of Mudros (October 1918) between Vice Admiral Calthorpe and Turkey's Huseyn Rauf Bey provided for the cessation of hostilities and British access to the strategic positions along the Dardenelles and Bosphorous. The demand for the evacuation of Turkish troops from certain territories and the exclusion of French officials from the talks fuelled Turkish suspicions that the old Ottoman Empire lands were to be dismembered. Nationalists did manage to retain some territory, but relations were bad. When the peace conference revealed that Smyrna would be handed over to Greece, Mustapha Kemal organised resistance which developed into a revolutionary movement.[28] Having established a provisional government at Ankara in 1920 and defeated the Armenians in the east, the Turks seemed poised to continue the war with Greece across the Dardenelles into the former Ottoman territories. The prospect that this might involve a clash with British troops, the so-called Chanak Crisis, almost led to a renewal of war. Lloyd George reinforced the British garrisons, but the standoff was resolved by a Convention which, through the Treaty of Lausanne, returned Eastern Thrace and Adrianople to the Turks in return for a neutralisation of the Dardenelles.[29]

The focus of British concern soon shifted further south. At San Remo in 1920, France and Britain were awarded League of Nations mandates over territories in the Middle East; the French sphere being in the north, the British in the south nearer the Suez Canal. Britain took over the new countries of Iraq and

Palestine, and the Arabs were left with territories in the Arabian Peninsula. However, at Cairo in 1921 Hussein's son Abdullah was placed at the head of Transjordan, a region severed from Palestine. The French ejected Feisal, another of Hussein's sons, from Syria, but he was installed by Britain as king of Iraq. Iraq was nominally independent, but the minority Christian Assyrians and the Kurds, who supported the British, were resented by the Muslim Arab majority. Soon after the war, the Arabs massacred or drove out thousands of Kurds and Assyrians. In June 1920, an Arab rebellion in southern Iraq had to be suppressed by force. Britain abandoned full control of Iraq in the 1920s, but retained rights to military and air force bases in the country by the terms of the British–Iraqi Treaty (1930).

In Palestine, Jewish immigration led to rioting in 1921 that intensified because of disputes over religious sites in 1929. Two commissions, under Sir Walter Shaw and Sir John Hope-Simpson, both concluded that Arab fear of Jewish immigration and land settlement had been the primary cause of the disturbances. Yet the World Zionist Organisation lobbied the British government to put no limitations on Jews entering or settling in the country. There were three reasons why the British chose to support the Jews. First, they appeared to be a loyal minority in the region, which was particularly important when Egypt was relinquished in 1922. Second, the Zionists, regardless of their religious convictions, appeared to be a settler population that could bring energy, expertise and European influence to develop the Middle East. Third, the Jews had a moral claim to the region. Like the white settlers of Africa, these migrants had made considerable sacrifices for the sake of land ownership and its development. However, Arab resistance that had begun in 1919 developed into a revolt in 1936, which prompted another commission by Lord Peel.[30] Its recommendation, that Palestine be partitioned, fuelled further Arab resentment of Britain and subsequent negotiations failed to produce a solution.

When Mussolini invaded Abyssinia in 1935, there was a possibility that the Fascist dictator would close off the Red Sea and thus sever the route to the East. Indeed, with Palestine in turmoil, there was a chance Britain might lose control of the whole region. Neville Chamberlain therefore reversed British policy: Jewish immigrants were to be limited to 75,000 over five years, after which the Arabs must give their consent to future numbers. Britain also offered the Arabs a degree of independence within ten years, but the British Empire was unable to contain the tide of Arab–Jewish antagonism.

Ultimately, it was external threats from Italy and Germany rather than the internal disputes that changed its policies, for in the Second World War, the region required a considerable garrison that could perhaps have been deployed elsewhere. On the other hand, British control of the Middle East and North Africa prevented Nazi Germany reaching the oil fields of the Persian Gulf.[31] Although initially the German plan had been to leave the region to the Italians, the development of a threat to the oil fields led to a joint Anglo-Soviet invasion of Iran in August 1941 (coupled with fears that Reza Shah was pro-Nazi) and this occupation lasted until 1946.

The end of the war brought little respite and both Arabs and Jews turned their attention to the removal of British troops. The Israeli terrorist organisation, the *Irgun*, had been formed in 1931, but it achieved its notoriety in 1946 by bombing the King David Hotel and carrying out an execution of two captured British soldiers in 1947. These events indicated that the territorial disputes of the region would not subside.

The British economy and imperial defence

Historians have disagreed on the point of origin of Britain's imperial decline, but the British Empire itself appeared as resilient as ever in 1918.[32] Corelli Barnett argued that by 1939, the British Empire had become a 'colossal burden', but the origin of this attitude was the result of the 'fundamental anomalies and weaknesses' exposed by the First World War.[33] The dominions certainly had no wish to become embroiled in another European war, but they did not seek complete separation either.[34] The evidence for decline is usually centred on the metropolitan core: British military and industrial power eclipsed by America, the decline of invisible earnings, political and social change in Britain, and the inevitable recovery of her Russian and German competitors.[35] Paul Kennedy argued that whilst British governments and chiefs of staff were 'excessively gloomy about their country's prospects', by the 1930s Britain had an overstretched global empire and only 9 or 10 per cent of the world's manufacturing strength and 'war potential'.[36] However, in the 1920s Britain retained the ability to command the loyalty of millions of its imperial subjects, it still had the military and naval capacity to protect its possessions, it emerged from the war with more territory, and there was little sign of any 'loss of will' to govern the Empire amongst the elites in London or in the colonies themselves. P. J. Cain and A. G. Hopkins argue that the City of London's financial strength gave the Empire its longevity.[37] It is this that challenges the idea of a break in continuity in 1914 or 1918. As P. J. Marshall put it, after the Great War the Empire continued to do 'business as usual'.[38]

The simultaneous outbreak of disturbances in Ireland, Egypt, Turkey, Iraq and India and the outbreak of a war with Afghanistan in 1919 raised serious concerns about the cost of imperial defence. Defence spending stood at £568 million in 1920, falling to £114.7 million in 1925. According to Patrick O'Brien, of all Britain's possessions only India paid in full for its defence.[39] The dominions paid only an average of 10 per cent of the costs that taxpayers in Britain paid. Lance Davis and Robert Huttenback estimated that, even before the First World War, if the colonies had paid for their defence costs commensurate with a comparable level of development, then Britain's taxes might have been 40 per cent lower, although this calculation has subsequently been disputed.[40] However, the relative decline of the British economy compared with the rest of the world was a cause for concern when its imperial commitments, and therefore the costs of Empire, were still growing.

After the First World War (and after the wartime contracts ended in 1921), production in the old staple industries was in decline and growth in the new industries was sluggish. Britain's foreign trade was declining relative to its European rivals and relative to its total production. In 1938, Britain's share of world trade had fallen to 14 per cent, from 17 per cent in 1913 and 25 per cent in 1860.[41] The return to the gold standard in 1925 made the pound less competitive, which also affected overseas trade. Invisible earnings fell since investments had been sold off during the war. Investment incomes were lower too. However, the Empire's share of trade with Britain increased.

Britain's weakened economic position meant that, as Bernard Porter put it, 'it was no longer a question of finding new worlds to conquer, but of digging in and defending those she had'.[42] The development of the colonies seemed an attractive option because if Britain was unable to influence foreign markets, it would have exclusive control over those in the British Empire. Leo Amery, the Colonial Secretary from 1924 to 1929, planned 'an imperial economic policy based on the mutual development of our common resources of nature and human skill, and on the maintenance of a standard of living which we set for ourselves, and are not simply content to have set for us by the unlimited and unregulated competition of the world outside'.[43]

This thinking helps toward an understanding of why Britain was so determined to hang on to the colonies in the inter-war years and to suppress nationalist agitation. The aim was to bind together a world-wide federation of white self-governing dominions, supported by a number of non-white dependencies and colonies, which would progressively develop into consumer markets as well as producers of primary products. It was not entirely negative in a political or military sense either. The British knew that collaboration was vital and a limited participation was encouraged. For example, 'Indianisation' in the Indian Army meant that the officer corps was no longer limited to British personnel.

The pace of colonial development was slow, being dictated by what seemed possible at the time. Amery was also kept short of the very money he felt he needed to tackle the 'boundless potentialities [that] call urgently for development in the interests of their own inhabitants, of the British Empire as a whole, and of the impoverished and wasted world'.[44] Nevertheless, Amery managed to fund railways in East Africa, roads in Nigeria and harbours at Kilindini in Kenya, Takoradi on the Gold Coast and Haifa in Palestine. He also set up the Colonial Medical Research Committee (1927) and the Agriculture Advisory Council. To persuade the British to buy imperial goods, he set up the Empire Marketing Board in 1926 and subsidised commercial development in the Empire Cotton Growing Corporation (1921). Nevertheless, funding was small and development was uneven since both were still dependent on the demand for products that could be exported. Moreover, spending on welfare tended to lag some way behind spending on other improvements in the infrastructure. For example, in 1938 there were still only 1300 hospital beds in Nigeria for a population of 3 million.[45] That same year, only 10 to 15 per cent of Kenyan African children went to school. This was not really related to any conscious discrimination since Rhodesia, with a worse record of racial prejudice, had more African children attending schools. The Colonial Under-Secretary summed up the problem in 1921: 'However willing may be the spirit, the flesh, interpreted in terms of ready money and rigidly bound by economic laws, is sadly weak.'[46]

From 1919, the Treasury managed to persuade the government to reduce military and naval expenditure with the argument that the greater accumulation of wealth in peacetime would not jeopardise Britain's ability to rearm if a new threat emerged. Limits of £135 million were set and to justify its decision the Cabinet decided that no war was likely within ten years. By 1920, the army had been reduced to 370,000 men but the navy was maintained at a size 60 per cent greater than the next largest fleet, excluding the United States. Moreover, air power was regarded as a cheap alternative to maintaining army garrisons in the Empire.

The Slump forced Britain to abandon the gold standard in 1931 and free trade through the Import Duties Act in 1932. Protectionism was reapplied to imports, and through the Ottawa Agreement, a form of Imperial Preference was created, excluding the territories of the British Empire from import duties. This was supported by the creation of the Sterling Area, where Britain and the colonies used the pound as their primary reserve and trading currency. In addition, some other countries outside of the British Empire, which were dependent on British trade, also came within the Sterling Area.[47] This area helped Britain survive the Depression and checked the decline in its share of world trade. It also maintained the City of London's reputation as a viable financial service centre in a period of economic crisis. However, the Empire was never big enough and therefore was not influential enough to draw the world out of the depression. Moreover, in the longer term, it was unable to change the fundamental problem of Britain's exports: they were becoming less competitive. The import trade recovered quickly, despite protectionism, through the concessions made to the dominions at Ottawa, but as Cain and Hopkins point out, the balance of payments began to show persistent deficits from the mid-1930s. This meant that America replaced Britain as the world's leading financial service provider. The prospect of another war in Europe in the 1930s caused further financial weakness through the flight of capital.

Britain's economic weakness in the 1930s coincided with growing disquiet about Britain's strategic position. The armed forces agreed that Britain suffered from a military and naval 'overstretch'. The burden of imperial defence was greater, but the currency was less secure, the gold reserves smaller and the balance of payments were less favourable than in 1914. Britain's potential enemies were also formidable: Japan and Germany had rapidly built up their armed forces by 1937, although Italy remained a paper tiger. By contrast, Britain's allies appeared to be weak: France was plagued by internal division; the Soviet Union was ideologically opposed to Britain and somewhat isolationist; the United States was unwilling to involve itself in European affairs; and even the dominions were opposed to any aggressive policies against Germany or Japan that might lead to war. Indeed, they were the strongest advocates of appeasement.[48]

When rearmament began, it began cautiously because of fears that it would create inflation, destroy the economic stability that had just been achieved in Britain and wreck the Sterling Area by initiating another financial crash. The Treasury also believed that taxation would increase, savings would be diverted and investments would fall. Moreover, it was feared that inflation would drive up prices and lead to a crisis in industrial relations worse than the General Strike of 1926. The decision to cut military and naval expenditure had had widespread pubic support in the 1920s. There was universal revulsion at the idea that Britain might have to fight another Great War and Neville Chamberlain was aware that the British people expected him to find a diplomatic solution.

Despite the gloomy economic and strategic position of the inter-war years, the British Empire still had the appearance of a leading world power. In 1921, plans were laid for the construction of a vast new naval base at Singapore and it was completed in 1938 at a cost of £60 million. The global presence of British ships, aircraft and garrisons was designed to act as a deterrent to both internal and external enemies. However, Britain's economic strength had ebbed since 1914 and, given the scattered nature of its imperial possessions, Britain could only deal with a limited number of threats. For example, although imperial policing had become more important in light of unrest in the Middle East and India, other solutions were found in Egypt, Iraq and Ireland. The potential Soviet threat to India compelled Britain to maintain a large force there and a mobilisation plan in 1927 envisaged the despatch of 11 divisions from the United Kingdom, even though this would denude Britain's defences in Europe and entail conscription.[49] Both Conservative and Labour governments were committed to disarmament and work on Singapore was suspended until 1931 when the invasion of Manchuria signalled the development of a new threat in the East. The DRC (Defence Requirement Committee) of 1933 concluded that Germany was the main threat, although up to 1939 the Royal Navy still regarded the Italian fleet in the Mediterranean as its greatest hazard. Even when the threats in Europe became more obvious, rearmament was constrained by cost and capacity.[50] From a strategic point of view, Neville Chamberlain wrote in 1934: 'we cannot provide simultaneously for hostilities with Japan *and* Germany'.[51] The DRC confirmed the following year that the armed forces could not preserve Britain's security in a three-front war. Thus, when Britain went to war in 1939 in Europe and found itself under attack in the Far East in 1941, it was initially unable to stem the tide. Consequently, once again, Britain turned to the Empire and to the United States for assistance.

The challenges to imperialism: conclusions

There were some significant changes to the British Empire after the First World War. Despite the acquisition of mandated territories, in the 1920s there was a desire to avoid further expansion because of economic and strategic 'overstretch'. Initially, the Empire defended itself aggressively against internal threats.

Ireland, Iraq and India were subjected to firm measures, but by the 1930s, minimum force was the preferred approach. Disarmament was strongly advocated and international co-operation through the League of Nations seemed to offer some prospect of cutting the burden of defence costs.

In the 1920s, the contrasts in political arrangements in the British Empire were thrown into sharp relief. Whilst the dominions gained greater autonomy, the hold on India was only grudgingly weakened for fear of wholesale anarchy and communal violence. The Amritsar Massacre was an ugly reminder not that the British could wield considerable power, but that their power could be so misused. The British were shocked that the Empire was not fulfilling its mission as a force for good, and many Indian moderates came to believe that the British had lost the moral right to govern India. Consequently, attempts to reach a compromise on constitutional arrangements failed.

In the new mandated territories of the Middle East, the British found themselves caught between Arab and Jewish rioters, reaping the legacy of short-term arrangements made during the First World War. David Fromkin asserts that the British destruction of the old order in the former Ottoman Empire led to the: 'crisis of political civilisation that the Middle East endures today'.[52] Despite this assertion, the political turmoil of the periods before and after the war suggests that there would have been violent changes in the Middle East anyway. However, there was a striking contrast in the idea that Britain could contemplate war as a last resort to resist invaders and uphold self-determination in Europe, yet would deny the same privilege to nationalist leaders across the Middle East and the Empire. The Labour Party called for steps towards colonial self-government in the 1920s, but even in 1943, it was felt this was still a long way off. Some areas (such as Ireland, Egypt, Iraq) were granted a very large measure of independence and it was the Conservatives who made concessions to India, but it took a second world war to convince Labour they should proceed quickly towards independence for the Indian subcontinent.

Above all, the inter-war years were marked by a sense of caution and deliberation. The emphasis was on stability and consolidation which, given the financial crises of the Slump, the deterioration in British trade, and the City of London's struggle to maintain its leadership role in financial services, was not surprising. The best that can be said is that this was a period of transition from formal rule to partnership. To nationalists it appeared that the British were hardly the 'reluctant imperialists' they had claimed to be, and they served no other interests but their own.

12

What effect did the Second World War have on British imperialism?

Perhaps the key difference between the First and Second World Wars is that throughout the Great War, the British Empire was engaged in offensive operations, whereas in the period 1939 to 1943 it found itself on the defensive. Although it was able to extricate the British Expeditionary Force from France and defeat Italian forces in North Africa (thus saving Egypt), it faced the onslaught of Germany's armed forces in the West and Japanese attacks in the East. In the First World War, the threats were limited to specific geographical areas: Africa, the Middle East, Europe and the Atlantic. Yet, in the Second World War, Britain's imperial resources were scattered across the globe, and the Empire was forced to defend itself against three major military powers. The priority, particularly after the fall of Europe, was the defence of the United Kingdom.

Although Britain could call on vast manpower resources, an invasion would have had a dramatic impact on Britain's control of the Empire. The Nazi occupation of France meant that French colonial possessions were transferred to the administration of the Vichy regime, a fact which presents us with an interesting counter-factual: if Britain had been invaded and occupied, would the same have been true of British possessions? The autonomy of the dominions of Canada, South Africa, New Zealand and Australia, and their approval of the war against the Axis powers, suggests that resistance against Germany and Japan would have continued from these bases.[1] The fact that the war was initially confined to Europe (with the exception of the Japanese attack on China) gave Britain the chance to concentrate its resources. Even so, in 1940 Britain was the only state in Europe still fighting the Nazis (as the Soviet Union was an ally

171

of Germany under the Nazi-Soviet Pact of August 1939). Britain survived due to its continued dominance of the sea, its victory in the air and the presence of the world's greatest anti-tank ditch, the English Channel. The Middle East and Egypt also formed a barrier to the Axis powers, denying them access to the oil fields of Persia and Iraq.

The Japanese attacks on South-East Asia in 1941 forced the British to redirect their resources, split between Britain itself, North Africa and aid to the Soviet Union following the German invasion in July that year. In addition, the setbacks to the Royal Navy, the loss of air superiority, and the fall of Hong Kong and Singapore placed Britain under intense strain. Australians were surprised by the suddenness of the British collapse and, ever since, there have been accusations that Britain was only concerned to save itself. This argument has formed the basis of republican calls for the severing of all ties with Britain and an independent, self-reliant security policy.

The only consolation of 1941–2 was the fact that America, a Pacific power, was fighting alongside the Empire. However, America's support was not unconditional. The Atlantic Charter hinted at America's desire to see the British Empire broken up (a view later modified by the Communist threat during the Cold War). Even so, Britain already knew that to retain the support of the colonies and dominions, it would have to make concessions. Promises of self-government and development were given to Indians and Africans quite early on. Nevertheless, some nationalists in India were prepared to negotiate with the Japanese and a 'fifth column' developed. The Japanese approach, close to the Indian border, was a critical moment for the Raj. Yet, the British Indian Army recovered from its early setbacks so that by the war's end, Burma had been reoccupied. The British Empire managed to survive, and, as a partner in the 'Big Three' (Britain, USA and USSR), it went on to defeat Italy, Germany and Japan in 1945. However, although the former colonial possessions were everywhere restored to Britain (whilst France lost Syria and Lebanon, and the Dutch were restored in Indonesia), a new international climate prevailed at the end of the war. A combination of financial and moral changes began to sweep the Empire away, and with it much of its informal influence.

India and Burma

At the outbreak of war, Indian Congress leaders resigned in protest from the provincial assemblies of India. They were angry that they had not been consulted over India's declaration of war (made by the Viceroy Lord Linlithgow) and by the despatch of Indian troops overseas. In fact, it seems likely that Congress would have opposed the British decision even if they had been consulted, since the Tripuri resolution (March 1938) urged non-cooperation with the British. Governors took over the running of the provinces and the other parties supported the Defence of India Act. Despite the demand for independence made by the Congress Working Committee, there was some reluctance to forgo control of the provinces amongst rank and file Congress members. Traditional objections to the cost of the Indian Army were neutralised when Britain agreed in November 1939 to pay for the Indian Army, its expansion, its supplies and equipment for the duration, which was a reversal of peacetime practice.

The Indian Army was successful in North Africa and in Abyssinia in 1940, but beyond that, it was too small a force to do any more than augment the garrisons of the Middle East. All volunteers, the Indian Army numbered just 158,000 Indian and 57,000 British troops in 1939. Despite the non-cooperation of Congress, recruiting continued to be on a voluntary basis and by 1942, the Indian Army had grown to one million men drawn from all classes and communities. It was the largest volunteer army in history, but it could never have been raised if opposition to British rule was as universal as Congress claimed. Whilst some have pointed to the fact that 'quotas' of recruits were demanded from villages of the 'martial races', it appears this affected only a minority.[2]

To try to encourage Congress to co-operate with the imperial war effort, Linlithgow made the 'August Offer' in 1940. It consisted of five points:

1. to confirm that India would be a free and equal partner after the war;
2. to set up a body, drawn from all parties, to decide on a new constitution;

3. power was to be withheld from any party if it did not guarantee the interests of the minorities;
4. as constitutional change was undesirable in wartime, representatives were invited to join the Viceroy's Executive Council and War Advisory Council;
5. preliminary constitutional discussions were to begin immediately.

Congress rejected the proposal with 'pain and indignation' and Gandhi began a campaign of individual civil disobedience, but it got little support. The Muslim League rejected the proposal in 1941 on the grounds that it made no provision for a separate Islamic state. Mohammed Ali Jinnah, the leader of the League, had been somewhat discredited during the 1937 elections. Although the League claimed to represent all Muslims, it had failed to secure any more than two (of 84) seats in the Punjab, and none in the North-West Frontier Province. Therefore, in March 1940 Jinnah made the Lahore Resolution that called for separate and autonomous states where there were Muslim majorities. It is often suggested that the League benefited from Congress's absence from the provincial governments.

The idea that Hindus and Muslims had been united before British rule – and intentionally set against each other in a deliberate policy of 'divide and rule' by the Raj – was put forward by nationalist historians after the war. It became a useful way of explaining the continued weakness of the nationalist cause without acknowledging the collaboration of the majority. S. Gopal wrote: 'There is no doubt that one main reason for the introduction of a system, which violated democratic principles and was calculated to destroy the attempts to build Indian nationalism on the models of nineteenth-century Europe, was to perpetuate British rule.'[3] The contradiction of this can be seen in light of the beliefs of Gandhi himself. As a devout Hindu promoting a revival of Hinduism, and despite gestures of unity, Gandhi would only promote his own faith. Moreover, it is difficult to find evidence of a 'calculated' British policy of division. With the exception of the Princely States where sovereignty was preserved, the British united India as a single entity. This made the Congress claim of 1930 that Britain had 'deprived the Indian people of their freedom' supremely ironic, as there was no such thing as a united 'Indian people' before the arrival of the British. Indeed, even in 1947, Indians spoke at least 15 separate languages (not including the 700 minor languages and dialects). It was the use of English and the introduction of British communications technology that had made greater unity possible.

According to Gopal, Gandhi rejected the changes which may have united society and modernised it on nationalist lines. His only contribution to unity was to speak out against the treatment of 'untouchables'. However, Gandhi did try to win over Muslims once. He urged Congress to join Islamic theologians in united criticism of the fall of the Caliph in Turkey (1922), but when Muslims themselves condemned the Caliph, Gandhi's campaign fell flat. Jawaharlal Nehru believed that economic progress would eventually wipe out religious differences, but Gopal failed to mention in his account that it was Nehru's very *insistence* on a united Indian state which alienated the Muslims, perhaps worsening sectarian fears. Jinnah had begun with an ideal of a united India, but when Congress was only prepared to reserve seats for minorities at provincial and not national level, he retreated towards the protection of Muslims interests. Gopal condemned: 'his regressive career, from westernised, secular twentieth-century attitudes to medieval, theocratic obscurantism . . . his split personality ultimately split India'.[4] Ayesha Jalal argues that Jinnah only advocated a separate Pakistan as a 'bargaining counter' to force Congress to accept Muslim interests at the centre.[5] However, it seems much more likely that Jinnah wanted to unite the separate Muslim organisations. The desire for a separate state, argues Judith Brown, came as a result of the communal violence.[6]

The Japanese offensive in December 1941 led to the rapid collapse of Hong Kong and Singapore (where 60,000 British and Indian troops were captured). Burma was attacked and Rangoon fell in March 1942. On 29 April, Mandalay was lost and British troops and civilians began a tortuous retreat through Burma's jungle during the monsoon. By the autumn, the Japanese had reached the borders of Assam. Faced with invasion and the possible collapse of British rule, Sir Tej Bahadur Sapru (representing Indian Liberals) sought confirmation of Britain's position on the Atlantic Charter. Churchill replied that the liberation of the oppressed applied *primarily* to the people of

Europe, which had indeed been the emphasis of the meeting. Congress seized upon the apparent contradiction and Churchill sent Sir Stafford Cripps in March 1942 to clothe the 'August Offer' with more detail in an attempt to satisfy Congress. In addition to the previous concessions, Cripps offered an immediate participation in the Executive, and the inclusion of the Princely States in the new constitution.

The Cripps proposals offered a final chance for co-operation, but with the exception of the Liberals, each group found making objections far easier than running the risk of being branded traitors. Gandhi described the proposals as 'drawing a post-dated cheque on a crashing bank'.[7] The Muslim League rejected them because a separate state was not 'unequivocally accepted'. The Sikhs feared they would be left to the mercy of the Muslim League and wanted greater protection. The Mahasabha (Hindu Orthodox Party) opposed the 'vivisection' of India. Congress could see an advantage in the inclusion of the Indian States and in the powers of an Indian defence minister, so it responded with a demand for the immediate establishment of Cabinet government (abolishing the Viceroy's Council). Cripps replied that this was a constitutional change that must come after the war had been won, and that proper provision had to be made for the minorities. The talks therefore collapsed on 11 April 1942, all sides blaming each other.

Yet despite this, the Viceroy went ahead with an enlarged Executive (5 British and 11 Indian members). Meanwhile, Congress faced division. Gandhi advocated passive resistance against the Japanese and C. Rajgopalachari wanted union with the Muslim League, while Nehru wanted to form a Home Guard. Some extremists sided with the Japanese. Finally, on 14 July 1942 the Congress Working Committee demanded the immediate abdication of British rule. Gandhi called for a civil disobedience campaign and 'open rebellion', exhorting his followers to 'do or die'. When, on 8 August, the All-India Congress Committee backed the 'Quit India' resolution, the Viceroy's Executive (with the unanimous support of the Indian members) declared Congress illegal. Internment of the leaders provoked bombings, attacks on railways and communications, arson against government buildings, destruction of bridges, and assassinations: 300 died and 200 were wounded before the disturbances were crushed, but in the circumstances of wartime, the action was not accompanied by the soul searching of Amritsar.[8] To make matters worse, a cyclone and tidal wave caused famine in Bengal (and Burmese rice, the usual source of relief food, was feeding the Japanese). Despite the efforts of the Indian Army, one million people died. Nevertheless, the tide of the war began to turn. By 1944, the Indian Army was making counter-attacks through Burma as well as contributing to the Allied war effort in Europe. In 1945, there were two and a half million Indian troops and 15,740 Indian officers serving in the war. The air force expanded to ten squadrons and the navy to 30,000 men.

The absence of Congress in the decision-making process of the war gave the Muslim League a chance to promote itself as the sole voice of Muslim interests. In the 1945–6 elections it won all the Muslims seats in the central legislature and 439 out of 494 seats in the provinces. For the Hindu majority, a satisfactory political settlement seemed further away than ever. The trial of 'Indian National Army' saboteurs provoked violence in the major cities and even a mutiny in the Indian Navy. The political situation was aggravated in southern India by a failure of the rains. After the war, Congress swept up eight of the 11 provinces, a ringing endorsement of Congress' insistence on independence. Unable to balance the conflicting interests in the subcontinent any longer, Atlee despatched a mission to India with the sole purpose of granting 'freedom as speedily and as soon as possible'. Britain had always predicted it would be unable to hold India by military force alone if the Indian population opposed them. That time had come, and the negotiations that followed led to India's independence in August 1947.[9]

British military setbacks and the retreat through Burma had not brought British rule in India or South-East Asia to an end in 1944. Indeed, the success of Japan, an Asian power, inspired relatively few to join the INA. This stemmed, in part, from the Indians' wish to achieve independence – not an exchange of overlords. In addition, Japanese rule was accompanied by widespread brutality. On the notorious Thailand–Burma railway, the 'Death Railway', 12,000 allied prisoners of war and 100,000 Asian labourers, mainly Burmese, Tamils and Malays, died as a result of murder, disease, sickness, malnutrition and exhaustion.[10] A further 100,000 Asian workers died in support of the railways project in Thailand. British and Commonwealth veterans continue to insist that Japan should apologise for the disregard of the Geneva Convention and the unnecessary violence inflicted on them. In China, the Japanese atrocities were even worse. The myths of the Japanese 'liberation' and the 'Co-Prosperity Sphere' in Asia were quickly exposed as a blatant exploitation of labour and resources for their war effort.

Africa and the Middle East

In 1938, Lord Hailey, a former member of the Indian civil service and expert on Africa, published the *African Survey*. In it he advocated economic and social development, and some resolution between direct colonial rule and parliamentary democracy. The report coincided with the appointment of Malcolm MacDonald as Colonial Secretary, a man who agreed with Hailey's findings. In 1940, in response to riots in the West Indies, he pushed through the Colonial Development and Welfare Act, allocating £55 million over ten years for the African colonies (although £3 million was spent in the first four years because of the costs of the war). To some extent, it built on the concept of 'Dual Mandate' (an argument for development and trusteeship) advocated by Sir Frederick Lugard in Nigeria, but this was a reversal of the imperialist maxim that colonies should be self-supporting financially.[11] It was made at a critical point in the war. MacDonald was making a clear distinction between British generosity and Fascist/Nazi expropriation.[12]

There was certainly widespread African support for Britain during the war, which Keith Jeffrey attributed to: 'the general nature of British imperialism, with its peacetime free press, civil rights, habeas corpus, cultivation of the elites, and promises, however vague, of ultimate self-government'.[13] There were messages of support from the African colonies, including Sierra Leone and the Legislative Council of Nigeria.[14] The Colonial Office calculated that by 1945, 374,000 Africans had been recruited into the armed forces. In addition, thousands of labourers were conscripted, including 100,000 in the open-cast mines of northern Nigeria alone.[15]

After the fall of Singapore, which was the greatest blow to British imperial prestige, there was some reluctance amongst colonial subjects to stand by the British Empire. Yet there may have been a greater awareness of the paradox of the British imperial war effort: Britain called upon its colonial subjects to fight a war of liberation. *The Nigerian Eastern Mail* demanded: 'What purpose does it serve to remind us that Hitler regards us as semi-apes if the Empire for which we are ready to suffer and die . . . can tolerate racial discrimination against us.'[16] G. O. Olusanya noted that Nigerians expected that the 'war that was being fought for freedom should be extended to them'.[17] This feeling led to further British promises that the future would not be one of trusteeship, but partnership. In July 1943, Oliver Stanley, the Colonial Secretary, stated that Britain aimed to: 'guide Colonial people along the road to self-government within the framework of the British Empire'.[18] Despite Churchill's interpretation of the Atlantic Charter (that liberation applied only to Europe), Britain was forced to address its responsibility as a colonial power. In March 1945, its second Colonial Development and Welfare Act made £120 million available to the colonies over ten years. Further acts followed in 1956 and 1959.

Even during the war, Britain was eager to develop Africa in a mutually beneficial relationship, particularly as the eastern portion of the Empire had temporarily fallen under Japanese control. In 1942, Lord Cranborne (then serving as Colonial Secretary) stated: 'Now that we have lost Malaya, the main problem before our African administrators . . . is to make good as far as the resources of their Territories allow the commodities formerly drawn from the Far East.' It could be argued that this was therefore an exploitative relationship, but Britain's priority was to win the war and it was prepared to utilise any resources to do so. Those involved in industries in demand, such as Rhodesian copper, benefited from the wartime boom. By contrast, the war was a financial drain for Britain. Exports fell by between 31 per cent and 40 per cent.[19] Foreign assets were wiped out by accumulated war debts. Britain paid a heavy price for ultimate victory and in 1945, economist John Maynard Keynes warned that Britain was facing a 'financial Dunkirk'. It was therefore not surprising that after the war,

Britain should look to its African colonies to assist in the financial reconstruction of Britain's wealth. Nor was this policy to be one way: Africans were to benefit as much as the British. The orientation of British colonial policy in 1945 was to the achievement of this aim.

Britain's control of the Middle East also came to an end after the war, even though there had been some enthusiasm for the fight against the Axis powers.[20] The Middle East had been garrisoned throughout the conflict, but the revelation of Nazi death camps destroyed, on moral grounds, the policy of denying Jews a homeland. The American president Harry Truman demanded access for 100,000 Jewish settlers and the British government responded with the establishment of a joint Anglo-American Commission of Enquiry in November 1945. But the delays and American support for the Jews encouraged Jewish terrorism to flourish. The Haganah's campaign of violence in 1946 meant that a garrison of 80,000 had to be maintained in Palestine. The cost of this force was £40 million, which was simply unsustainable, and so in 1947, Britain appealed to the United Nations for support, before quitting the region in 1948. However, a different arrangement was made over Suez. Although Britain had unilaterally declared Egypt independent of the Empire in 1922, it retained control of foreign policy and defence. The Anglo–Egyptian Treaty of 1936 ended military occupation, but in fact control of the strategic Suez Canal was to be retained for 20 years. The war had forced Britain to re-enter Egypt but the country was successfully defended. Negotiations after the war centred on the continued British military presence in the Canal Zone, a point that was apparently resolved by the British withdrawal in 1955, but which was to develop into bitter enmity in the Suez Crisis of 1956.

The dominions

The Second World War exposed the difficulty in defending a scattered Empire and the acute need for the dominions to share in the burden of imperial defence. The collapse of France and the U-boat threat to the Atlantic shipping lanes meant that Britain had to acknowledge that it could no longer protect

Canada. Security now lay in the hands of the United States and this was recognised under the terms of the Ogdensburg Agreement of August 1940.

The greatest challenge to imperial security in the east followed the Japanese assault on South-East Asia. The Pacific islands were immediately threatened by the Japanese in December 1941. In January 1942, Borneo and the Dutch East Indies came under attack, Australian troops engaged the Japanese on the Kokoda Trail in New Guinea in 1942, and in February, Australian troops were amongst those captured when Singapore fell. Extreme republicans believe the British knew that Singapore would fall and deliberately misled the Australians who were posted there, but there is, in fact, no evidence for this.[21] Another opinion is that the British exploited Australian naivety: the British had no intention of ever supporting Australia and they abandoned them at the moment of crisis. Both of these views take little note of the reality of the situation and give almost no credit to the Japanese for the skill of their operations.[22] In the attack on Singapore, the rapid seizure of the Malay Peninsula was critically important. Although the British forces had a slight numerical superiority (88,000 to the Japanese 70,000), the British had little training in jungle warfare and they were either dispersed in the defence of airfields or stretched across the 175-mile-wide front. Japanese forces infiltrated, bypassed and enveloped the British and Indian units. The Japanese soon achieved air superiority, but British ships, some converted First World War vessels, lacked adequate air defences. The capture of the island fortress itself was concluded quickly when Japanese troops cut off the water supply at Tengah. Singapore is often thought to have been a land battle, but, in fact, the defences had relied on air power and naval supremacy. The Japanese defeated these elements, which left the land forces isolated.

John Curtin, the Australian Prime Minister, blamed Churchill for the 'inexcusable betrayal' of Singapore. He had earlier criticised Churchill for the fall of Tobruk in the same terms: namely a lack of preparation. Yet it was ironic that Curtin stubbornly refused to introduce the conscription that was necessary for the defence of Australia. He accused the British of abandoning Australia in the *Melbourne Herald* in December 1941 and promised that the United States would be the keystone of its defence plan.[23] However, as the fall of the Philippines showed, the Americans had their own problems in 1941–2. At the end of February 1942, the Japanese had reached Timor and an air raid on Darwin brought the war to the shores of Australia. The British knew they would be unable to support Australia, and despite the accusations of betrayal, Clement Atlee, then Dominions Secretary, told the Australian Prime Minister plainly: 'Your greatest support in this hour of peril must be drawn from the United States.'[24] This was accurate, if hardly encouraging. With reluctance, Churchill agreed that Australian troops, which he had hoped could be sent to the defence of Burma, must return to Australia. It was clear that no British or Indian troops could be spared because the situation in Burma was deteriorating rapidly. Indeed, Burma not Australia was the target of Japanese strategy. Oil and other natural resources were the prizes for the Japanese, but severing the 'Burma road' and thus the supply routes of Chiang Kai Shek's Chinese forces were regarded as objectives of great strategic importance. Nevertheless, for the Empire, Curtin's declaration of transferred dependence was significant. Curtin stated: 'Australia looks to America, free of any pangs as to our traditional links or kinship with the United Kingdom.' However, as Carl Bridge argued, Australia's shift into the American Pacific orbit was 'not nearly so simple or absolute', and he condemned the 'Labour patriotic myths' of Britain's abandonment of Australia as a 'travesty of justice'.[25]

American forces gradually cleared the South-East Asian islands of Japanese occupiers between 1942 and 1945. Australian troops fought their way back through New Guinea in August 1942, paving the way for a period of closer co-operation with America in South-East Asia. Britain chose to reinforce and re-equip its forces on the Indo-Burmese front, but it was still a low priority for resources. Yet the British and Indian troops, supported by the Americans, defeated Japanese forces at Imphal and Kohima, and again at Meiktila and Mandalay (April–May 1944). In May 1945, Japanese forces had been expelled from Burma, and the Americans' island-hopping campaign finally brought Japan within bomber range. Defeated in the field, deprived of resources and subjected to atomic attack by the Americans at home, the Japanese surrendered.

Nemesis of Empire?

The British Empire survived the Second World War, but it was financially crippled by it. John Gallagher argued that whilst the British world system was in decay before 1939, the war gave it a brief revival but finally brought it down.[26] The Japanese victories proved that Asians could overthrow British rule by force of arms. Morally, it broke the mystique of perpetual and invincible British power. Indian nationalists had been inspired by Japan's victory over Russia in 1905, but that had been a remote concept for the majority of Indians. In 1942, the British themselves were humiliated at Singapore and their forces driven from Burma. The Indian National Army and the 1942 campaign of sabotage in the subcontinent were directly related to the Japanese victories, and the Quit India movement enjoyed more widespread support than it might otherwise have received, at least at that point in India's historic journey towards independence. Curtin's belief that Australia should look to America for its future support was given a fillip by the British setbacks, and accusations of betrayal have formed a potent part in the shaping of republican Australian identity. The war had shown that Britain was unable to defend Canada and Australia, at least not at the same time as fighting a war in Europe, South-East Asia and North Africa.

However, the Indian Army and Australian troops continued fighting alongside the British, demonstrating that the Empire was still a military force to be reckoned with. Allied victories in South-East Asia from late 1942 reinforce the point. Indeed, imperial solidarity remained strong: 5.5 million imperial soldiers fought in the war. British troops died defending Burma, Malaya and India, even though it was clear from the 1930s that India, at least, would soon be self-governing. This fact is all the more remarkable when it is remembered that the United Kingdom itself was still under a considerable threat. What some saw as betrayal was, in reality, little more than the product of a shortage of resources and a series of stinging defeats. The second of these, particularly, should be credited more to Japanese prowess than British perfidy.

In addition, although Congress had widespread support, their refusal to participate in the British system during the war opened the way for the Muslim League to assert itself as the only legitimate voice of the Islamic communities. The war thus made the recognition of a separate state of Pakistan – their primary aim – inevitable. Congress still insisted on a unified state and blamed Britain for the communal conflict that followed. The idea that Britain pursued a deliberate policy of 'divide and rule' is still contested. Moreover, nationalists believe that they forced concessions out of the British by direct action, whilst the British believed they could satisfy nationalists with concessions and thus keep India, and Pakistan, in the Commonwealth when self-government was eventually granted. This followed a pattern that had begun with the granting of responsible government to Canada in 1848.

Economically, the Empire enabled the British to survive the war, but by 1945, it was left bankrupt. Trade with Europe and the Far East was severed early on, so greater emphasis was placed on Canada and African colonies. Sales of colonial goods enabled Britain to buy raw materials and munitions from the United States. Britain's Food Ministry also fixed prices and tried to increase production in the colonies, which in many cases represented its greatest intervention throughout the whole history of the Empire. There were winners and losers in this process. High wartime prices benefited those in war industries, but fixed prices on some crops, like cocoa, appeared unfair to others. A wartime shortage of capital and an inability to provide the goods the colonies required in return for its food, meant that credit was frozen in London accounts, a situation that lasted until the 1950s. However, loans for development were made to the colonies in 1940 and 1945 for mutual benefit. The colonies would be able to boost production and develop for a secure basis of self-government, but Britain would be able to use the goods to exchange for American materials. Britain also rationed the colonies' imports (for protection), which caused shortages of consumer goods and thus inflation. Whilst critics would point to Britain's self-interested approach in this situation, it should be acknowledged that the primary aim was the defeat of the Axis powers and Britain lacked the resources to do this. In the end, therefore, the Empire contributed not to Britain's accumulation of wealth, but to the final defeat of Fascism in Europe and Japanese militarism in Asia. This victory came at a price: a loss of prestige, a great cost, and ultimately, the acceleration of the process of decolonisation.

13 Decolonisation after 1945: how did British imperialism end?

Decolonisation was a term that came into general use in the 1950s, but it has been challenged since it implies the initiative for the relinquishing of the empire emanated from the metropolis. Nationalists have preferred to use 'liberation struggle' or 'resumption of independence', although the latter claim (implying complete continuity) is tenuous.[1] The date for the origin of decolonisation is also debated. Paul Kennedy argued that the European empires had always contained the seeds of their own destruction.[2] Muriel Chamberlain believes that the loss of India in 1947 marked the turning point for the British Empire, but George Boyce notes that the British had always had a sense of contingency, they had adapted to changing conditions and drew upon these experiences rather than any rigid theories.[3] This flexibility was a strength; it helped them to avoid destructive ideological wars and to withdraw from the imperial experience relatively unscathed. It also provided useful justifications to excuse actions that had been forced upon them. It was easy to see a trend towards eventual self-government in the writings of Liberals and radicals. In 1838, Charles Treveleyan wrote: 'The existing connection between two such distant countries as England and India cannot, in the nature of things, be permanent: no effort of policy can prevent the natives from ultimately regaining their independence.'[4] The Whig view of history, with its emphasis on linear progress, lent itself perfectly to the idea. However, whilst such liberal views can be criticised as too determinist (and in the case of the American colonies clearly misleading), the granting of responsible government to the colonies of settlement does indicate that, in some cases, the realisation of democratic institutions and autonomy within the framework of the Empire was the logical end.

The timing of decolonisation was driven by a number of factors. In the nineteenth century, although colonies were frequently decried as financial burdens, there was little consideration given to the abandonment of the Empire.[5] This can be explained in part by the importance of prestige. Great Power status could be maintained by the possession of territory that might yield something of value in the future. The emergence of the great territorial states such as the USA, Russia and Germany prompted Joseph Chamberlain to speculate that the future would be dominated by the largest powers. The colonies of settlement achieved the status of dominions, as defined by the imperial conference of 1907, because it was felt that they had reached a level of development that enabled them to be 'independent' of the United Kingdom. Although the dominions were to be consulted on foreign policy, before the Second World War Britain shouldered the defence costs and provided much of the manpower. Progress elsewhere was limited. India's move to self-government was firmly established by the Montagu Declaration (1917), but the steps were cautious as the British aimed to ensure fair representation for minorities and refused to give way to agitators. The delays added to the frustration of the nationalists.

British control over the Middle East was shared through the League of Nations and granted autonomy or independence before the Second World War in accordance with the mandate system. Iraq became independent in 1932, but in Palestine, the difficulties of finding a solution to the rival claims of Jews and Arabs, and the outbreak of war, delayed independence. Egypt was formally classed as a protectorate in 1914, but the title was relinquished in 1922 following the Milner Mission into the causes of a serious uprising there in 1919. Although Egypt became an independent monarchy, British military occupation continued because of concerns for the security of the Suez Canal. In the 1936 Anglo–Egyptian Treaty, formal intervention was ended, but Britain pressured Egypt into an anti-German stance in 1939 in order to defend North Africa. Class B and C Mandates, covering former German colonies in Africa and the Pacific, had been handed over to France, Britain and the dominions in 1919. There was no obligation to move these territories towards independence, but a League of Nations Commission supervised the governance of these areas.

Decolonisation in Asia

The desire for power-sharing or independence in India was rooted in the nineteenth century. Dadabhai Naoroji was among the delegation that petitioned the British government for devolved institutions as early as August 1852, and the Bombay Association, formed that year, used the arguments they had derived from British history and Western philosophy to justify their cause. Although it was an Englishman, Alan Hume, who founded the Indian National Congress in 1885, this body was seen as a useful mouthpiece to reach the government of India and complemented Surendranath Banerjea's Indian National Conference, itself a movement that stood on foundations of Western notions of nationalism; 'the conception of a united India, derived from the inspiration of Mazzini [the Italian patriot and liberal]'.[6] India had never before been a nation state, even the Mughal rulers had presided over an empire which did not unite the subcontinent, but the English language and British-built communications linked Indians as never before. The country remained divided, despite the nationalists' claims to represent all India as if it were a united front. Muslims and Untouchables sought their own representation, and the Muslim League was established as early as 1906. Rivalry between these groups led to widespread violence of increasing magnitude.

Whilst attempts to find moderate political solutions in the inter-war years had failed, the outbreak of the war in 1939 merely hardened the nationalists' resolve and made compromise less likely. The British were eager to shelve the issue of Indian power-sharing until the war was over, but the setbacks in Europe in 1940 and the Japanese onslaught in South-East Asia undermined the British position. It was evident to the nationalists that Britain was weakened by its defeats, and the British government recognised as much by despatching Sir Stafford Cripps in 1942 to renew British offers in return for three things: support during the war, guarantees for racial and religious minorities, and the right to secede from the Indian union.[7] The British accepted that India's withdrawal from the Empire-Commonwealth was likely. These factors suggest that the move towards India's independence was dependent on the defeats Britain suffered in the war. This had the dual psychological effect of accelerating

Britain's belief that it would relinquish India and of encouraging the nationalists to believe that they could liberate India themselves. The Japanese had provided stark evidence that Europeans, now lined up in prison camps in their thousands, could be defeated by Asians.

After the war, the Cabinet Mission of 1946 came close to agreement on a federal India, but Jinnah's decision to demonstrate the strength of the Muslim League through the 'Direct Action Day' (16 August 1946) led to the death of 4000 people and inflicted permanent damage on Hindu–Muslim relations. The Viceroy, Lord Wavell, argued that Atlee must either commit Britain to a further ten years of rule or fix a date for withdrawal, but Atlee initially rejected the idea as a counsel of despair. Nevertheless, Wavell's replacement, Mountbatten, urged the same conclusion and the initial date fixed for the transfer of power was June 1948. Withdrawal would leave the decision about the jurisdiction of each interest group to the Indians themselves, but there was little prospect of agreement and partition was likely. The immediate problems this would cause included the severing of the Punjab irrigation system, the separation of Muslim heartlands (later known as East and West Pakistan) by one thousand miles, and the division of producing areas and their neighbouring processing plants. Yet the greatest tragedy was still to unfold. Mountbatten knew the British no longer had either the means to retain control or the will to do so. Hoping for the emergence of a quasi-federation as proposed by the 1946 mission, Mountbatten brought forward the date for withdrawal to 14 August 1947.[8] However, communal violence raged across the regions affected by the potential new boundaries in the autumn of 1947. It is thought that as many as 500,000 died, and ten million people were displaced. Gandhi himself was assassinated when he attempted to stem the violence.

There was much criticism of the transfer of power, but interestingly enough, the violence that developed was not directed at the British. Mountbatten was probably right to assume the British had lost the ability to resolve the disputes between Hindu and Muslim. They had also lost the legitimacy to chair the negotiations. However, the violence of 1947 has overshadowed what was achieved by British and South Asian leaders.

The emergence of a united India and a united Pakistan (and later Bangladesh in 1971) was clearly preferable to civil war, or a return to the large number of rival states that characterised the pre-colonial period.

Since the transfer of power in 1947, Pakistan has periodically turned to military rule, but India remains the world's largest democracy. Congress dominated the first 40 years of Indian politics, but it was defeated in 1998 by a coalition that was led by the BJP, a Hindu traditionalist party. This party has alarmed minority groups – and some Western observers – by its uncompromising line on religion and education. Moreover, relations between India and Pakistan have been punctuated by suspicion, and in the 1960s by war. In Kashmir, Muslim separatists dispute a borderline settled in 1962, and desultory fighting, punctuated by more severe crises, has continued until the present day.

The transfer of power in Ceylon contrasted with the India experience. Ceylon was a Crown Colony controlled by a Governor with an executive and legislative council. From 1923, the legislative council had had an elected majority and the colony had a wide franchise. Despite the presence of ethnic tensions between the majority Sinhalese and the minority Tamils, power was transferred smoothly and its prosperity, based on tea and rubber exports, seemed assured. It was not until the 1980s that Tamil guerrillas began to seriously challenge the homogeneity of Sri Lanka.

The handover of Burma was equally rapid. Despite having to fight their way painstakingly back through the jungles of the north in 1944–5, the British did not intend to retain the country. Power was transferred to a former lawyer, Aung San, who had been selected by the Japanese as their puppet ruler in 1942. Aung San had skilfully changed sides in 1944 and had won an overwhelming mandate to govern in elections after the war. When he was assassinated in July 1947, his successor, Thakin Nu, took Burma to independence on 4 January 1948. Burma, or Myanmar, has been under military dictatorship since 1962.[9]

Ethnic difficulties assisted the British only in Malaya. The federated states, some brought under British protection from Thailand as late as 1909, were major suppliers of rubber and tin and the profits had been used to support the viability of the Sterling Area from 1939. Independence was delayed by the convergence of two issues. First, the British were eager to foster Malaya as a bulwark against communism in Asia. Second, the Malays were determined to prevent the unpopular Chinese minority from seizing the key assets of the country (or becoming a vassal of Communist China) and therefore welcomed British military support. Lieutenant-General Sir Gerald Templer defended the Malay communities by pooling the people in protected villages. This deprived the communist insurgents of supplies and any potential support from the local Chinese population. Systematic and patient operations, through patrolling and ambushes, gradually wore down the guerrillas. Power was transferred to Tunku Abdul Rahman (the Chief Minister of the legislature) through elections in 1956, a fact that further undermined the communists' 'anti-imperialist' cause. British military discipline, training and the flexibility offered by helicopters for deployment and supplies paid dividends. The Malaya Scouts, which later became an SAS unit, specialised in successful deep penetration operations. Above all, the emphasis was on winning the 'hearts and minds' of the local population rather than putting more troops into the country.[10] A local police force was organised by Sir Arthur Young, with the same object in mind. It was this ethos which created an atmosphere of close co-operation and avoided the difficulties that had accompanied the Indian handover. On 31 August 1957, Malaya became independent, and in 1963 Singapore, Sarawak and Sabah (formerly British North Borneo) came together to form Malaysia. In 1965, Singapore broke away as a separate island republic. Brunei gained its independence in February 1984.

Decolonisation in Africa

India's independence did, as many nineteenth-century commentators had predicted, mark the beginning of the end of the British Empire. In just 20 years, the majority of colonies had been relinquished. The Congress movement was an inspiration to several groups in Africa. The South African Native National Congress (formed in 1912 and becoming the African National Congress in 1925) was a direct imitation of the Indian Model. J. E. Casely Hayford formed the National Congress of British

West Africa. The attraction lay not just in successful methods, but also the charisma and popularity of Gandhi.

Yet, once again, the pace of change was determined by the metropolis rather than by pressure groups. When colonies had been taken over there was a general expectation that they would, under British rule or 'protection', develop into modernised states. In an era of minimal state intervention, the bulk of this development relied on the influence of capitalism. However, the idea that the colonies should be developed using government funding was put forward as early as the 1890s by Joseph Chamberlain. He began with the Colonial Loans Act (1899) which made borrowing easier. The 1929 Colonial Development Act, which actually committed government money, was reduced by the Slump and then by the Second World War. The post-war Colonial Development and Welfare Acts took up where the previous acts had left off, and looked forward to the development of the colonies to strengthen the empire, and its finances, as a whole.

The problems the British faced when they considered relinquishing power included setting the time scale and deciding on the groups to whom power would be transferred. The basis of 'indirect rule' had been traditional rulers, often the direct descendants of the leaders the British had first encountered. However, the modernisation of the colonies had led to the emergence of African middle classes, usually educated along Western lines. These men included the radical nationalists who, after the Pan-African Conference in Manchester in 1945, endorsed a programme of 'African socialism based on the tactics of positive action without violence'. The Pan-Africanists had first come together in 1919 and they met periodically in the inter-war years, led by black Americans. As this organisation prepared to fight colonial rule, the British were, at the same time, prepared to grant greater representation in order to implement development more efficiently. The priority, Lord Hailey observed, was not 'constitution-mongering' (which had failed in India), but the training of new African elites to assume government roles.

Africans already played an important part in the running of the colonies. As well as the administrators, the Gold Coast had had two nominated African representatives on the Legislative

Council from 1888. The Gold Coast became more prosperous during the inter-war years through cocoa plantations, and became the world's largest producer after 1945. This wealth continued to alter the social structure and led to increased spending on health and education. The benefits naturally extended to Britain, and the profits from cocoa supported the Sterling Area. After the war, a new constitution ensured the majority of the Governor's Council were elected Africans. To the British it seemed as if the policy of gradually widening the African participation in government to ensure the continued development of the colony was being successful. The formation of J. B. Danquah's moderate United Gold Coast Convention in 1947 seemed to confirm the view.

However, the situation changed when Danquah invited Kwame Nkrumah to be the party secretary. Having absorbed the ideas of British communists, Nkrumah had joined 'The Circle', a secret organisation pledged to revolutionary action across Africa. On his return to Gold Coast from London, Nkrumah's tours through Accra and Kumasi were accompanied by serious rioting and 29 died in the fighting. An enquiry into the violence concluded that the 1946 concessions were now redundant and an African judge, Mr Justice Coussey, worked out a new arrangement. In 1949, Nkrumah set up his own party, the Convention People's Party, the core of which consisted of the Westernised 'Youth Section'. Their strategy was to mobilise mass support through strikes, boycotts and non-cooperation. This led in 1950 to Nkrumah's imprisonment, but he was permitted to run his party from within prison and the CPP was the largest single party in the elections of 1951. With this mandate, Sir Charles Arden-Clarke, the Governor, released Nkrumah and he effectively became prime minister. However, the Gold Coast was not yet ready for independence: the cocoa crop had been devastated by disease and Nkrumah knew a socialist agenda would drive away much-needed investment. Moreover, there were still too few Africans with experience of government, and Nkrumah's greatest problem was still convincing other Africans to support him. However, even before the 1956 election, Lennox-Boyd, the British Colonial Secretary, had pledged to grant Gold Coast its independence on 6 March 1957.

The division of Africans continued to plague Nkrumah in the independent Ghana. He was determined to rule Ghana as a single state and he imposed a dictatorship soon after independence. Opposition leaders were arrested and the new constitution of 1960 gave him considerable powers. From 1961 he began to align the country with the communist bloc. Nor had he forgotten the ideals of the Pan-African Conference; he devoted some effort to urging all Africans to unite. However, his rule and his profligate spending made him unpopular and he was deposed in a military coup in 1966. The precedent of centralised planning and control has damaged Ghana's politics ever since and episodes of democracy have been interrupted by army rule.

Ethnic divisions made the independence of Nigeria even more problematic than Ghana. The frontier established by the Royal Niger Company had incorporated the Yorubas of the western region, the Ibos of the eastern region and the Muslim Emirates of the north. Lord Lugard had permitted indirect rule in the north, but the south was less conservative. The development of Nigeria was slower than the Gold Coast and there was a smaller Westernised elite, but the nationalist leader Nmandi Azikiwe successfully protested against the constitution of 1946 and gained greater concessions in the 1951 version. The emergence of three distinct parties, each representing one of the three regions, and concerns for the fate of minorities in an independent Nigeria led the British to propose a federalist constitution in 1954. In the elections that followed, each of the parties relied on its heartlands for electoral support although the prospect of independence created a unity of purpose. Chief Awolowo of the western region warned that independence raised expectations: 'There is a popular illusion among educated young Nigerians about self-government. They believe it is like the Kingdom of God and his righteousness which, once attained, brings unmixed blessing. They therefore seek it as a first objective. It is a clever way of evading the immediate problems which confront the country.'[11]

The discovery of oil and natural gas could have forged a greater unity in Nigeria through prosperity, but after independence on 1 October 1960, the old fissures remained. In 1964, all sides accused the other of election rigging, and in January 1966, the army of the eastern region staged a *coup d'état* in the west. This prompted a counter-coup by the north and the installation of a compromise president. However, massacres of Ibos pushed the eastern region to declare itself an independent state called Biafra in May 1967. Military rule continued after the three-year civil war and the country was divided into 19 regions. So far, attempts to restore civilian government have failed.

Military rule also affected Sierra Leone. The transfer of power took place in 1961 and Dr Milton Margai's party won a democratic majority in 1962, but he was overthrown by the army in 1967 and a one-party state emerged in 1978. Attempts to restore civilian government in the 1990s provoked a civil war in 1997. In contrast, Gambia, independent in 1965, managed to escape military dictatorship after the intervention of Senegalese troops in 1981–2.

Uganda had no single nationalist movement and Britain's dealings were through the Kabaka of the Bagandans, Mutesa II. Mutesa had little interest in the rival kingdoms of Bunvoro, Toro and Ankole that, with Buganda, made up the Protectorate of Uganda. In addition, he was eager to prevent the incorporation of Buganda into an East African federation. In 1952, the new British Governor, Cohen, declared that Uganda must be transferred as a 'unitary form of central Government on parliamentary lines'.[12] Mutesa's continued opposition compelled Cohen to deport him to London, an act which provoked considerable debate in the House of Commons. The idea of an East African federation was dropped, but the Namirembe conference of 1954 worked out a compromise for the incorporation of Buganda with the rest of Uganda. After independence in 1962, the Kabaka was overthrown by Milton Obote, the Prime Minister, in 1966. The leader of the palace coup was Idi Amin and he seized power for himself in 1971. His bloody dictatorial regime was only brought to an end with the help of Tanzanian troops. Obote returned to power but was overthrown in 1985. Nevertheless, Uganda has returned to democracy, plagued only by rebels in the north. By contrast, Julius Nyerere combined the traditional credentials as son of a chief with a Western education to lead Tanganyika successfully in its first 20 years as independent Tanzania from 1961. In 1964, it united with Zanzibar, restoring a historic link between the island and the hinterland.

Kenya, North and South Rhodesia and Nyasaland presented the British with some difficulties because the ethnic divisions of Africans were further complicated by the presence of white settlers. The moderate climate and sparse population were attractive 'pull' factors in east Africa, but the flow of settlers increased after the Second World War in response to the 'austerity' programme in Britain. White plantation owners ploughed their savings into coffee and tea production, just as whites developed modern farming in southern Africa. In Kenya there was an expectation that the whites would be treated the same way as the Australians, with the assumption that they now owned the land and should be given representation accordingly. The British government felt differently. The Devonshire White Paper (1923) concluded that Kenya was 'an African territory' where 'the interests of the African natives must be paramount, and that if and when those interests and the interests of the immigrant races should conflict the former should prevail.' Resentment reached boiling point as settlers organised themselves and threatened a loyalist rebellion along the lines of Ulster's struggle in Ireland.[13] The large Asian population, who had migrated into the country, primarily as traders, were agitating for representation too. The Africans themselves tolerated the Europeans, but there was widespread hatred of the Asians. One chief stated: 'if the *wazungu* (whites) will only sleep for two days, there would be no Indian Question.'[14]

Until 1948, four nominated members of the Legislative Council represented Africans in Kenya. Tribal chiefs made direct representations to the colonial authorities but once again, the most radical leaders were those who had received some Western education. The Kikuyu Association was formed in 1920, but this moderate body was supplemented in 1921 by the Young Kikuyu Association (later the Kikuyu Central Association). In the 1950s, Jomo Kenyatta emerged as a leading spokesman of the Kikuyu Central Association, but, having fostered communist affiliations in Britain, he was suspected of connections with the Mau Mau guerrilla organisation and was arrested. The Mau Mau, drawn from the Kikuyu people, were driven by a mixture of motives, including fears about land ownership. They ensured loyalty through a series of shocking oaths, some of which relied on committing atrocities.[15] The settler population could not contain their brutal tactics and British troops were called in. This ended any chances the settlers had of claiming the right to govern Kenya independently.

Operations against the Mau Mau lasted from 1952–6, and there was condemnation of British forces in left-wing circles for what appeared to be a typical example of colonial brutality. In fact, the military effort was not to sustain British rule. It was already clear that Britain would pull out of Kenya, but they aimed to leave behind a constitution that would safeguard the interests of all races. Moreover, they would not permit the terror gangs to succeed. The Mau Mau killed 2,465 people, most of them cut to pieces by *pangas*, but it did not become the fighting organisation that Kenyatta had hoped for and it failed to drive the settlers out. Kenyatta set up the Kenya African National Union (KANU) to pursue a political path to power. The opposition, Kenya African Democratic Union (KADU) preferred a federal system, primarily to safeguard their interests against the Kikuyu-dominated KANU. Many unrealistic promises were made by KANU to attract support, telling voters that they would all get luxurious homes or the vehicles of the white settlers. Nevertheless, KANU won the elections prior to independence in 1963. For ten years from 1982, Kenya became a one-party state, and despite the return to pluralism, accusations of vote-rigging and intimidation have increased.

The British South Africa Company, which had run Northern and Southern Rhodesia, was wound up in 1923 and 1924 in both territories. The North became a Crown Colony, but, having rejected union with South Africa, Southern Rhodesia became a 'self-governing colony'. This exceptional arrangement meant that Southern Rhodesia was not a dominion, and therefore the British government could intervene if necessary to protect the interests of Africans against a substantial settler population. In 1953, Southern Rhodesia joined Northern Rhodesia and Nyasaland to form the Central African Federation, which brought together the mineral-based economy of the North with the booming agriculture of the South. However, Africans opposed the federation. Kenneth Kaunda emerged as the leader in Northern Rhodesia in the wake of labour disputes. Dr Hastings Banda became the spokesman of the Nyasaland population and in Southern Rhodesia, Joshua Nkomo led the

Zimbabwe African People's Union against his rival Reverend Ndabaningi Sithole and the Zimbabwe African National Union. The federation was therefore broken up in 1963 and independence was granted to Nyasaland (Malawi) and Northern Rhodesia (Zambia) in 1964.

Britain would not grant Southern Rhodesia its independence until there was black majority rule and a new constitution in 1961 had only allocated 15 out of 65 seats to Africans along with a 'Bill of Rights'. The settler population argued that the division of the black Africans proved that civil war would result (as had occurred in neighbouring Zaire) if majority rule were granted. Rhodesians looked instead to South Africa's restrictions on Africans as its model. Ian Smith then announced a Unilateral Declaration of Independence in 1965 in the interests of whites in Rhodesia. Harold Wilson's government impotently imposed sanctions whilst South Africa and Mozambique supported the UDI. Africans organised a guerrilla war, but it was the withdrawal of support by South Africa in 1979 that compelled the Rhodesian government to capitulate. After elections in 1980, the Crown Colony of Rhodesia was formally granted its independence. Nevertheless, the African voters split between the ZANU (led by Robert Mugabe) which represented the Shona, and the minorities of the south and west who supported Nkomo. Mugabe's one-party regime inherited thriving farming and tourism industries, but in 2000–1 farm occupations and murders of white farmers and their workers by 'war veterans' added to Zimbabwe's economic disaster. Elections have been accompanied by considerable voter intimidation.

Decolonisation of the islands and the Suez crisis

Changes in the West Indies were dominated by economic crisis after 1929 in two staple crops, sugar and bananas. On one side, the growers organised themselves as a lobby group, whilst workers began to organise trade unions. Amongst the union leaders were future politicians, Norman Manley and W. A. Bustamente (Jamaica) and Grantly Adams (Barbardos). The British, conscious of the economic weakness of the islands if granted independence on their own, established a federation in 1958.

However, the richer islands of Trinadad (with Tobago) and Jamaica resented having to support the poorer islands and became independent in 1962. Britain's solution was to set up an arrangement called 'Associated States'. Internal self-government was supported by Britain (in that Britain assumed responsibility for defence and foreign affairs). However, each of the islands gradually shed British rule: Barbados, 1966; Grenada, 1974; Dominica, 1978; St Lucia and St Vincent, 1979; Antigua, 1981; and St Kitts-Nevis, 1983. The loss of British protection left Grenada powerless against American military intervention in 1983. British Guiana was granted its independence in 1966 and British Honduras in 1981, although Britain was called upon to provide military support against Guatemala. The Bahamas became independent in 1973, but Bermuda voted against independence in 1995.

There were two contrasting examples of decolonisation in the Mediterranean. Malta was granted independence in 1964, but only after some consideration had been given to direct representation in Westminster. In this respect, Malta was regarded as akin to the Channel Islands or Gibraltar. Gibralterians were determined not to come under the heel of General Franco, despite Spanish claims to the colony, and in a referendum they voted firmly against incorporation with Spain. Cyprus had been of strategic importance to Britain, but ethnic divisions were the greatest concern for Britain after the Second World War. The majority Greek population wanted *enosis* (union) with Greece, but it was clear that the minority Turkish population would be under pressure the moment the British relinquished control. Michael Mouskos ('Makarios') became the militant leader of the *enosis* campaign, even after he was exiled to the Seychelles, and Colonel Grivas organised a guerrilla movement. Unable to contain the movement, Harold Macmillan handed Cyprus over in 1960. In Britain, the resignation of Lord Salisbury from the Cabinet in protest attracted little sympathy: imperialism was clearly unfashionable.

The Suez Crisis of 1956 had highlighted the disillusionment with imperial matters. Early in the year, British troops had been withdrawn from Egypt and the Sudan was granted its independence. President Nasser announced in July that he intended to nationalise the Suez Canal, but his hostility to Israel and his communist sympathies also determined the British and French response. When negotiations over the free passage of the canal failed, British and French troops poured into the Egyptian Canal Zone, whilst Israeli troops drove into Sinai. Anthony Eden's motive was to prevent the emergence of another Hitler, as he had been appalled by the appeasement of the 1930s.

The hostile reaction of the USSR and the United States indicated that British world hegemony was truly at an end. In one month, British and French troops had been withdrawn and Britain's ability to exert its power or influence was seriously curbed. The Second World War had left Britain economically weak. The retreat from India, and from Palestine in June 1948, was evidence of the new world order. Britain was not under pressure from the United States, but was eager to avoid repression or the condemnation of other countries, and keen to maintain American support.

There was even a desire not to be 'left behind' when it came to the granting of independence to the colonies. Britain's international standing could be greatly enhanced if it appeared to take the lead in offering freedom. A Cabinet Committee paper in 1959 was concerned that: 'our past record of benevolent government will be forgotten and it will be the French and Belgians who will be regarded by world opinion as the leaders, while we may be classed with the Portuguese as obstacles to further advance.'[16]

When the military junta of Argentina invaded the Falkland Islands in 1982 to regain popularity after its inept economic policies, Britain's independent action was largely supported by America. Unlike Cyprus or Suez, the British armed forces were acting on behalf of a sympathetic settler population. This was not a colonial operation, but a conflict fought under the rules of the United Nations: UN Resolution 502 opposed the Argentine occupation. British troops were engaged in a war of liberation. This limited conflict also indicated that Britain was still prepared to fight for its possessions, or rather the protection and self-determination of the population there.

Hong Kong was held on lease from China through an agreement drawn up in 1898. China was determined to regain the colony and to wipe out the embarrassment of colonial rule, but also to acquire one of the most successful of all of Britain's imperial possessions. There were reservations about the hand-over, particularly as the Chinese pro-democracy movement had been fired on in Tiannamen Square in 1989, and the Chinese negotiators did not want the establishment of any democratic institutions before the British left. Moreover, the British armed forces had been kept busy on the border rounding up Chinese men and women trying to escape communist rule. The compromise was that after the handover on 1 July 1997, Hong Kong would be a 'special administrative region'. As China's own economy geared itself along capitalist lines in the 1990s, the bright future of the former colony seemed assured. Despite several announcements that this was the final end of the British Empire, Britain in 2002 still retains possession of Anguilla, Montserrat, Ascension Island, St Helena, the Caymen Islands, the British Virgin Islands, Pitcairn, Tristan de Cunha, Gibraltar, Bermuda, the Turks and Caicos Islands, the British Indian Ocean Territory, British Antarctic Territory, South Georgia, South Sandwich Islands and the Falklands.

The Commonwealth

Balfour's declaration defining dominion status in 1926, referred to such states enjoying 'a common allegiance to the Crown' as 'freely associated members of the British Commonwealth of Nations', and this was enshrined in the Statute of Westminster (1931). Ireland's change to a republic in 1949, and the independence of India and Pakistan (who wanted to remain in the Commonwealth) demanded an alteration in the status of the British monarchy. George VI was thus the 'Head of the Commonwealth' and the 'symbol of the free association'. The degree to which these freely associated states would work together was tested in 1961 when South Africa became a republic and left the Commonwealth. Its record on race relations meant that South Africa became the 'pariah state' whose membership would not have been welcome. In a similar way, Fiji was ejected in 1987 when a military *coup d'état* overthrew the civilian government (it was reinstated in 1997). Nigeria was suspended in 1995 because of a poor human rights record. In 1991, the Commonwealth formally established that it stood for democracy, the rule of law, good government and social justice. On this basis, Mozambique, which had never been a British colony, joined the Commonwealth in 1995. This suggests that the Commonwealth has a future, particularly as a lobby for the protection of human rights. In this, Britain will provide a valuable link between the developing and developed nations of the world.

Co-operation has not been extended to common citizenship, as each state has chosen to define its own criteria. British citizenship was not defined until 1948 and it was not until 1962 that barriers to immigration by Commonwealth peoples were erected. Moreover, membership of other international organisations seems to have superseded the purpose of the Commonwealth. Britain's part in the North Atlantic Treaty Organisation does not stand at odds with the Commonwealth, but its entry into the EEC in 1973 caused some remarks from Commonwealth partners that Britain was turning its back on its responsibilities. In fact, it was perhaps logical that there would be an economic realignment of Canada and Australia with the United States and Japan. Moreover, Britain's membership of the EEC was hesitant and merely reflected the country's weakened economic position. Membership of the EU continues to create discussion, but not because Britain harks back to its imperial past. Rather, the subsuming of British law, currency and administration reflects concerns that British sovereignty, or independence, is at stake.

In 1994, Roger Louis and Ronald Robinson suggested that decolonisation was an attempt by Britain to return to 'informal empire' with the backing of the USA.[17] Certainly, Britain was eager to retain its connections with former colonies as partners in the Commonwealth and to promote its own economic recovery after the Second World War. Corelli Barnett argued that Atlee's desire to retain African colonies as a 'New Jerusalem' was an expensive illusion.[18] However, the emergence of the super-powers, the demands of alignment with the North Atlantic Treaty Organisation (and its most powerful member the United States, which provided substantial loans), the inability to act independently over Suez, the desire to focus on welfare at home and an awareness of the new, post-imperial climate of world opinion, all converged to bring any aspirations of continued global influence through imperialism to an end. This was a gradual process which culminated in the decolonisation of the African states in an atmosphere aptly summed up by Harold Macmillan: 'The wind of change is blowing through this continent [Africa], and whether we like it or not, this growth of national consciousness is a political fact. We must all accept it as a fact, and our national policies must take account of it.'[19]

John Gallagher described three factors that caused British decolonisation: first, the growth of political movements in the colonies; second, the domestic constraints in the metropolis; and third, international pressures.[20] Ronald Robinson believed it had been due to Indian nationalism, British social democracy and American anti-imperialism.[21] David Birmingham, in referring to African decolonisation, attributed it to nationalist campaigning for independence and the pressure of superpowers for access to a continent dominated by Europeans at an opportune moment of imperial retreat (due to internal weaknesses).[22] Anthony Low agreed that nationalist movements and the imperial response was significant, but argued the international dimension was rarely as important.[23] John Darwin concluded that the three factors identified by John Gallagher, entitled 'domestic, international and peripheral', were the most important, but he argued that the metropolitan case needed further subdivision. Britain's economic and military strength declined relative to its commitment (and other powers), but there was also a post-war indifference to Empire in Britain and the emergence of a post-imperial economy.[24] The idea of political indifference is supported by the findings of Stephen Howe, whose examination of the left wing found that it was a marginal issue that rarely divided the political parties.[25]

The key difficulties Britain had faced included the selection of who should inherit British rule. In some cases, the transfer of power was to a selected elite, but this was not universal. Wherever possible, the British sought to transfer power to democratic institutions, but some of these collapsed soon after independence. Independence was often complicated by the existence of ethnic divisions and political rivalry between groups that had been thrown together by the construction of artificial colonial frontiers. The British frequently tried to prevent violent groups from gaining power, from the Mau Mau to the communist terrorists of Malaya. However, where the tide of violence was overwhelming and combined with determined anti-colonial sympathies in the population, as in India and Cyprus, then the British pulled out more rapidly. The financial aspect of decolonisation remains unresolved. Although Macmillan drew up a 'profit and loss' account of the Empire, its findings were inconclusive. In the decolonisation of India, financial considerations were perhaps quite significant, but they were less important elsewhere.[26]

The partnership of the Commonwealth replaced British imperialism, and its members asserted their equality with Britain, even removing 'British' from the title 'British Commonwealth'. This agency has proved several times in its short history that it is guided by a moral philosophy that favours human rights. Ironically, in this respect it has directly inherited the ambitions of the British who advocated imperialism as a force for good. From an economic perspective, the Commonwealth continues to support the development of former colonial territories, again inheriting a process that began with the Colonial Development Loans, and perhaps even before that. However, the Commonwealth clearly marks the end of the British Empire. It is a free association of nations that share a worldview rather than a common development. Moreover, the inequality of wealth between developed nations (which include the former colonies of settlement) and the old colonies remains unresolved. Nevertheless, as one Colonial Office official remarked in 1948, the Commonwealth was 'the boldest stroke of political idealism which the world has yet witnessed, and on by far the grandest scale'.[27]

14 What was the cultural legacy of imperialism?

In recent years there has been renewed interest in the relationship between culture and imperialism, part of a wider post-modernist approach to the connections between language, imagery and power. Whilst the Orientalist debate has dominated the field, culture is undoubtedly a feature of the imperialist landscape that stretches far beyond the narrow horizons of language and power. Culture helped to define British imperialism as distinct from other European versions. It was an agency for propagating support for the imperialist enterprise. It also created idealised notions of the British themselves. Moreover, it raised the concept of Empire beyond trade and conquest to a realm of adventure, chivalric duty and sacrifice. The culture of imperialism promoted 'Britishness' but also embraced aspects of the civilisations it came across. Chinese, Indian and Middle Eastern designs became part of the British imperial culture. There was a cultural exchange on a global scale, often accompanied by greater population mobility and migration. This exchange is visible in all forms of media, from art to film. But cultural aspects of imperialism also affected education, youth movements, religion and sport, both for the British and for the peoples of the Empire. Many regard this legacy as an unhappy one, but the impact varied from place to place. Frequently it was a case that people adopted what they wanted from the Empire, and rejected the rest: it is more difficult to find where British culture was imposed successfully.

Popular imperialism

Public support for imperialism emerged as an extension of British patriotism. The growth of mass communications made this public support more visible, and that made it attractive to advertisers and writers. There was no central direction to the popularisation of imperialism, although there were many notable advocates for it, and there was no propaganda ministry (except in wartime). Public support also grew with the expansion of the Empire in the second half of the nineteenth century, but it was by no means universal. There were important distinctions in response to the Empire which were based on class, or, in the case of the colonies themselves, on the level of benefit which individuals had accrued.

Imperial themes abounded in popular culture at the end of the nineteenth century, but Empire consciousness reached its peak after the First World War. Imperial enthusiasts tried to promote the empire in new ways, Lord Beaverbrook with press coverage, Leo Amery with emigration schemes and the Empire Marketing Board.[1] A number of societies also sprang up, such as the Royal Empire Society, the British Empire Union and the British Empire League. However, their impact amongst the working class was often disappointing. Whilst the Empire was a popular setting for stories in novels, it was often the exotic settings that attracted readers rather than the idea of Empire itself. Books on the 'Wild West' of America were as popular amongst young people as those about Africa and India, and in some cases, more so. Popular entertainments, such as music halls, well-known songs and poems, often returned to the imperial theme. Patriotic pride was the unifying sentiment, and it provided a social cement between classes in Britain at a time when class distinctions were at their most marked.[2] In advertising, the imperial theme offered distinction, credibility and a sense of the exotic. Consumer goods came from all over the world and reminded the British of their world-wide status: tea from Ceylon, sugar from the West Indies, rubber from Malaya, cotton from India and palm oil from West Africa. The great diversity of Empire, and its global sprawl, made the British feel that they commanded a world-wide system. It transferred their identity from an island nation to a cosmopolitan Great Power.

Popular imperialism became more institutionalised in the early twentieth century.[3] However, European affairs assumed a greater importance when British lives were at stake in the world wars, and there was an expectation that the League of Nations would resolve international disputes without involving the British or the Empire in the inter-war years. Nevertheless, popular culture continued to embrace the imperial and the patriotic theme well beyond the heyday of the empire itself.

Imperialism often gathered a popular following because of the way that colonial wars and events were reported in the press. When Britain appeared to be poised to fight Russia in 1878 in defence of the Turks, the government called for Indian troops to be sent to Malta as a staging post. This gesture graphically illustrated the solidarity and global reach of the Empire, and it was seized upon by the newspapers and music halls. The term 'Jingoism', a bombastic form of patriotic pride, stemmed from the popular refrain of the time: 'We don't want to fight, but, by Jingo, if we do, we've got the men, we got the ships, we've got the money too'. What made the concept 'imperial' in British minds was that Queen Victoria had become Empress of India only the year before, marked by the pageant of the Dehli Durbar, and thus Britain was an imperial power able to match the Russian Empire. In a similar fashion, the relief of Mafeking in the South African War produced a popular reaction in Britain and the new verb: to maffick. This was only partly an expression of pride. It was a release of tension after the setbacks of the first few months of the fighting and it signalled the beginning of the end of the war (or so it was thought). Jan Morris regarded popular imperialism not as a 'Jingoistic shout of self-satisfaction but an injunction to greatness. The Empire itself was not simply a display of power, or an opportunity to profit, but an impulse to achievement.'[4] However, Morris acknowledged that the British were still 'essentially insular' and 'saw the whole wide Empire, even the world itself, only as a response to themselves'.[5]

Education, literature and film

Given the slow spread of educational opportunity in Britain, it is not surprising that the impact of European-style education in the Empire was patchy. Whites did not necessarily have all the advantages either. In areas where Islamic education had traditionally dominated, the *madrassahs* (seminaries) continued to thrive. In New Zealand, the dispersed nature of settler communities meant that there was no formal education, unless a church school was available. Until the 1930s, Maoris were offered a primary education, but no more than that, and often under the auspices of churches. Missionaries saw education as vital as it enabled their target congregation to read the Bible, but non-whites regarded the ability to read as a prerequisite for better jobs, wages and prospects. Missionaries in India were deliberately restricted by the authorities for fear of provoking hostile reactions to proselytising, and Indians took advantage of the education without conversion. Gradually, church schools were outnumbered and then superseded by the state in India, and the pattern was repeated across the Empire. Universities also sprang up, in parallel with Britain's own. Freetown (Fourah Bay College) was established in 1827 and Cape Town (South African College) in 1829. New Zealand's first university was Otago (1869).

Schooling for the masses was a different matter, particularly as it was felt that agricultural communities had little need of academic work. In 1900, four-fifths of Indian children of school age were illiterate and three-quarters of all villages had no school. These statistics prompted Curzon to make generous grants to the existing primary and secondary sectors, and he set up technical education training colleges. Significantly, about 270,000 girls were at school in 1899, challenging their traditional relegation to *purdah*. In the same period there were some 30,000 Indian graduates and the key issue was the exclusion of educated Indians from the administration of their own country. In 1900, there were 1142 members of the Indian Civil Service but only 60 of them were Indians. There was considerable hostility to the 'educated Babu' who was seen as disloyal or 'partially qualified' and therefore unfit to govern.[6] Thomas Anstey Guthrie ridiculed the Babu in the form of fictional 'Hurry Bungsho Jabberjee, B.A., Calcutta University' (1897). However, there were occasions where the British sought to select leaders from the indigenous population and mould them with the same values as themselves. Terence Ranger has shown how, in King's College of Budo in Uganda, the Public School system was faithfully replicated to fit Gandan pupils for the role of leadership within the framework of the Empire.[7] There seems to be broad agreement amongst historians that the Empire was a vast educational enterprise designed to fit each section of society into its role of service.

As an educational tool, historical fiction, romances and children's books were similarly affected by themes of patriotism and the modernist superiority of the British race, but imperialist values in literature did not always demand an imperial setting or plot. British characters were stereotypically heroic and moral, with courage, deference to tradition, and decorum. Their opponents, regardless of race, were often untrustworthy, savage, brutal, effeminate, cowardly and immoral. Fiction presented, as the medium demands, idealised versions of the world.[8] In children's literature, this reached the point of caricature. The *Boys Own Paper* (a journal published from 1880) was filled with emblems of the Empire and pull-out sections offered a range of imperial or patriotic themes, from big game hunting to badges of British Army regiments. Historical figures, from Clive of Plassey to Horatio Nelson, were held up as role models.

It was perhaps inevitable that film makers would turn to the exotic settings of the Empire to make popular movies. The endeavour and suffering of the Empire builders offered an opportunity to make films of adventure and romance. Reality was unimportant, and stories could be based very loosely on truth to make them credible. Documentaries, which would eventually become more popular during the Second World War, were harder and more expensive to make. Nevertheless, 'imperial' films were enjoyed by British audiences, but not because of their imperialism. The greater attendance at American movies suggests that it was the escapist value of the films, rather than any acceptance of an imperial message, which was important.

Government intervention in film-making was tacit. There was no policy of propaganda, but censorship was imposed. The independence of film makers was frequently evident in the subject matter. Sir Robert Vansittart, former Under-Secretary of the Foreign Office and a critic of appeasement, turned to film-making when he fell foul of the Chamberlain government. His *Sixty Glorious Years* (1938) placed Queen Victoria's imperial reign in a positive light and made references to Britain's military readiness, highlighting the folly of the government's line on appeasement. By contrast, the BBFC (British Board of Film Censors), with government backing, prevented two films being made on the Indian Mutiny for fear of inciting the Indian people at a delicate point in the progress towards self-government. Six of the 11 film scripts submitted on imperial themes in the 1930s were rejected because they put the British Army, colonial administration or whites in a bad light.[9]

Architecture: a reciprocal influence

Colonial architecture reflected fashions in Britain but it was often adapted to incorporate local designs. Hence, the Classical or Gothic style from the 1840s was preferred, but some buildings in India took on Oriental domes, towers and doorways from the 1850s. Government buildings were frequently on a grandiose scale, designed to impress the subject peoples and represent power. On the other hand, the high spaces found in public buildings fulfilled a rather practical purpose of circulating air in stifling tropical heat. Colonial buildings also conveyed a self-confidence and permanence that local, indigenous architecture sometimes did not. Railway stations and bridges were potent symbols of British industrial strength. However, in rural areas, the Indian bungalow, with a distinctive thatched roof and veranda, was replicated across the Empire more frequently than the Greek temple, English country house or Gothic cathedral. Thomas Metcalfe believes that the bungalow 'advanced a political purpose – that of social distancing' because of its walls, sweeping drive, watchmen and gates.[10] Yet Metcalfe neglects to mention that in India the British were never distant from their servants, whilst visitors were received on the veranda, that is, within the walls. The social distancing was not racial, but class-based and reflected the suburban attitudes of Britain's middle classes.

Sport and the Empire

To the British, sport and sportsmanship were defining elements of their national identity. Fair play, applauding the heroic underdogs, courtesy on the pitch and following the rules of the game were cherished values. Sportsmen were thought to make good soldiers because of the emphasis on physical endurance, but it was equally important that 'good character' be displayed. 'Character' was essential to put up with hostile climates, insects and disgruntled local populations in the colonies. It was also vital to obey the rules of etiquette so that there was a sense of decorum and no embarrassment when meeting unknown but fellow colonial workers. The teamwork and comradeship of the sports field was thought to be a vital part of the colonial order.

These were the ideals, but sport served a practical purpose for the colonial British as a release from the tedium of work. It was a way of bringing people of the same class or race together. It was a way of keeping fit and was thought to ward off disease.[11] Sport was a useful way to cross class barriers, as officers found when they played sports with their men. Soldiers confessed to be sport mad, as there was little else to do. E. F. Knight, a *Times* correspondent, covered the war in Hunza in 1891 and played golf during lulls in the fighting.[12] Women played sport as vigorously as the men. It could even cross racial divides. Christopher Masterman, a revenue collector, got to know educated Indians through playing tennis.[13] Horse riding was universal in India, Australia and South Africa, but the image that polo was played by everyone or that all Anglo-Indians went hunting in India was, in fact, a myth.

The British took their favoured sports with them and they were often adopted by the colonised, but it was a cross-fertilisation. Polo was adapted from the original Asian game that used sheep carcasses. Snooker was invented as a game for the club in India and cricket was enthusiastically taken up across the Empire. In 1882, Australia's 'Test' team defeated the England side and took home the 'Ashes' of England's game as a souvenir. In 1905, the New Zealand 'All Blacks' toured Britain and quickly established their formidable reputation in Rugby. The Scots took with them their Highland Games, whilst the English settlers recreated the Hunt. Some criticised the passion for sport, but others, like Lord Bryce, saw an advantage in its ability to define Englishness and thus maintain unity amongst the colonial populations of the Empire. In Rhodesia he found: 'in the character of the climate a justification for devotion to cricket. Our countrymen are not to be scared by the sun from the pursuit of the national game. They are as much Englishmen in Africa as in England.'[14]

The popularity of sport was transferred to the dominions of 'Greater Britain' so that South Africa, Australia, New Zealand and the British nations are still the main competitors in Rugby Union, although the sport has spread with equal passion through Canada, Argentina, Japan, Samoa and Fiji. Cricket, by contrast, has been transferred beyond the old Dominions to India, Pakistan and the West Indies. Their teams, followed with great enthusiasm in their own populations, continue to provide England with formidable test matches. English soccer has a world following, greater even than the American pastimes of baseball and American Football, and athletics, which can trace its origins beyond the British Empire, is now also a global phenomenon. The imperial legacy survives in the Commonwealth Games, which is still regarded as an important testing ground for athletes pursuing world titles. The legacy of sport is therefore perhaps the happiest and most popular of all.

Democracy and imperialism

A paradox of British Imperialism was the development of democracy in Britain at the same time as the continuation, even extension, of authoritarian rule over others. Generally, this was resolved by the idea that the British, a free people, were exercising a trusteeship over violent and savage people or populations as yet unable to resist the rule of native tyrants. Distinctions were drawn between the way that the British ruled, with minimum force, under Christian and paternal ethics and whose long-term aim was the improvement of the land they had inherited, with other European powers. King Leopold's brutal regime in the Congo and 'Prussian frightfulness' in Africa (and during the First World War) seemed confirmation that the British had got it right and the rest of Europe had not. It was because of this view that the Amritsar Massacre (1919) came as a profound shock. In the 1920s, liberal views of the Empire (as essentially progressive and modernising in a benign sense) grew in popularity. Missionary work, with its roots in the nineteenth century, illustrated the 'good works' of Empire too.

However, radicals in Britain, and later the left-wing, saw little benefit in the Empire and many were struck by the contradiction of imperial rule and British democracy. Imperialism, nationalism (at least in the British Isles if not in Ireland) and militarism were regarded in intellectual circles as partners that had caused the heavy losses of the First World War and the strongest criticisms came from these quarters in the 1930s. The famous Oxford Union debate, where students rejected the idea of fighting for their country 'right or wrong' in 1933, illustrated the change taking place.[15] Pride in the Empire was thus based on its size, the heroism of the Empire-builders, the fact that imperial subjects were loyal to Britain, missionary work, the improvements taking place in the social and economic life of the colonies, and its military strength. Criticisms of Empire were focused on its cost, the greed of capitalists and traders ('Nabobs', 'planters' and 'Randlords'), the denial of freedom to subject peoples, or the occasional excesses of plantation owners or soldiers.

The fixed point in the bewildering array of colonies and constitutional arrangements and the enduring institution around which the Empire clustered was the monarchy. Raised to the position of Empress of India after the long period of mourning for Albert, Victoria was converted, as John MacKenzie put it, from 'petulant widow to imperial matriarch'.[16] The monarchy was the emblem of the Empire and its unity. Victoria was remote enough to retain the mystique of royalty, but her face was well known enough to be recognised as an imperial icon. The monarchy was able to touch the lives of individuals too, as towns, schools and hospitals were named after her. Victoria took a keen personal interest in her sailors and troops, always enquiring about their welfare and casualties on campaign. This culminated in her despatch of tins of chocolate to all soldiers in the South African War, which became souvenirs cherished long after the event.

The monarchy also gave pomp and pageantry to the Empire. This was particularly loved by the press, a medium rapidly expanding in the last quarter of the nineteenth century with a mass reading public for the first time. Bernard S. Cohn has shown how the Imperial Assemblage in India in 1877, a durbar of great pomp to proclaim Victoria the Empress of India, was designed to demonstrate a transfer of authority from the Mughal emperors to Britain. Although it was a British interpretation of Mughal traditions (designed to appeal to the 'Oriental mind'),

Cohn concluded that it was successful in creating a new idea of authority until it was challenged by Gandhi in the 1920s.[17] David Cannadine points out that whereas the rituals of monarchy also served as a symbol of competitiveness with other Great Powers, in the period 1914–53 its emphasis turned to an 'expression of continuity'.[18] The coronation of George VI, for example, 'generated an increased feeling of security, stability and permanence of the British Empire'.[19] However, the monarchy grew in popularity in Britain even though the Empire began to fall away, or, at least, convert itself into the Commonwealth. This was in part due to the monarchs themselves: Victoria, Edward VII, George V and George VI had adapted to the changed circumstances of greater democracy and placed service to the country before self-interest, playing the roles required of them by the politicians and the public. The stark exception to this rule was Edward VIII who was widely condemned for his abdication in favour of marriage to Wallace Simpson.

The long-term constitutional effects of imperialism on Britain were limited. Although Crown Colonies had existed, there was no question of them becoming the personal property of the monarch, as had happened with the Belgian Congo. When the British Empire became the British Commonwealth, the title of King-Emperor was terminated and the monarchy under Queen Elizabeth II reverted to its previous titles. In spite of the Empire, democracy in Britain flourished and Britain's monarchy remained a limited and constitutional branch of the executive. Some idiosyncrasies remain, the most striking of which is the Honours List where even the least affluent, but hard-working members of British society can find themselves awarded a medal entitled Member of the British Empire.

The effects of imperialism on Britain

There was concern amongst intellectuals about the effects imperialism might have on the British people. Fear and dislike of foreigners in Britain predated the Empire, but knowledge of attacks on settlers in southern Africa, the murder of women and children in the Indian Mutiny or the mutilation of wounded men by the Pathans on the North-West Frontier of India, for example, gave the British people the impression that what differentiated them from the 'savage' or the foreigner was their restraint, their courage and their respect for the law. This sense of superiority was most marked at the end of the nineteenth century when the British rationalised their rule as a product of their racial attributes. Social Darwinism, the application of the ideas of competitive evolution and 'survival of the fittest' to the human race, coincided with the supremacist notions that prevailed. However, there were plenty of critics who deplored this arrogance. As awareness of British poverty spread at the beginning of the twentieth century, and after recruitment for the Boer War had revealed that large numbers of urban men were undernourished, concerns grew for the future of the race. Gloomy predictions of racial degeneration were aired. Yet alongside this, others spoke of the debilitating effects of luxury and wealth which would sap the warlike and manly vitality of the British race. 'Materialism' was condemned. Analogies were drawn with the Roman Empire, allegedly defeated by barbarians because of corruption and decadence. This pessimism has been labelled 'cultural despair'.[20]

The left argued that it was the popular enthusiasm for Empire and the material benefits of imperialism that were turning the British working class away from revolutionary politics. George Orwell was particularly critical of the working classes during the Second World War for their loyalty to the Empire. However, although many products came from the Empire, and some industries such as cotton manufacturing had big imperial markets, working-class ideas on imperialism were based on patriotism. Their growing demand for consumer goods and material improvement had little to do with the Empire itself. The aristocracy and wealthy middle class also seem to have made their fortunes not from the Empire, but in finance, manufacturing and land. There were obvious exceptions to this, such as Cecil Rhodes, but it was not the rule. Even Cain and Hopkins's concept of 'Gentlemanly Capitalism' actually examines the existing elites rather than people who gained their fortunes from imperialism on the periphery. Professionals in law, medicine, the armed forces and engineering were employed in the Empire, but it was in fact only a minority of the British middle class who benefited through the careers they took up and the pensions they received. In 1900, there were only 1500 employed in government service, rising to 20,000 after 1945. Indeed, it could be argued that the costs sometimes outweighed the benefits: death in service was higher in the tropics than in Britain.

Support for the Empire was drawn from across the classes and acted as a bridge across social divisions. The singing of the national anthem was an expression of solidarity rather than solely an outburst of pride. Pride in the Empire had a genuine cross-class appeal and it was a point of contact that the British, from whatever background, could share. The Victorian and Edwardian eras are usually most associated with rigid class boundaries, but social mobility was still possible and expressions of class were strongest in the upwardly mobile. In the colonies themselves, improved status was common. Even British soldiers, either despised or patronised at home, had their own servant in India. Ed Davis of the Dorset Regiment (1924–36) related how the 'nappy wallah' would shave a man whilst he was still in bed. There were myriad servants for the different tasks: barbers, cleaners, 'Dhobi' men, even men who stencilled names on kit-bags; each had their specialism.[21] Soldiers were referred to as *sahib* by Indians, which increased morale: 'after about four years in India they [the British soldiers] were four feet off the ground.' Yet the Other Ranks got on well with the 'sweepers' who had no caste. The Dorsets, who had been given great hospitality by the civilians of Sudan, found that the British community in India ignored their existence: class barriers were therefore stronger than race in some cases.[22]

It is often generally assumed that education in Britain was designed to train young people for imperial rule. However, recruitment for imperial posts did not demand training for any region. The earliest institution for specific training was Fort William College in Calcutta, set up by Wellesley in 1800. There, the aim was to provide an education in oriental languages, history and law. The East India Company certainly recruited its officials at a young age. John Malcolm was interviewed for a cadetship aged 12. He was described as 'a careless, good-humoured fellow, quite illiterate' but, aged only 15, he was placed in command of a cavalry unit. The company's establishment of Haileybury College in Britain in 1805 addressed the obvious weaknesses for administrators, if not the soldiers. Nevertheless, appointments relied, not on qualifications, but on personal contacts, introductions and references of good character.

The tough life of colonial administration did not require academic ability, but self-confidence and endurance. The public schools focused on the values that might be required for colonial rule rather than detailed knowledge of the Empire itself. Physical training and sport were to induce courage and fair play. Classical history gave the impression that the British had inherited a new Roman Empire, yet it was tempered by the precepts of Christianity which promoted sacrifice, selfless duty and generosity of spirit.

Young people in Britain were exposed to a great deal of imperial literature and organisation. The main point of contact for the majority of young people who were not in the private sector was in their local state school. Robert Roberts relates how, as a schoolboy in Salford around 1913, his headmaster proudly pointed to the areas of the world splashed with pink on the map that marked the British Empire. Each child received 'a medal, a bun, an orange, a banana and a small box of chocolates: King George V had no more loyal subjects in his Empire [than us]'.[23] The children sang patriotic songs on Empire Day (24 May), which was the date of Queen Victoria's birthday. History and geography were two subjects particularly closely linked to the British Empire. Alongside the fiction of G. A. Henty and Rudyard Kipling or the films of the 1930s, children might also join the youth organisations that had imperial origins: the Boys Brigade (1883), the Boy Scouts (1908) and the Girl Guides (1912).

Public schools, and some universities, set up Cadet or Officer Training detachments which were more overtly designed to give boys training in weapon handling and drill. Yet, although the ultimate goal was to fit some aristocratic and middle-class young men for service in the Empire, the cadet forces actually reinforced the discipline of the school. It was acknowledged that education was for the preparation of gentlemen, but many of these (four-fifths in fact), equipped with the approved standards of behaviour, would go on to other professions not directly linked to the Empire. The schools and universities were focused on themselves, their discipline, identity and ethos, rather than the abstraction of the wider world. Although young men were educated in mathematics and the classics, 'old hands' in the Empire were critical of the system that gave no grounding in the problems of government, racial antagonism and conflict resolution. The specialist subjects, such as geology, forestry and anthropology, were less popular – even though it was often expertise in these areas that was needed.

Ex imperio immigration

Readjusting to the United Kingdom was a disorientating experience for some returning imperial and commonwealth workers. One British official in India felt, like many others, that he was 'leaving a task half finished'.[24] Many were disillusioned because 'much of what they'd served for seemed to be breaking up'. Few stayed on in India after 1947 because of this disillusionment, particularly in the separatism that 'was contrary to everything we thought right or possible'.[25] There was a mixture of looking forward to seeing friends and families back in Britain, but also a sense of nostalgia, which grew as the years went by. Some found England a strange place as it had changed so much from the schooldays that were their only experience of it. Former Anglo-Indians found it hard to convey what India had meant to them and what their work had been about. They found their fellow Britons uninterested. Moreover, there were insurmountable stereotypical images to contend with. The British Empire was gradually portrayed as an exploitative and immoral episode of history, which had perpetuated poverty, beggary, squalor, hunger and filth.[26] It was an image that Norman Watney, a railway engineer, did not recognise: 'it seemed to me that I had a job, it was a tough one and that was all there was to it . . . There was absolutely no feeling of exploitation.'[27]

The flow of post-imperial immigrants into Britain was partly the result of post-war economic growth, as in the case of many West Indian migrants; or flight from unrest such as the Asian refugees from Uganda in the 1960s. However, migration to the British Isles predates the colonial epoch and may be only partly related to the development of a global empire. In fact, migrants from different parts of the empire had been settling in Britain, sometimes temporarily, from the eighteenth century. At the end of the 1700s, it is thought that there were between 5000 and 10,000 black people living in London. In the late nineteenth century too, a steady trickle of Indian scholars arrived in the metropolis. In 1961, the numbers of immigrants increased to 115,000. The scale of the flow prompted the government to pass the Commonwealth Immigration Act in 1962, in order to absorb and integrate the existing immigrant population.

However, the extent of that integration is debatable since British governments have sought to encourage immigrant minorities to retain their cultural identity, whilst integrating them into British society. To ensure equality of opportunity, both Conservative and Labour governments supported Race Relations Acts, but the Conservative MP Enoch Powell criticised immigration policies in 1968, arguing that Britain would soon face race riots and social conflict. The issue degenerated into ideological arguments on racism and national identity, but whilst these disputes were part of the imperial legacy, few references to the empire were made at the time. Indeed, the contemporary far right does not invoke any imperial nostalgia, preferring to play on fears of a greater burden on taxpayers, undercutting jobs through cheap labour and 'foreign' colonisation of residential areas. Hostility to foreigners in Britain also has a long and pre-colonial history. Jews in the thirteenth century were a target for punitive taxation by the state and widespread (but by no means universal) hostility from the population, which culminated in a massacre at Queensborough.[28] The French and the Irish were also targets of loathing and ridicule for centuries.

On the receiving end, many Afro-Caribbean and Asian British endure the worst of the racist *provocateurs* with remarkable stoicism. Inevitably, misunderstanding and suspicion occasionally erupt in a depressing cycle of violence. The early 1980s was a notable nadir in this respect, with rioting in London's Notting Hill, Liverpool's Toxteth and St Paul's in Bristol. In light of the unrest, community leaders and the police made a concerted effort to improve mutual understanding and the annual Notting Hill Carnival is a success story for race relations. However, black and Asian British still feel there is indifference – if not outright hostility – from many whites, which they feel needs to be addressed. Police forces are sometimes accused of 'institutionalised racism' and the family of black teenager Stephen Lawrence

charged the police with unnecessary delays in pursuing the mur-
derers of their son in what appears to have been a racially motivated attack. The acquittal of three white men after the assault of
an Asian in Leeds, due to lack of conclusive evidence, led to several days of rioting in 2001. New waves of immigrants, now universally described as 'asylum–seekers', continue to pose fresh
challenges for the government. These issues are unlikely to be
resolved in the short term.

British imperialism has left both former colonisers and
colonised with an important legacy. Whilst the imperial epoch is
regarded as either an embarrassment or a painful and humiliating episode, the lasting influence of contact between Britain and
the wider world may be turned to mutual advantage in the end.
A closer understanding of each other's culture and history, and a
willingness to work for the same values in the Commonwealth,
may ultimately prove to be the most precious and valuable outcomes of all.

Chronology

1497	John Cabot reaches Newfoundland
1564	First slaving voyages begin
1585	First Virginia settlement
1600	The East India Company chartered
1607	Jamestown founded
1612	Settlement of Bermuda
1627	Colonisation of Barbados
1639	Grant of Madras to England
1655	Jamaica taken from Spain
1661	England receives Bombay
1670	Hudson's Bay Company chartered
1690	Fort William established (Calcutta)
1698	Slave trade opened to private traders
1744	Anglo–French conflict in India
1756	Calcutta captured by the Newab of Bengal; start of Seven Years' War
1757	Defeat of Newab of Bengal by Robert Clive at Plassey
1761	Capture of Pondicherry
1765	Stamp Tax provoked riots in America
1773	Boston 'Tea Party'
1775	Outbreak of the American War of Independence
1783	Loss of America
1784	India Act imposed limited government control
1786	British trading post established at Penang
1787	Sierra Leone established as a colony for freed slaves
1788	New South Wales established; Warren Hastings tried for misgovernment
1791	Canada Act divides Upper and Lower Canada
1793	Revolutionary War begins in Europe
1795	British capture of Cape of Good Hope
1807	Abolition of the slave trade
1812	War with America over Canadian border
1813	East India Company Charter Act opens India to private traders and missionaries

1815   Cape Colony, islands of Berbice, Demerara and Essequibo assigned to Britain at close of Napoleonic Wars; Java restored to the Dutch; Reunion restored to France

1816   Treaty of Segauli ends war in Nepal; suppression of piracy at Algiers; Guadaloupe restored to France

1817   Third Maratha War (to 1818); Uva Rebellion (Ceylon); Fifth Cape Frontier War against Xhosa (to 1819)

1818   Rajput States and Poona brought under British control

1819   Raffles acquired island of Singapore for East India Company

1820   Wave of settlers arrive in Cape Colony

1821   Crown took over holdings of the African Company of Merchants on Gold Coast

1822   Gambia coastline annexed into Sierra Leone

1823   Monroe Doctrine prevents further colonisation of the Americas

1824   Burma War (to 1825); Anglo–Siamese Treaty re-established independence of Perak; First Ashanti War to 1826 (Gold Coast); Malacca acquired from Dutch in exchange for Bencoolen

1825   Creation of autonomous adminstration for Van Dieman's Land (Tasmania)

1826   Defeat and annexation of Bhurtpore (India); Gold Coast administered by London merchants from the Crown; establishment of the Straits Settlement (Malay Peninsula); settlements with Spain over British Honduras (completed 1859)

1827   Royal Navy destroys Turkish and Egyptian fleets at Navarino Bay

1828   Declaration of equal rights for all 'coloureds' in Cape

1829   *Suttee* abolished in Bengal (extended to the rest of British India)

1830   Mysore brought under British control; Royal Geographical Society founded

1831   Rebellion in Jamaica (the Baptist Insurrection); formation of British Guiana

1832   Establishment of settlement on the Falkland Islands

1833   Emancipation Act: abolition of slavery in the colonies (abolished in Britain in 1807)

1834   Sixth Cape Frontier War against Xhosa invasion (to
         1835); Boers trek and settle north of the Orange River;
         St Helena transferred to Crown from East India
         Company; South Australia Act permits new colony to be
         established
1835   T. B. Macaulay's *Minute on Education* (India) published
1836   The Great Trek (southern Africa); creation of the state
         of South Australia
1837   Rebellions in Upper and Lower Canada (to 1838);
         Coorg Rebellion (India); Singapore became capital of
         Straits Settlement (replacing Penang)
1838   Abolition of apprenticeship for former slaves; invasion of
         Afghanistan
1839   Durham Report; despatch of Wakefield's settlers to New
         Zealand; First Opium War (China) to 1842; Aden
         acquired; Boers establish Natal
1840   Treaty of Waitangi; Lower and Upper Canada united
1841   Thomas Buxton's Niger Expedition failed to establish
         trade to replace slave traffic; British sovereignty
         established over Hong Kong; New Zealand recognised
         as a colony; Thomas Cook tours begin.
1842   Retreat from Afghanistan; Crown control reimposed on
         Gold Coast; end of the Opium War (opens Treaty
         Ports)
1843   Annexation of Natal; annexation of Sind; defeat of
         Marathas of Gwalior (India); establishment of Gambia
         as a separate colony; Maori revolt
1844   Southern Maratha campaign; Morse telegraph invented
1845   First Sikh War (to 1846); First New Zealand War (to
         1846)
1846   Repeal of the Corn Laws (progress towards free trade);
         James Brooke acquired mining rights for Brunei,
         control of Sarawak and annexed Labuan; Seventh Cape
         Frontier War (to 1847); famine in Ireland
1847   Liberia established
1848   Canada received 'Responsible Government'; annexation
         of Orange River Sovereignty; Second Sikh War (to 1849)
1849   Annexation of the Punjab; campaigns on the North-
         West Frontier begin (to 1890s); Livingstone crosses the
         Kalahari; repeal of the Navigation Acts

1850 Eighth Cape Frontier War (to 1853)

1851 Lagos bombarded in anti-slavery operations; autonomous administration for Victoria (Australia) and gold rush begins; Burma War; Basuto War (to 1853)

1852 Self-government for New Zealand; Second Burmese War, Pegu annexed; Livingstone explores Zambezi

1853 Second Burma War ends with annexation of Lower Burma; East India Company annexes Nagpur; first telegraph in India

1854 Bloemfontein Convention establishes Orange Free State; Crimean War (to 1856); Ballarat miners revolt (Australia); agreements between the United States and Britain on Canadian trade

1855 Santal Rebellion (India); Britain and Afghanistan declare war on Persia (to 1857)

1856 Outbreak of the Second Chinese War (to 1858); annexation of Oudh; bombardment of Bushire (Persia); Natal becomes a crown colony; Tasmania and Australian states gain self-government; riots in British Guiana

1857 Indian Mutiny (to 1858)

1858 Abolition of the East India Company; Burton and Speke discover Lake Tanganyika and Lake Victoria

1859 Autonomous administration for Queensland; Fijians appeal for British control

1860 Second New Zealand War (to 1870); operations against the Chinese concluded

1861 Indian Councils Act; coastal influence established in Nigeria; outbreak of American Civil War led to 'cotton famine'; gold discovered in New Zealand; Sikkim War; refrigeration begins in Australia

1862 Belize colony established; first English Cricket tour of Australia

1863 Lagos became a Crown Colony; conflict with Shogunates of Japan; Third New Zealand War (to 1864)

1864 Baker discovers Lake Albert

1865 Morant Bay Rebellion in Jamaica; trade treaties opened up Japan

1866 Establishment of the united West African Settlements centred on Sierra Leone; Fenian attack on Canadian border

1867   Fenian terrorism in Britain; British North America Act
        created federated Dominion of Canada; diamonds
        discovered in South Africa
1868   Expedition against Abyssinia; annexation of Basutoland;
        guerrilla warfare in New Zealand (to 1872); Ambela
        Campaign on North-West Frontier of India;
        Livingstone explores the Congo
1869   Opening of the Suez Canal; rebellion in Canada
1870   Defeat of Fenian raiders and suppression of Riel's
        rebellion (Canada); Manitoba established; Western
        Australia granted Responsible Government
1871   Anglo–Dutch Treaty recognised Dutch supremacy of
        Sumatra; British Honduras established as a Crown
        colony; diamond fields at Kimberley annexed; Stanley
        meets Livingstone at Ujiji
1872   Cape Colony granted self-government;
1873   Expedition against Ashanti; Gold Coast re-established as
        a separate colony; famine in Bengal; abolition of slavery
        in Zanzibar.
1874   Lagos re-established as a separate colony; Chinese
        workers of Perak protected by installation of pro-British
        regime; Fiji annexed
1875   Purchase of Suez Canal shares; operations against Perak
        rebellion; Selangor accepted a British Resident (Malay
        states)
1876   Victoria becomes Empress of India; indigenous
        Tasmanians died out
1877   Walvis Bay acquired; Ninth Cape Frontier War;
        neutralisation of Samoa agreed by Britain, Germany and
        the United States; famine in Bengal
1878   Eastern Crisis; Britain acquired Cyprus from Berlin
        Congress; Zulu War (to 1879); Second Afghan War (to
        1880)
1879   British West African traders combined in the United
        African Company; Khedive Ismail deposed and
        replaced by Tewfik; Australian frozen meat arrives in
        London
1880   Annexation of Griqualand (South Africa), federation
        plan rejected by Cape parliament; 'gun war' rebellion
        against disarmament in Basutoland

1881   Defeat in First Anglo–Boer War and Pretoria
         Convention; Land War in Ireland

1882   Resolution on local self-government in India by Lord
         Ripon; occupation of Egypt and Suakin expedition;
         formation of British North Borneo Company; civil
         disobedience over land ownership by Maoris; Maxim
         machine-gun invented

1883   Ilbert Bill controversy (India); J. R. Seeley publishes *The
         Expansion of England*

1884   British Somaliland acquired; Convention of London
         confirms Transvaal's independence; Gordon besieged at
         Khartoum (killed in 1885)

1885   Formation of Indian National Congress; Berlin West
         Africa Conference; expedition to Sudan; Bechuanaland
         Protectorate established; Nigeria declared a
         protectorate; southern New Guinea declared a
         protectorate; Third Burma War; suppression of North-
         Western Rebellion (Canada); Penjdeh Incident

1886   Discovery of gold on Witwatersrand (Transvaal); Lagos
         established as a separate colony from Gold Coast; Niger
         Company received royal title and control of Nigerian
         coast; self-government for Ireland rejected; Burma
         annexed to India; completion of the Canadian Pacific
         Railway

1887   Baluchistan incorporated into India; first states
         incorporated into Malay states federation; Victoria's
         Golden Jubilee; first Colonial Conference

1888   Gambia designated a separate Crown colony (dissolving
         the West African settlements of 1866); Sarawak and
         North Borneo became British protectorates; Sikkim
         War; Matabele accepted British protection and granted
         mining rights to Rhodes

1889   Rhodesia conquered (named in 1895); pacification of
         Upper Burma (to 1893)

1890   Zanzibar acquired in exchange for Heligoland; Uganda
         protectorate established; British East Africa/Kenya
         formed; Labuan transferred to British North Borneo
         Company from the Crown; Western Australia
         established as an independent colony; Rhodes becomes
         Cape Prime Minister

1891   Suppression of slavery in Nyasaland (to 1896) and
       upper Gambia (to 1900); expeditions to Manipur,
       Saminar and Nagar
1892   Partition of Cameroon agreed with Germany; Chin Hills
       expedition; railways link from Cape to Johannesburg
       completed
1893   Gandhi begins work in South Africa; operations against
       tribes in Sierra Leone (to 1899); Natal granted
       self-government; expedition against the Matabele;
       Imperial Institute founded in London
1894   Northern Rhodesia created; Gambia expedition;
       Waziristan expedition
1895   North-western Nigeria acquired; Jameson Raid;
       expedition against the Ashanti; Chitral expedition
1896   Matabele Uprising; Mashona Uprising; formal
       establishment of Federation for the Malay States; Rhodes
       resigns as Cape Premier; Klondike gold rush in Canada
1897   Victoria's Diamond Jubilee and Colonial Conference;
       Pathan uprising (India); Royal Niger Company defeat
       the Fula Empire; suppression of guerrillas in North
       Borneo; famine in India;
1898   Conquest of Sudan, Fashoda Incident; lease begins on
       Wei Hei Wei, Kowloon and New Territories
1899   Bloemfontein Conference; outbreak of the South
       African War (to 1902); Benin annexed (Nigeria); Sudan
       becomes a condominion
1900   Boxer Rebellion (China); Ashanti War; Crown
       Protectorates established over Northern and Southern
       Nigeria replacing the Royal Niger Company; Britain
       withdraws claims to Samoa; annexation of Orange Free
       State and Transvaal
1901   First expedition against Somali guerrillas (to 1920);
       abolition of slave trade in Northern Nigeria; federation
       of Australia; railway from Mombasa to Lake Victoria
       completed
1902   Anglo–Japanese Alliance; Colonial Conference
1903   Northern Nigeria pacified and slavery abolished;
       coronation durbar in India; Tariff Reform campaign
1904   Tibet expedition; creation of the *entente cordiale*;
       Empire Day begins

1905   Bengal Partition; Borneo, Sarawak and Labuan brought
        under Straits settlement control; Botha and Het Volk
        demand self-government for the Transvaal; Alberta and
        Saskatchewan formed
1906   Muslim League formed; formalisation of measures to
        abolish slavery in Gambia; Lagos incorporated into
        Nigeria; Sinai ceded by Turkey to Egypt
1907   Self-government for South African states;
        Anglo–Russian Convention; Britain and France agree to
        guarantee independence of Siam; Imperial Conference
        agrees to confer the term 'dominion' to certain
        federated and self-governing colonies
1908   Scouting movement launched
1909   Morley-Minto Reforms; Non-Federated Malay States
        brought under British protection; Anglo-Persian Oil
        Company formed
1910   Union of South Africa
1911   Delhi durbar for coronation of George V
1912   Initiation of Home Rule Bill for Ireland
1913   Suffragette agitation
1914   Outbreak of the First World War; invasion of
        Mesopotamia; Boer rebellion in South Africa
1915   Mutiny of Indian troops at Singapore; Ghadr campaign;
        landings at Gallipoli
1916   Easter Rising; Battle of the Somme
1917   Imperial War Cabinet set up; declaration by Montagu
        on Indian self-government; Balfour Declaration (Middle
        East); Bolshevik revolution in Russia
1918   Battle of Amiens; defeat of Germany
1919   Montagu-Chelmsford Reforms (dyarchy) and Rowlatt
        Act; Amritsar Massacre; Troubles in Ireland; Mandates
        given to League of Nations powers; Afghan War
1920   First non-cooperation campaign (India); San Remo
        Conference (Middle East); Government of Ireland
        Act
1921   Anglo–Irish Treaty; Imperial Conference
1922   Chanak Crisis; Irish Civil War (to 1923); Gandhi
        imprisoned; formation of the Irish Free State
1923   Devonshire Declaration affirms that Kenya is 'African
        Territory'

1924	Rand strike, Hertzog becomes prime minister of South Africa; Gandhi fasts against Hindu–Muslim conflicts; British Empire Exhibition at Wembley; British Imperial Airways begin flights
1925	Dominions Office set up in London
1926	Balfour Report on dominion status
1927	Simon Commission on Montagu-Chelmsford Reforms
1928	Unrest in India caused by Simon Commission
1929	First Round Table Conference; Lord Irwin's declaration on realisation of dominion status for India; Arab–Jewish fighting in Palestine
1930	Civil disobedience campaign (India) to 1931; Canada offers preferential tariff to Britain; Empire Games first held
1931	Statute of Westminster; Japanese annexation of Manchuria; Gandhi–Irwin Pact; Ceylon self-government measures; Bitain abandons the gold standard and sets up the Sterling Area
1932	Ottawa Imperial Conference introduces preferential tariffs; civil disobedience campaign in India (to 1934), Congress declared illegal
1933	White Paper on Indian Reforms published
1934	Gandhi suspends civil disobedience campaigns; Japan rejects naval limits
1935	Government of India Act; Italian invasion of Abyssinia
1936	Anglo–Egyptian Treaty
1937	First elections under the Government of India Act; Peel Commission on Middle East; riots in West Indies; Japanese invasion of China; Aden becomes a Crown colony
1938	Nazi annexation of Austria and Sudetenland
1939	Restrictions placed on Jewish immigration; outbreak of Second World War in Europe; Congress provincial governments resign
1940	Ogdensburg Agreement; Lahore Resolution; Colonial Development and Welfare Act; defeat of the Italians in North Africa
1941	Atlantic Charter; Japanese attack on East Indies and fall of Hong Kong; Nazi invasion of Balkans and Soviet Union

1942	Creation of 'Quit India' movement; Stafford Cripps Mission; fall of Singapore; Battle of El Alamein
1943	Defeat of German forces in North Africa and invasion of Italy; famine in Bengal
1944	Normandy landings; Indian Army clears northern Burma
1945	Defeat of Germany and Japan
1947	India and Pakistan independent
1948	Apartheid in South Africa; British withdrawal from Palestine; Gold Coast riots
1950	Second Colonial Development and Welfare Act passed
1952	Mau Mau rebellion
1956	Suez crisis
1957	Ghana and Malaya independent
1960	Nigeria independent
1961	Sierra Leone and Tanzania independent; South Africa left the Commonwealth
1962	Jamaica, Trinidad, Uganda, Western Samoa independent
1963	Kenya and Zanzibar independent
1964	Malawi and Zambia independent
1965	Gambia, Lesotho and Cook Islands independent
1966	Guyana, Barbados, Botswana independent
1968	Mauritius, Swaziland and Nauru independent
1970	Fiji independent
1978	Tuvalu independent
1979	Kiribati independent
1980	Vanuatu independent; Rhodesia declared UDI
1982	Britain defeats Argentina after Falklands invaded
1994	South Africa rejoined Commonwealth
1997	Hong Kong returned to China

Notes

1 Introduction: what was British imperialism ?

1 Benjamin J. Cohen, *The Question of Imperialism* (New York, 1974), pp. 242–3.
2 See Raymond E. Dummett, *Gentlemanly Capitalism and British Imperialism: The New Debate on Empire* (London, 1999), p. 18.
3 C. C. Eldridge, *Victorian Imperialism* (London, 1978), p. 1.
4 Cited in ibid.
5 See J. M. MacKenzie, *Propaganda and Empire* (Manchester, 1984).
6 See John Darwin, 'Imperialism and the Victorians: The Dynamics of Territorial Expansion' *English Historical Review* 447, CXII (1997), p. 615.
7 See Wm Roger Louis, 'Introduction', in Judith M. Brown and Louis, eds, *The Oxford History of the British Empire* IV *The Twentieth Century* (Oxford, 1999), p. 31.
8 See, for example, Glen Balfour-Paul, 'Britain's Informal Empire in the Middle East', in Brown and Louis, eds, *The Oxford History of the British Empire* IV op. cit. and Peter Sluglett, 'Formal and Informal Empire in the Middle East', in Robin Winks, ed., *The Oxford History of the British Empire* V op. cit., ch. 27.
9 See Philip D. Curtin, *The Atlantic Slave Trade: A Census* (Madison, 1969). The controversy over the numbers involved is covered in J. D. Fage, 'African Societies and the Atlantic Slave Trade' *Past and Present* 125 (November 1989): 97–115. An attempt to move beyond the argument over numbers can be found in James Walvin, *Making the Black Atlantic: Britain and the African Diaspora* (London, 2000).
10 P. J. Marshall, *The British Empire* (Cambridge, 1996), p. 37 and 42.
11 J. Brown, *Modern India: The Origins of an Asian Democracy* (2nd edn, Oxford, 1994), p. 118
12 See C. A. Bayly, ed., *Atlas of the British Empire, 1558–1995* (London, 1989), pp. 170–1.
13 Ibid., p. 236. Different conclusions are reached by Andre G. Frank, *Dependent Accumulation and Underdevelopment* (London, 1978).
14 See D. Fieldhouse, *Black Africa, 1945–1980: Economic Decolonisation and Arrested Development* (London, 1986), p. 233.
15 S. Gopal, *Modern India* (Historical Association, 1967), p. 8; and D. Fieldhouse, 'For Richer, for poorer', in Marshall, *The British Empire*, op. cit., pp. 142–6.
16 Robert McCrum, Robert MacNeil and William Cran, *The Story of English* (revised edn, London, 1992)

17 British imperialism introduced words, new cuisine and ideas into British culture, which accounts for the modern usage of 'juggernaut', 'veranda' and 'bungalow', or the popularity of Indian and Chinese food. Bernard Porter felt that these counter-flows had been somewhat negligible, partly because the British had been so determined *not* to be influenced by the cultures they encountered. Nevertheless, the presence of British Asians, West Indians and Africans is, retrospectively, beginning to make itself felt on 'multi-cultural' Britain. B. Porter, *The Lion's Share: A Short History of British Imperialism, 1850–1983* (2nd edn, London, 1984), pp. 349–50 and 361.

18 Darwin, 'Imperialism and the Victorians', op. cit., p. 618.

19 The idea of 'empire on the cheap' was not restricted to material value, but could include 'risks' posed by other Great Powers. See ibid., pp. 618 and 625.

20 John S. Galbraith, *Reluctant Empire: British Policy on the South African Frontier, 1834–54* (Berkeley, 1963), pp. 128–54.

21 *Africa: The Next Ten Years* Cabinet Official Committee on Africa, 3 June 1959 Public Record Office (PRO) AF (59) 28 CAB 134/1355.

22 Thomas Pakenham, *The Scramble for Africa* (London, 1991), p. 654.

23 John Nottingham, entry in the *Museum of the British Empire and Commonwealth*, Bristol.

2 What was the nature of imperialism in the early nineteenth century?

1 Vincent T. Harlow, *The Founding of the Second British Empire, 1763–1793*, 2 vols (London, 1952) II, pp. 1–11.

2 Ronald Hyam and Ged Martin, *Reappraisals in British Imperial History* (London, 1975) ch. 1.

3 P. J. Marshall, 'British Expansion in India in the Eighteenth Century' *History* 60 (1975), p. 42; Jac Weller, *Wellington in India* (London, 2000).

4 The Magna Carta (1215), perhaps the foundation of English liberalism, stated: 'to none will we deny or delay right or justice'. However, the concept of liberty was applied only to the king's subjects, and even then, without consistency. The Magna Carta failed to protect men and women from Charles I's arbitrary policies. In 1628, parliamentarians appealed against unlimited royal power in the Petition of Right using the Magna Carta, but it took a Civil War to curb absolutist government. Another appeal in 1679 was necessary to protect men and women from arbitrary imprisonment.

5 James Walvin, *Making the Black Atlantic: Britain and the African Diaspora* (London, 2000), pp. 162–3.

6 R. Pares, *A West Indian Fortune* (London, 1950).

7   Philip D. Curtin, *The Atlantic Slave Trade: A Census* (Madison, 1969).
8   Julian Hoppit, *A Land of Liberty? England 1689–1727* (Oxford, 2000), pp. 266–8.
9   See Gad Heuman, 'Slavery, The Slave Trade, and Abolition', in Robin Winks, ed., *The Oxford History of the British Empire* v (Oxford, 1999), pp. 315–25.
10 P. J. Marshall, ed., *The British Empire* (Cambridge, 1996), p. 284.
11 Donald Southgate, *The Most English Minister* (London, 1966), p. 152.
12 Sir Reginald Coupland, *The British Anti-Slavery Movement* (London, 1933).
13 Eric Williams, *Capitalism and Slavery* (London, 1944).
14 See also William Darity, 'British Industry and the West Indies Plantations', in Joseph E. Inikori and Stanley L. Engerman, eds, *The Atlantic Slave Trade* (Durham, NC, 1992), pp. 205–79.
15 Seymour Drescher, *Econocide: British Slavery in the Era of Abolition* (Pittsburgh, 1977).
16 J. R. Ward, 'The British West Indies in the Age of Abolition, 1748–1815', in P. J. Marshall, ed., *The Oxford History of the British Empire* II (Oxford, 1998), p. 426.
17 David Richardson, 'The British Empire and the Atlantic Slave Trade, 1660–1807', in Marshall, *The Oxford History of the British Empire* II, op. cit., p. 461.
18 See Herbert S. Klein, *The Atlantic Slave Trade* (Cambridge, 1999).
19 David Eltis, *The Rise of African Slavery in the Americas* (Cambridge, 2000).
20 C. A. Bayly, *Imperial Meridian: the British Empire and the World, 1780–1830* (London, 1989).
21 John Gallagher and John Robinson, 'The Imperialism of Free Trade' *Economic History Review* 2nd ser., VI (1953), p. 3.
22 D. C. M. Platt, 'The Imperialism of Free Trade: Some Reservations' *Economic History Review* 2nd ser., XXI (1968), pp. 296–306 and 'Further Objections to an "Imperialism of Free Trade", 1830–1860' *Economic History Review* 2nd ser., XXVI (1973), pp. 71–91; P. J. Cain and A. G. Hopkins, *British Imperialism* 2 vols, I (London, 1993), p. 312.
23 R. Ben Jones, *The Hanoverians* (London, 1972), p. 15.
24 Tom Pocock, *Battle for Empire* (London, 1998), p. 13.
25 C. A. Bayly, 'The Second British Empire', in Winks, *The Oxford History of the British Empire* v, op. cit., pp. 61–2; and C. A. Bayly, *Imperial Meridian: The British Empire and the World, 1780–1830* (London, 1989).
26 Colonel John Gurwood, *Despatches of the Duke of Wellington* (1852), pp. 832–34, in George Boyce, 'From Assaye to *The Assaye*' *Journal of Military History* 63, 3, (1999), p. 645.
27 David Washbrook, 'India, 1818–1860: The Two Faces of Colonialism', in Andrew Porter, ed., *The Oxford History of the British Empire* III (Oxford, 1999), p. 404.

28   Marshall, *The British Empire*, op. cit., p. 29.
29   These included The British North Borneo Company (1882–1941), the Royal Niger Company (1886–98), The Imperial British East Africa Company (1888–93) and the British South Africa Company (1889–1923).
30   Martin Lynn, 'British Policy, Trade, and Informal Empire in the Mid-Nineteenth Century' in Porter, *The Oxford History of the British Empire* III, op. cit., p. 103.
31   J. Bright and J. E. T. Rogers, eds, *Speeches by Richard Cobden* (1880).
32   Martin Lynn, 'Policy, Trade, and Informal Empire', op. cit., p. 105.
33   Ibid., p. 110.
34   Ibid., p. 105.
35   Marshall, *The British Empire*, op. cit., p. 23.
36   These ideologies could be traced back into earlier periods. See Anthony Pagden, *Lords of all the World: Ideologies of Empire in Spain, Britain and France, c.1500-c.1850* (New Haven, 1995); Peter N. Miller, *Defining the Common Good: Empire, Religion and Philosophy in Eighteenth Century Britain* (Cambridge, 1994); and David Armitage, *The Ideological Origins of the British Empire* (Cambridge, 2000).

3 What was the nature of British rule in India, c.1770–1858?

1   R. A. Huttenback, *British Relations with Sind, 1799–1843* (Berkeley, 1962), pp. 105–6; M. Yapp, *Strategies of British India* (Oxford, 1980), pp. 560–72; Judith M. Brown, *Modern India: The Making of an Asian Democracy* (Oxford, 1985), pp. 32 and 47.
2   P. J. Marshall, 'British Expansion in India in the Eighteenth Century' *History* 60 (1975), p. 42.
3   Percival Spear, *A History of India* II, 1979 edn (London, 1979), pp. 112–15.
4   C. A. Bayly, *Rulers, Townsmen and Bazaars: North Indian Society in the Age of British Expansion, 1770–1870* (Cambridge, 1989); Burton Stein, *Thomas Munro: The Origins of the Colonial State and His Vision of Empire* (Delhi, 1989).
5   J. Darwin, 'Imperialism and the Victorians: The Dynamics of Territorial Expansion' *English Historical Review* CXII, 447 (1997), p. 626.
6   *Select Committee of Enquiry into the affairs of the East India Company*, 17 April 1832, Parliamentary Papers XIV, 1831–2, p. 36.
7   David Kopf, *British Orientalism and the Bengal Renaissance* (Berkeley and Los Angeles, 1969); Satya A. Pachori, *Sir William Jones: A Reader* (Delhi, 1993), pp. 170–2.
8   Eric Stokes, *The English Utilitarians and India* (Oxford, 1959), p. 45.

9 Bernard S. Cohn, 'Representing Authority in Victorian India', in T. O. Ranger and Eric Hobsbawm, eds, *The Invention of Tradition* (Cambridge, 1983), pp. 165–78.

10 J. K. Majumdar, ed., *Indian Speeches and Documents on British Rule, 1821–1918* (Calcutta, 1937), pp. 48–9.

11 Brown, *Modern India*, op. cit., p. 66.

12 Peter Stanlis, *Edmund Burke; The Enlightenment and Revolution* (New Brunswick, 1991), p. 20.

13 Robert Frykenburg, 'India to 1858', in Robin Winks, ed., *The Oxford History of the British Empire* V (Oxford, 1999), p. 204.

14 Brown, *Modern India*, op. cit., p. 85.

15 Edward Said, *Orientalism* (New York, 1979), p. 215.

16 Ibid., p. 78., Javed Maheed, *Ungoverned Imaginings*, (Oxford, 1992), p. 15.

17 Syed Nurullah and J. P. Naik, *A History of Education in India* (Calcutta, 1951).

18 Das Veena, 'Subaltern as Perspective', in Ranajit Guha, ed., *Subaltern Studies: Writings on South Asian History and Society* IV (Delhi, 1989).

19 Garland Cannon and Kevin R. Brine, eds, *Objects of Enquiry: The Life, Contributions, and Influences of Sir William Jones (1746–1794)* (New York and London, 1994), p. 78. There are several works that are therefore worthy of consideration on this issue; the sympathetic work of Garland Cannon and Kevin Brine, *Objects of Enquiry*; the critical S. N. Mukherjee's, *Sir William Jones: A Study in Eighteenth-Century Attitudes To India*, (Cambridge, 1968); Javed Maheed's *Ungoverned Imaginings*; and Said's *Orientalism*, op. cit.

20 John Mackenzie, *Orientalism* (Manchester, 1975), p. 215.

21 H. V. Bowen, 'British India, 1765–1813: The Metropolitan Context', in P. J. Marshall, ed., *The Oxford History of the British Empire* II (Oxford, 1998), p. 541.

22 Rajat Kanta Ray, 'Indian Society and the Establishment of British Supremacy, 1765–1818', in ibid., p. 515.

23 P. J. Marshall, 'The British in Asia: Trade to Dominion, 1700–1765', in Marshall, *The Oxford History of the British Empire* II p. 493.

24 C. A. Bayly, *The New Cambridge History of India* II (Cambridge, 1988), pp. 32–8.

25 Marshall, 'The British in Asia', op. cit., p. 497. The conspiracy theory, that the East India Company plotted the takeover of Bengal by creating instability, can be found in Susil Chaudhury, *From Prosperity to Decline: Eighteenth Century Bengal* (New Delhi, 1995), pp. 306–26.

26 Barbara Harlow and Mia Carter, *Imperialism and Orientalism* (Massachusetts, 1999), p. 36.

27 Douglas M. Peers, *Between Mars and Mammon: Colonial Armies and the Garrison State in Early Nineteenth-Century India* (London, 1995), p. 172.

28 H. G. Rawlinson, *The British Achievement in India* (London, 1948), p. 65.
29 *Select Committee Report on East India Produce, Parliamentary Papers* VIII, 1840, pp. 272–4.
30 Romesh Dutt, *The Economic History of India under early British Rule* (London, 1950), pp. v–xxi.
31 Rajat K. Ray, *Industrialisation in India: Growth and Conflict in the Private Corporate Sector* (Dehli, Oxford University Press, 1979), pp. 349.
32 Tapan Raychaudhuri, 'British Rule: An Assessment', in P. J. Marshall, ed., *The British Empire* (Cambridge, 1996) p. 363. For a provocative new view that El Nino climatic effects were worsened by European imperialism and were tantamount to genocide, see Mike Davies, *Late Victorian Holocausts* (London, 2001).
33 M. E. Chamberlain, *Britain and India: The Interaction of Two Peoples* (Newton Abbot, 1974), p. 131.
34 Neil Charlesworth, *British Rule and the Indian Economy, 1800–1914* (London, 1982), pp. 36–7.
35 Eric Stokes, *The Peasant and the Raj: Studies in Agrarian Society and Peasant Rebellion in Colonial India* (Cambridge, 1968).
36 Thomas R. Metcalfe, *Land, Landlords and the British Raj: Northern India in the Nineteenth Century* (Berkeley, 1979).
37 Ratna Ray, 'Land Transfer and Social Change Under the Permanent Settlement' *IESHR* XI (1974), pp. 1–45.
38 Frank Conlon, *A Caste in a Changing World: The Chitrapur Saraswat Brahmans, 1700–1935* (Berkeley, 1977); Henny Sender, *The Kashmiri Pandits: A Study of Cultural Choice in North India* (Delhi, 1988).
39 Brown, *Modern India*, op. cit., p. 86.
40 Philip Mason in *A Matter of Honour: An Account of the Indian Army, Its Officers and Men* (London, 1974) argued that the oath of loyalty was a crucial factor in why so many troops remained faithful to their British allies. Amiya Barat argued that it was the neglect of that loyalty, and mismanagement, which caused the mutiny in *The Bengal Native Infantry: Its Organisation and Discipline, 1796–1852* (Calcutta, 1962).
41 David Omissi, *The Sepoy and the Raj* (London, 1994), pp. 4 and 6.
42 C. Chester, The Adjutant General of the Army to Major-General Hearsey, *Final Orders to the Musketry Schools*, 13 April 1857, in John William Kaye, *The History of the Sepoy War in India, 1857–58* (London, 1880), pp. 639–41.
43 Martin Richard Gubbins, *An Account of the Mutinies in Oudh and of the Siege of the Lucknow Residency* (London, 1858), pp. 99–100. Oriental and India Office Collection, British Library (OIOC).
44 T. R. Metcalfe, *The Aftermath of Revolt. India, 1857–70* (Princeton, 1964).
45 Stokes, *The Peasant and the Raj*, op. cit.

46 A. Dashe, letter on Measures to Suppress the Mutiny in Kiyalpore District, 11 May 1858, in Harlow and Carter, *Imperialism and Orientalism*, op. cit., p. 181.

47 Charles Ball, *History of the Indian Mutiny* II (London, 1859), pp. 630–2. OIOC.

48 Lord Canning found that it had been perceived reforms by the government rather than the Evangelicals themselves that had caused resentment. H. Edwardes and H. Merivale, *The Life of Sir Henry Lawrence* (London, 1872), in Victor Sutcliffe, 'The Causes of the Indian Mutiny' *Soldiers of the Queen: The Journal of the Victorian Military Society* 82 (1985), pp. 13–16.

49 Lord Roberts, *Forty-One Years in India* (London, 1896), p. 251.

50 Syed Ahmed Khan, *The Causes of the Indian Revolt* (Benares, 1873), pp. 14–15. OIOC.

51 T. Rice Holmes, *A History of the Indian Mutiny* (5th edn, London, 1904) p. 243.

52 Emma Ewart, letters to her sister, OIOC Mss Eur B 267.

53 Brown, *Modern India*, op. cit., p. 86.

54 Ibid., pp. 94–5.

55 Tapan Raychaudhuri, 'British Rule in India', op. cit., p. 359.

56 Ibid., p. 359.

57 D. A. Washbrook, 'India, 1818–1860', in Andrew Porter, ed., *The Oxford History of the British Empire* III (Oxford, 1999), p. 418.

58 Cited in Rawlinson, op. cit., p. 51.

59 Lady Trevelyan, ed., *Macaulay: Miscellaneous Works* 5 (New York, 1880), p. 141.

60 Rawlinson, op. cit., p. 51.

61 Partha Chatterjee, *Nationalist Thought and the Colonial World: A Derivative Discourse?* (London, 1986).

4 'New Imperialism' and 'Gentlemanly Capitalism': did the flag follow trade?

1 John Darwin, 'Imperialism and the Victorians: The Dynamics of Territorial Expansion' *English Historical Review* CXII, 447 (1997), p. 629.

2 Wm. Roger Louis, 'Introduction', in Robin Winks, ed., *The Oxford History of the British Empire* V (Oxford, 1999), p. 36.

3 Sir John Seeley, *The Expansion of England: Two Courses of Lectures* (2nd edn, London, 1891), p. 8.

4 R. D. Long, ed., *The Man on the Spot: Essays on British Empire History* (London, 1995).

5 Darwin, 'Imperialism and the Victorians', op. cit., pp. 614–42.

6 J. A. Hobson, *Imperialism: A Study* (3rd edn, London, 1938), pp. 53–4.

7 Anthony Brewer, *Marxist Theories of Imperialism: A Critical Survey* (2nd edn, London, 1980).

8 This idea was developed by Paul Kennedy in *The Realities behind Diplomacy: Background Influences on British External Policy 1865–1980* (London, 1981), pp. 59–65.

9 J. S. Galbraith, *Mackinnon and East Africa, 1875–78: A Study in the 'New Imperialism'* (Cambridge, 1972) and *Crown and Charter: The Early Years of the British South Africa Company* (Berkeley, 1974).

10 J. S. Marais, *The Fall of Kruger's Republic* (Oxford, 1961), p. 324; Iain R. Smith, *The Origins of the South African War* (London, 1996), p. 397.

11 Darwin, 'Imperialism and the Victorians', op. cit., pp. 614–22.

12 Robert I. Rotberg, *Cecil Rhodes and the Pursuit of Power* (Oxford, 1988).

13 J. S. Galbraith, 'Cecil Rhodes and his 'Cosmic Dreams': A Reassessment' *JICH* II (1973), pp. 173–89.

14 Robert I. Rotberg, 'Joseph Thomson: Energy, Humanism, and Imperialism', in *Africa and its Explorers* (Cambridge, 1970), p. 300.

15 Darwin, 'Imperialism and the Victorians', op. cit., p. 624.

16 Darwin, ibid., p. 629.

17 David B. Abernethy, *The Dynamics of Global Dominance: European Overseas Empires, 1415–1980* (New Haven and London, 2000), pp. 95–6.

18 Paul Bairoch and Maurice Levy-Leboyer, eds, *Disparities in Economic Development since the Industrial Revolution* (New York, 1981), pp. 8–14.

19 David S. Landes, *The Unbound Prometheus: Technological Change and Industrial Development in Western Europe from 1750 to the Present* (Cambridge, 1969), p. 42.

20 Paul Bairoch, 'International Industrialisation levels from 1750 to 1980' *Journal of European Economic History* II (1982), p. 275.

21 R. Robinson and J. Gallagher, 'The Imperialism of Free Trade' *Economic History Review* 6 (1953), p. 11.

22 Ibid., p. 8.

23 Ibid.

24 Ibid., p. 13.

25 D. C. M. Platt, 'Further Objections to an "Imperialism of Free Trade", 1830–60' *Economic History Review* 26 (1970).

26 Britten Dean, 'Britain's Informal Empire: The Case of China' *Journal of Commonwealth and Comparative Politics* 14 (1976).

27 Louis, in Winks, *The Oxford History of the British Empire*, op. cit., p. 39.

28 P. J. Marshall, ed., *The Oxford History of the British Empire* II (Oxford, 1999), p. 25.

29 Martin Lynn, 'Policy, Trade and Informal Empire in the Mid-Nineteenth Century', in Andrew Porter, ed., *The Oxford History of the British Empire* III (Oxford, 1999), pp. 119–20.

30 R. Robinson and J. Gallagher, with Alice Denny, *Africa and the Victorians: The Official Mind of Imperialism* (2nd edn, London, 1981), p. 465.

31 A. G. Hopkins, 'The Victorians and Africa: A Reconsideration of the Occupation of Egypt, 1882' *Journal of African History* 27 (1986), p. 389.

32 B. Porter, *The Lion's Share: A Short History of British Imperialism* (2nd edn, London, 1984), p. 163.

33 G. N Sanderson 'The European Partition of Africa: Coincidence or Conjuncture?' *JICH* 3 (1974).

34 Robinson and Gallagher, *Africa and the Victorians*, op. cit., p. 499.

35 D. Fieldhouse, *Economics and Empire* (London, 1976), pp. 337–8.

36 D. Fieldhouse, '"Imperialism": An Historiographical Revision', *Economic History Review* 6 (1961–2), p. 205.

37 Anne McClintlock, *Imperial Leather: Race, Gender, and Sexuality in the Colonial Context* (New York, 1995), p. 254.

38 A. C. Hopkins, ed., *Globalisation in World History* (London, 2002).

39 Abernethy, *Dynamics*, op. cit., pp. 12–17, 363–86.

40 P. O'Brien, 'The Costs and Benefits of British Imperialism' *Past and Present* 120 (1988), p. 186.

41 P. J. Cain and A. G. Hopkins, 'New Imperialism: Gentlemanly Capitalism and British Expansion Overseas, II, New Imperialism 1850–1945' *Economic History Review* 40 (1987), p. 6.

42 P. J. Cain and A. G. Hopkins, *British Imperialism* I (London, 1993), p. 369.

43 Fieldhouse, *Economics and Empire*, op. cit., pp. 55.

44 Cain and Hopkins, *British Imperialism* I, pp. 56–8.

45 Raymond E. Dummett, 'Exploring the Cain/Hopkins Paradigm', in *Gentlemanly Capitalism and British Imperialism* (London, 1999), p. 8.

46 A. N. Porter, '"Gentlemanly Capitalism" and Empire: The British Experience since 1750?' *JICH* 18 (1990).

47 D. Cannadine, 'Review Article: The Empire Strikes Back' *Past and Present* 147 (1995).

48 M. J. Daunton, 'Gentlemanly Capitalism and British Industry, 1820–1914' *Past and Present* 122 (1989), pp. 119–58.

49 C. M. Turnbull, 'Formal and Informal Empire in East Asia', in Robin Winks, ed., *The Oxford History of the British Empire* V (Oxford University Press, 1999), pp. 390; see also D. K. Fieldhouse, *Economics and Empire*, op. cit., pp. 85–7.

50 Fieldhouse, 'Imperialism: An Historiographical Revision', op. cit., p. 203.

51 O'Brien, 'The Costs and Benefits of British Imperialism', op. cit., p. 173.

52 The railway, designed to protect the headwaters of the Nile, was begun in 1896 and reached Kampala in 1901. It cost £5 million. It was criticised in Britain because of the time taken over its construction.

53 M. E. Chamberlain, *New Imperialism*, Historical Association Pamphlet G73 (1970), pp. 22–3.

54 Darwin, 'Imperialism and the Victorians: The Dynamics of Territorial Expansion', op. cit., pp. 614–42.

55 For example, Iain Smith showed that there had been interaction between commercial, industrial and political lobbyists and decision-makers in the years before the outbreak of the South African War. However, he rejected a conspiracy of capitalists, or a 'war for gold', pointing instead to the ambitions of Sir Alfred Milner, who wanted a political settlement of British supremacy in South Africa, as the prime cause of war in 1899. Smith's research showed the tremendous value of detailed and local studies both at the periphery and in the metropolis. Iain R. Smith, *The Origins of the South African War (1899–1902)* (London, 1996), pp. 404–12.

56 E. H. H. Green, 'Gentlemanly Capitalism and British Economic Policy, 1880–1914: The Debate over Bimetallism and Protectionism', in Raymond Dummett, op. cit., p. 66.

57 Dummett, op. cit., pp. 24 and 41.

5 What were the motives and effects of colonisation and migration

1 Marc Ferro, *Colonization: A Global History* (London, 1997), p. 11.

2 John Keay, ed., *The Royal Geographical Society History of World Exploration* (London, 1991), pp. 212–13.

3 C. C. Eldridge, *Victorian Imperialism* (London, 1978), p. 48.

4 Edward Gibbon Wakefield, *A View of the Art of Colonization* (London, 1849) in ibid., p. 47.

5 Ged Martin, 'Canada from 1815', in Andrew Porter, ed., *The Oxford History of the British Empire* III (Oxford, 1999), pp. 537–8.

6 George Boyce, *Decolonisation and the British Empire, 1775–1997* (London, 1999), p. 23.

7 Ged Martin, *The Durham Report and British Policy: A Critical Essay* (Cambridge, 1972).

8 Martin, 'Canada', op. cit., p. 539.

9 John Manning Ward, *Colonial Self-Government: The British Experience* (London, 1976).

10 Simon C. Smith, *British Imperialism* (Cambridge, 1998), p. 29.

11 D. W. Brogan, *The English People: Impressions and Observations* (London, 1947), in Boyce, *Decolonisation*, op. cit., p. 43.

12 Boyce, *Decolonisation*, op. cit., p. 49; Martin Lynn, 'British Policy, Trade, and Informal Empire in the Mid-Nineteenth Century', in Porter, *The Oxford History of the British Empire* III, op. cit., p. 104.

13 *Report from the Select Committee on Africa* (Western Coast), Parliamentary Papers, V (1865), p. iii.

14 Marjory Harper, 'British Migration and the Peopling of the Empire', in Porter, *The Oxford History of the British Empire*, op. cit., p. 75.

15 Ged Martin and Benjamin E. Kline, 'British Emigration and New Identities', in P. J. Marshall, ed., *The British Empire* (Cambridge, 1996), p. 258.

16 P. J. Cain, 'Economics and Empire: The Metropolitan Context', in Porter, ed., *The Oxford History of the British Empire* III, op. cit., p. 47.

17 A poem by Charles Mackay, 'The Emigrants' (1856), was turned into a popular and catchy song by Sir Henry Bishop. See Chris Brooks and Peter Faulkner, *The White Man's Burdens* (Exeter, 1996), p. 177.

18 Martin and Kline, 'British Emigration', op. cit., p. 263.

19 James S. Donnelly, *The Great Irish Potato Famine* (London, 2001), p. 185. The introduction consists of an excellent historiographical review of this tortured debate.

20 David Fitzpatrick, *Oceans of Consolation: Personal Accounts of Irish Migration to Australia* (London, 1994).

21 Ferro, *Colonization*, op, cit., p. 150.

22 A controversial account of the early colonisation can be found in Harrison Wright, *New Zealand, 1769–1840: Early Years of Western Contact* (Cambridge, 1959).

23 Colonel Thomas Talbot settled 12,000 paupers near Lake Eyrie on 65,000 acres. Harper, 'British Migration' op. cit., p. 80.

24 Ferro, op. cit., p. 149.

25 A. Keppel-Jones, *South Africa: A Short History* (3rd edn, London, 1963), p. 85.

26 Cited in Eldridge, *Victorian Imperialism*, op. cit., p. 19.

27 Christopher Saunders and Iain R. Smith, 'Southern Africa, 1795–1910', in Porter, *The Oxford History of the British Empire* III, op. cit., p. 620.

28 Donald Denoon, *Southern Africa since 1800* (London, 1972), p. 104.

29 Shula Marks, 'Southern Africa', in Judith M. Brown and Wm Roger Louis, eds, *The Oxford History of the British Empire* IV (Oxford, 1999), p. 551.

30 Eric A. Walker, W. P. *Schreiner: A South African* (Oxford, 1937, reprntd 1969), pp. 288–303.

31 Thomas Pakenham, *The Scramble for Africa* (London, 1991), p. 654.

32 Gillian Wagner, *Children of the Empire* (London, 1982), p. xv.

6 Collaboration and resistance: was the Empire held by coercion or co-operation?

1 Quoted in David Killingray and David Omissi, eds, *Guardians of Empire: The Armed Forces of the Colonial Powers, c.1700–1964* (Manchester, 1999), p. 5.

2 Basil Davison, *The Story of Africa* (London, 1984), p. 190.
3 Ronald Robinson, 'Non-European Foundations of European Imperialism: Sketch for a Theory of Collaboration', in Roger Owen and Bob Sutcliffe, eds, *Studies in the Theory of Imperialism* (London, 1972), p. 133.
4 Charles Allen, *Plain Tales* (London, 1975), p. 246.
5 Ibid., p. 249.
6 Ronald Hyam, *Britain's Imperial Century, 1815–1914* (2nd edn, London, 1993), p. 306.
7 Allen, *Plain Tales from the Raj*, op. cit., p. 184.
8 David Gilmour, *Curzon* (London, 1994), p. 229. Curzon handled the incident badly: his vitriol only served to alienate even those officers who felt that the soldiers had been in the wrong.
9 Ibid., p. 171.
10 Lord Cromer to Curzon, 18 December 1898, Curzon Papers 111/218.
11 S. Orwell and I. Angus, eds, *The Collected Essays, Journalism and Letters of George Orwell* I (London, 1968), pp. 239 and 403.
12 Allen, *Plain Tales*, op. cit., p. 232.
13 T. R. Moreman, 'The British and Indian Armies and North-West Frontier Warfare, 1849–1914' *JICH* 1 (1992), p. 40; D. Killingray, 'Guardians of Empire', in Killingray and Omissi, *Guardians of Empire*, op. cit., p. 6.
14 T. A. Heathcote, *The Indian Army: The Garrison of British Imperial India, 1822–1922* (London, 1974), p. 201.
15 David French, *The British Way in Warfare, 1688–2000* (London, 1990), p. 144.
16 Killingray and Omissi, *Guardians of Empire*, op. cit., pp. 1–19.
17 Tony Gould, *Imperial Warriors: Britain and the Gurkhas* (London, 1999), p. 57.
18 David Omissi, *The Sepoy and the Raj* (London, 1994), p. 47.
19 Ibid., pp. 58–9.
20 Ibid., p. 55.
21 Robinson, 'Non-European foundations', op. cit., p. 132.
22 Ibid., p. 140.
23 Toyin Falola, 'Africa', in P. J. Marshall, ed., *The British Empire* (Cambridge, 1996), p. 350.
24 Marshall, *The British Empire*, op. cit., p. 8; I. N. Kimambo, *Penetration and Protest in Tanzania: The Impact of the World Economy on the Pare, 1860–1960* (London, 1991); Colin Bundy, *The Rise and Fall of the South African Peasantry* (London, 1979); William Beinhart, Peter Delius and Stanley Trapido, eds, *Putting a Plough to the Ground: Accumulation and Dispossession in Rural Africa, 1850–1930* (Johannesburg, 1986).
25 Charles Chenevix Trench, *Viceroy's Agent* (London, 1987).
26 Omissi, *Sepoy and Raj*, op. cit., p. 18.
27 Allen, *Plain Tales from the Raj*, op. cit., p. 220.
28 Ibid., p. 240.

29 Omissi, *The Sepoy and the Raj*, op. cit., p. 9.
30 Tapan Raychaudhuri, 'British Rule in India: An Assessment', in Marshall, *The British Empire*, op. cit., pp. 360–1.
31 A. J. Stockwell, 'Power, Authority, and Freedom', in Marshall, *The British Empire*, op. cit., pp. 163–4.
32 Robinson, 'Non-European foundations', op. cit., p. 134.
33 T. O. Ranger, *Revolt in Southern Rhodesia 1896–7* (London, 1967), pp. 142–55, and A. M. Keppel-Jones, *Rhodes and Rhodesia* (Montreal, 1983), pp. 435–9.
34 Bruce Vandervort, *Wars of Imperial Conquest in Africa* (London, 1998), p. 166.
35 J. Laband, *Kingdom in Crisis: The Zulu Response to the British Invasion of 1879* (Manchester, 1991).
36 Thomas Pakenham, *The Scramble for Africa* (London, 1991), p. 498.
37 Donald Denoon, *Southern Africa since 1800* (London, 1972), p. 142.
38 E. A. Ayendele, *Holy Johnson: Pioneer of African Nationalism, 1836–1917* (London, 1970), pp. 226–7.
39 Wm Theodore de Bary, *Sources of Indian Tradition* (New York: Columbia, 1958), p. 578.
40 Dennon, *Southern Africa*, op. cit., p. 128.
41 Michael Barthorp, *The North-West Frontier* (Blandford, 1982), pp. 170–2, 177.
42 Surendranath Benerjea, *A Nation in Making* (Madras, 1925), pp. 208–9.
43 Robinson, 'Non-European foundations', op. cit., pp. 135.
44 Ibid., p. 138.
45 Jeremy Black, *War and the World: Military Power and the Fate of Continents, 1450–2000* (New Haven and London, 1998), p. 170.

7 Colonial discourse: was there an ideology of imperialism?

1 John Warren, *The Past and its Presenters* (London, 1998), p. 4.
2 For a brilliant explanation and criticism of the concept of post-structuralism, see Richard J. Evans, *In Defence of History* (London, 1997), p. 4.
3 Andrew Wohl, 'Race and Class: Parallels in Racism and Class Prejudice' http://landow.stg.brown.edu/victorian/race/rcov.html.
4 Eric Hobsbawm and Terence Ranger, *The Invention of Tradition* (Cambridge, 1983), pp. 211–2.
5 M. Foucault, *Power/Knowledge: Selected Interviews and Other Writings, 1972–77* (Brighton, 1980), pp. 131–3.
6 Edward Said, *Orientalism* (London, 1978; 1995 edn contains Said's responses to his early critics).

7   S. Monas and H. Kozicki, eds, *Developments in Modern Historiography* (London, 1993), p. 3.

8   Anne McClintock, *Imperial Leather: Race, Gender and Sexuality in the Colonial Context* (London and New York, 1995), p. 5.

9   Ranajit Guha, 'On Aspects of the Historiography of Colonial India' *Subaltern Studies* I (Dehli, 1982). See also Rosalind O'Hanlon, '"Recovering the Subject", Subaltern Studies and Histories of Resistance in Colonial South Asia' *Modern Asia Studies* XXII, 1 (1988), pp. 189–224 and D. A. Washbrook, 'Orients and Occidents: Colonial Discourse Theory and the Historiography of the British Empire', in Robin W. Winks, ed., *The Oxford History of the British Empire* v (Oxford, 1999), p. 601.

10 Warren, *The Past and its Presenters*, op. cit., pp. 11–12.

11 Leela Gandhi, *Post-Colonial Theory* (Edinburgh, 1998), pp. 170–1.

12 McClintock, *Imperial Leather*, op. cit., p. 5.

13 Mrinalini Sinha, *Colonial Masculinity: The Manly Englishman and the Effeminate Bengali in the Late Nineteenth Century* (Manchester, 1995), p. 19.

14 Clare Midgley, *Gender and Imperialism* (Manchester, 1998), pp. 14–15.

15 Washbrook, 'Orients and Occidents' op. cit., p. 603; see also Kate Teltscher, *India Inscribed: European and British Writing on India, 1600–1800* (Oxford, 1995); and C. A. Bayly, *Empire and Information: Intelligence Gathering and Social Communication in India, 1780–1870* (Cambridge, 1996).

16 It is curious that post-colonial theorists tend to make no references to Romanticism, as this laid the foundations of their views: it was Foucault who resurrected the philosophical conclusions of Nietzsche, whilst 'deconstruction' might be traced back to the 'authenticity of being' in Heidigger and the 'anti-empiricism of knowledge' in Herder. Robert Young, *White Mythologies: Writing History and the West* (London and New York, 1990), pp. 12 and 15; and Warren, *The Past and its Presenters*, op. cit., p. 110.

17 Gyan Prakash, 'Writing Post-Orientalist Histories of the Third World: Perspectives from Indian Historiography' *Comparative Studies in Society and History* XXXII, 2 (1990), p. 384.

18 Washbrook, 'Orients and Occidents', op. cit., p. 604.

19 Sheldon Pollock, 'Deep Orientalism?', in Carol A. Breckenridge and Peter Van der Veer, eds., *Orientalism and the Post-Colonial Predicament: Perspectives on South Asia* (Philadelphia, 1993), p. 101.

20 John M. MacKenzie, *Orientalism: History, Theory and the Arts* (Manchester and New York, 1995), p. 214.

21 Ibid., p. xvii.

22 Ibid., pp. 214–15.

23 Kenan Malik, *The Meaning of Race: Race, History and Culture in Western Society* (Basingstoke, 1996).

24 Said, *Orientalism*, op. cit., p. 272.

25 Washbrook, 'Orients and Occidents', op. cit., p. 607.

26 Ajiz Ahmad, *In Theory: Classes, Nations and Literatures* (London, 1992), pp. 159–220.

27 Midgley, *Gender and Imperialism,* op. cit., p. 5.

28 Gandhi, *Postcolonial Theory,* op. cit., p. x.

29 Ibid., p. 2.

30 H. Bhabha, *The Location of Culture* (London, 1994) p. 63.

31 Dane Kennedy, 'Imperial History and Post-Colonial Theory' *JICH* 3 (1996), p. 356.

32 Ibid., p. 359.

33 C. A. Bayly, 'The Second British Empire', in Winks, *The Oxford History,* op. cit., p. 70.

34 This leaves some doubt over the interpretation of comments such as those in the novel by John Buchan, *A Lodge in the Wilderness* (1907), which are taken as *actual* imperial plans. His desire was to see the empire become: 'a closer organic connection under one crown of a number of autonomous nations of the same blood, who can spare something of their vitality for the administration of vast tracts inhabited by lower races – a racial aristocracy considered in their relation to subject peoples, a democracy in relation to each other.' Quoted in P. J. Marshall, ed., *The British Empire* (Cambridge, 1996), p. 60.

35 Eugene F. Irschick, *Dialogue and History: Constructing South India, 1795–1895* (Berkeley, 1994).

36 D. George Boyce, *Decolonisation and the British Empire, 1775–1997* (London, 1999), p. 269.

37 Neil Lazarus, *Resistance in Postcolonial African Fiction* (New Haven, 1990), p. ix.

38 Cited in Basil Davison, *The Story of Africa* (London, 1984), p. 167.

39 Andrew Porter, 'Religion, Missionary Enthusiasm and Empire', in Andrew Porter, ed., *The Oxford History of the British Empire* III (Oxford, 1999), p. 245.

40 Ibid., p. 225.

41 E. A. Ayendele, *The Missionary Impact on Modern Nigeria, 1842–1914* (London, 1966), p. 29.

42 Roland Oliver, *Sir Harry Johnston and the Scramble for Africa* (London, 1957), p. 182.

43 Andrew Porter, '"Cultural Imperialism" and Protestant Missionary Enterprise, 1780–1914' *JICH* xxv 3 (1997), pp. 367–91.

44 Cited in Charles Allen, *Soldier Sahibs: The Men Who Made the North-West Frontier* (London, 2000), p. 11.

45 Tom Gibson, *The Maori Wars* (Sydney and Auckland, 1974), pp. 245–6.

46 Denis Judd, *Empire: The British Imperial Experience from 1765 to the Present* (London, 1997), pp. 82–3.

47 *Daily News,* 12 December 1866.

48 Gad Heuman, *The Killing Time: The Morant Bay Rebellion in Jamaica* (London, 1994).

49 Judd, *Empire*, op. cit., p. 90.
50 Muriel Chamberlain, *The Scramble for Africa* (London, 1974), p. 25.
51 Dorothy Middleton, 'Africa', in John Keay, ed., *The History of World Exploration* (London, 1991), pp. 100–14.
52 Richard Burton, *Mission to Gelele, the King of Dahomey* (London, 1864).
53 David Livingstone, *Private Journals, 1851–53*, ed. I. Shapera (London, 1960), pp. 43–4.
54 P. D. Curtin, *The Image of Africa: British Ideas and Actions, 1780–1850* (London, 1965).
55 Ronald Robinson and John Gallagher with Alice Denny, *Africa and the Victorians* (London, 1961; 2nd edn, 1981), p. 50.

8 Was the British Empire racialist or racist?

1 See Les Back and John Solomos, eds, *Theories of Race and Racism: A Reader* (London, 2000).
2 Neil MacMaster, *Racism in Europe* (Basingstoke, 2001), pp. 1–11.
3 Ibid., p. 14
4 Michael Crowder, *West Africa under Colonial Rule* (London, 1968), pp. 11–12.
5 Mark Ferro, *Colonisation: A Global History* (London and New York, 1997), p. 18.
6 Mary Bennett, *The Ilberts in India, 1882–1886* (London, 1995), p. 50.
7 MacMaster, op. cit., p. 81.
8 Sir Harry Johnston, *Fortnightly Review* 1890, p. 705, cited in L. R. Gardiner and J. H. Davison, *British Imperialism in the Late Nineteenth Century* (London, 1968), pp. 12–13.
9 Cited in *The Times*, 27 July 1925.
10 Rhodes's 'Confession of Faith', cited in Antony Thomas, *Rhodes* (London, 1996), p. 8.
11 *The British Empire* III (London, 1973), p. 228.
12 David Livingstone, *Expedition to the Zambesi and Its Tributaries* (London, 1975), p. 141.
13 Cited in H. G. Rawlinson, *The British Achievement in India* (London, 1948), p. 104.
14 Henry Labouchere, *Truth* 16 November 1882, p. 693.
15 M. E. Chamberlain, *Decolonisation* (2nd edn, London, 1995), p. 50.
16 W. David McIntyre, *British Decolonisation, 1946–1997* (London, 1998), p. 22.
17 Robin Neillands, *Fighting Retreat: The British Empire, 1947–1997* (London, 1996), p. 10; Charles Allen, *Plain Tales from the Raj* (London, 1975), p. 119.

18 Neillands, *Fighting Retreat,* op. cit., p. 29.
19 Richard Holmes, *Firing Line* (London, 1985), p. 400.
20 Donald Denoon with Marivic Wyndham, 'Australia and the Western Pacific', in Andrew Porter, ed., *The Oxford History of the British Empire* III (Oxford, 1999), pp. 549, 557 and 571.
21 Karl Meyer and Shareen Brysac, *Tournament of Shadows: The Great Game and the Race for Empire in Asia* (London, 1999), p. 92.
22 Charles Allen, *Tales from the South China Seas* (London, 1983), p. 65.
23 Basil Davison, *The Story of Africa* (London, 1984), pp. 201–2; Nigel Worden, *The Making of Modern South Africa* (Oxford, 1994), p. 66.
24 David Cannadine, *Ornamentalism* (London, 2001).
25 Allen, *Plain Tales,* op. cit., p. 237.
26 Ibid., p. 238.
27 Mrinalini Sinha, *Colonial Masculinity: The Manly Englishman and the Effeminate Bengali in the Late Nineteenth Century* (Manchester, 1993), pp. 2–3, 35, 40–1, and 51.
28 John X. Merriman to Professor Goldwin Smith, 24 April 1904, in P. Lewsen, *Correspondence of John X. Merriman: Paradoxical South African Statesman* (New Haven, 1982), pp. 441–2.
29 Allen, *Plain Tales,* op. cit., p. 122.
30 Alice Pennell, *Pennell of the Afghan Frontier* (London, 1914).
31 Lawrence James, *Raj: The Making and Unmaking of British India* (London, 1997), p. 456.
32 Ferro, op. cit., pp. 144–5.
33 Worden, op. cit., pp. 90–3.
34 Wm Roger Louis, 'Introduction', in Judith Brown and Louis, eds, *The Oxford History of the British Empire* IV (Oxford, 1999), pp. 31–2.
35 Terence Ranger, 'The Invention of Tradition in Colonial Africa', in Eric Hobsbawm and Terence Ranger, *The Invention of Tradition* (Cambridge, 1983), pp. 261–2.
36 Ferro, *Colonisation,* op. cit., p. 184.
37 Ian Hernon, *The Savage Empire* (London, 2000), p. 86.
38 P. J. Marshall, *The British Empire* (Cambridge, 1996), p. 373.

9 What was the significance of gender to British imperialism ?

1 As Diana Wylie points out, advocates of the 'myth of the destructive female' were 'usually nameless', but included many male colonists in the twentieth century, as well as the novelist Somerset Maugham and film director David Lean. Diana Wylie, 'Disease, Diet and Gender: Late Twentieth-Century Perspectives on Empire', in Robin W. Winks, ed., *The Oxford History of the British Empire* V (Oxford, 1999), p. 285.

2   See L. H. Gann and Peter Duigan, *The Rulers of British Africa,*
    1870–1914 (Stanford, CA, 1978), pp. 141–57. John Morris, an
    Indian Army Officer, felt that it was the language barrier that made
    wives more dependent on their husbands, and therefore was: 'very
    largely responsible for the break-up of relations between the British
    and the Indians'. Cited in Charles Allen, *Plain Tales from the Raj*
    (London, 1975), pp. 212–13.
3   Ronald Hyam, *Empire and Sexuality: The British Experience*
    (Manchester, 1990), pp. 189–97. For an outline of the debate see
    Margaret Strobel, *European Women and the Second British Empire*
    (Bloomington, 1991), ch. 1.
4   Ibid., pp. 17–18, 208. See also Claudia Knapman, *White Women in*
    Fiji, 1835–1930: The Ruin of Empire (Sydney, 1986).
5   Claire Robertson and Iris Berger, eds., *Women and Class in Africa*
    (New York, 1986); Elizabeth Schmidt, *Peasants, Traders and*
    Wives: Shona Women in the History of Zimbabwe, 1870–1939
    (London, 1992).
6   Spivak, cited in Robert Young, *White Mythologies: Writing History*
    and the West (London and New York, 1990), p. 164.
7   Chandra Talpade Mohanty, 'Under Western Eyes: Feminist
    Scholarship and Colonial Discourses' *Boundary* 2 (1984), p. 333.
8   Lawrence James, *Raj: The Making and Unmaking of British India*
    (London, 1997), pp. 202, 327.
9   The important exception to this is Anne McClintock, *Imperial*
    Leather: Race, Gender and Sexuality in the Colonial Contest (New
    York, 1995), pp. 10–11.
10 Mrinlini Sinha, *Colonial Masculinity: The 'Manly Englishman' and*
    the 'Effeminate Bengali' in the Late Nineteenth Century
    (Manchester, 1995).
11 Wylie, 'Disease, Diet and Gender', op. cit., p. 287.
12 Kenneth Ballhatchet, *Race, Sex and Class under the Raj: Imperial*
    Attitudes and their Critics, 1793–1905 (London, 1980), pp. 115
    and 121.
13 Ronald Hyam, *Britain's Imperial Century, 1815–1914* (2nd edn,
    London, 1993), p. 294.
14 Ibid., pp. 285 and 292.
15 David Omissi, *The Sepoy and the Raj* (London, 1994), p. 14.
16 Tony Gould, *Imperial Warriors: Britain and the Gurkhas* (London,
    1999), p. 423.
17 McClintock, op. cit., p. 10.
18 See introduction to Midgley, *Gender and Imperialism*, op. cit.,
    p. vii.
19 Ibid., p. 2.
20 Ibid., p. 5.
21 Dane Kennedy, 'Imperial History and Post-Colonial Theory'
    JICH 3 (1996), pp. 350 and 353.
22 Jenny Sharpe, *Allegories of Empire: The Figure of Woman in the*
    Colonial Text (Minneapolis, 1993), p. 9.

23 Antoinette Burton, *Burden's of History: British Feminists, Indian Women, and Imperial Culture, 1865–1915* (Chapel Hill, NC, 1994); and Benita Perry, *Delusions and Discoveries: Studies on India and the British Imagination, 1880–1930* (London, 1972).

24 Margaret Strobel, *European Women and the Second British Empire* (Bloomington, 1991).

25 Rosalind O'Hanlon, 'Gender in the British Empire', in Judith Brown and Wm Roger Louis, eds, *The Oxford History of the British Empire* IV (Oxford, 1999), p. 380–2

26 Rozina Visram, *Women in Pakistan and India: The Struggle for Independence from British Rule* (Cambridge, 1992), pp. 16, 56–7. See also Vijay Agnew, *Elite Women in Indian Politics* (New Dehli, 1979).

27 Nancy L. Paxton, 'Mobilising Chivalry: Rape in British Novels about the Indian Uprising of 1857' *Victorian Studies* 1 (1992), pp. 5–30.

28 Neil MacMaster, *Racism in Europe, 1870–2000* (Basingstoke, 2001) p. 81.

29 Allen, *Plain Tales,* op. cit., p. 83.

30 Ibid., p. 191.

31 Lady Deborah Dring's first husband, Major General John Marshall, 45th Rattray Sikhs died in 1942. Allen, *Plain Tales,* op. cit., p. 215.

32 Strobel, *European Women,* op. cit.

33 Allen, *Plain Tales,* op. cit., p. 234.

10 The Great War: watershed or continuity ?

1 Robert Holland, 'The British Empire and the Great War, 1914–1918', in Judith M. Brown and Wm Roger Louis, eds, *The Oxford History of the British Empire* IV (Oxford, 1999), p. 116.

2 C. E. Carrington, 'The Empire at War, 1914–18', in E. A. Benians, James Butler and C. E. Carrington, eds, *The Cambridge History of the British Empire* III (Cambridge, 1929–59), p. 610.

3 David Omissi, *Indian Voices in the Great War: Soldiers' Letters, 1914–1918* (London, 1999), p. 3.

4 This view has been challenged by cultural historians. John Parker attacks Philip Mason's view of the father–son relationship in *The Gurkhas: The Inside Story of the World's Most Feared Soldiers* (London, 1999). Instead, Parker argues that homosexual relationships 'enhanced affection and battlefield cohesion', although he provides scant evidence. This view is refuted in Tony Gould's *Imperial Warriors: Britain and the Gurkhas* (London, 1999), p. 223.

5 Lyn MacDonald, *1915: The Death of Innocence* (London, 1993), pp. 75–143; Lt-Col. Merewether and Rt Hon. Sir Frederick Smith, Bart., *The Indian Corps in France* (London, 1929).

6 R. Millar, *Kut: The Death of an Army* (London, 1969).

7 Peter Hopkirk, *On Secret Service East of Constantinople* (Oxford, 1994), p. 181.

8 These figures exclude a total of 142,057 who were, at the time of compilation in 1923, missing (some who returned home are not recorded) and a further total of two million wounded. The total dead of the British Empire was therefore *c.*851,117. 'Spanish flu', which coincided with the end of the war, killed six million in 1919.

9 Judith M. Brown, *Modern India: The Origins of an Asian Democracy* (2nd edn, Oxford, 1994), pp. 204–5.

10 D. George Boyce, *Decolonisation and the British Empire, 1775–1997* (London, 1999), p. 89.

11 Ibid., p. 90.

12 Gerard J. de Groot, *The First World War* (London, 2001), p. 104.

13 C. E. Bean, *Official History of Australia in the War of 1914–18* (Sydney, 1921, 1933).

14 John Laffin, *Damn the Dardenelles! The Agony of Gallipoli* (London, 1980), p. 214.

15 Anon., Foreword by Sir William Birdwood, *The Anzac Book* (London, 1916), p. x.

16 De Groot, op. cit., p. 106.

17 K. S. Inglis, 'Australia', in Peter Marshall, ed., *The British Empire* (Cambridge, 1996), p. 343.

18 Holland, 'The British Empire and the Great War', op. cit., p. 126.

19 Anon., *Canada in the First World War and the Road to Vimy Ridge* (Ottawa, 1996), pp. 1 and 13.

20 H. W. Wilson and J. A. Hammerton, eds, *The Great War* III (London, 1915).

21 Glyn Harper, *The Massacre at Passchendaele: The New Zealand Story* (Auckland, 2001).

22 De Groot, op. cit., p. 110.

23 Sheila Lawlor, *Britain and Ireland, 1914–1923* (Dublin, 1983), pp. 87, 94.

24 Boyce, *Decolonisation*, op. cit., p. 73.

25 Michael Hughes, *Ireland Divided: The Roots of the Modern Irish Problem* (Cardiff, 1994), p. 51.

26 Ibid., p. 127.

27 Max Beloff, *Imperial Sunset: Britain's Liberal Empire* i (London, 1969), pp. 15 and 17.

28 W. David McIntyre, 'Europe and the World in the Age of Expansion', in *The Commonwealth of Nations: Origins and Impact, 1869–1971* (Minneapolis, 1977), p. 175.

29 Ronald Hyam, *Britain's Imperial Century, 1815–1914* (2nd edn London, 1993), p. 310.

11 How did British imperialism meet the challenges of the inter-war years?

1 T. O. Ranger, 'Connexions between Primary Resistance Movements and Modern Mass Nationalism in East and Central Africa' *Journal of African History* IX, 3 (1968), pp. 437–53, and IX, 4, pp. 631–41. Ranger's view has subsequently been regarded as largely erroneous.

2 Francis Robinson, 'The British Empire and the Muslim World', in Judith M. Brown and Wm Roger Louis, eds, *The Oxford History of the British Empire* IV (Oxford, 1999), pp. 412–14, 419.

3 D. George Boyce, *Decolonisation and the British Empire, 1775–1997* (London, 1999), p. 269.

4 V 13221, Report of the Commissioners appointed by the Punjab Sub-Commissioner of the INC (Indian National Congress), Bombay 1920, I, p. 14. Oriental and India Office Collection (OIOC), British Library.

5 Hunter Minority Report L/P&J/6/1669 OIOC vol. 3, pp. 117 and 126, and p. 203.

6 Ibid., vol. 3, p. 120.

7 Lawrence James, *Raj: The Making and Unmaking of British India* (London, 1997), p. 483.

8 D. George Boyce, 'From Assaye to the *Assaye*: Reflections on British government, Force and Moral Authority in India' *The Journal of Military History* 63, 3 (1999), pp. 660–8.

9 Brigadier General Dyer to Secretary, War Office, 3 July 1920, in *The Amritsar Massacre* (London, 1920, reprtd., 2000), p. 150.

10 Robin Neillands, *Fighting Retreat: The British Empire, 1947–97* (London, 1996), p. 3.

11 Ibid., pp. 43–4.

12 Sir Charles W. Gwynn, *Imperial Policing* (London, 1934), pp. 34–5.

13 Nirad C. Chaudhuri, *Thy Hand, Great Anarch: India, 1921–52* (London, 1987); Stephen Howe, 'The Slow Death and Strange Rebirths of Imperial History' *The Journal of Imperial and Commonwealth History* 29, 2 (2001), p. 135 and n. 5.

14 C. H. Philips, *The Evolution of India and Pakistan, 1858–1947* (Oxford, 1962), pp. 215–16.

15 See Judith M. Brown, *Gandhi's Rise to Power: Indian Politics, 1915–22* (Cambridge, 1972).

16 Tapan Raychaudhuri, 'India, 1858 to the 1930s', in Robin W. Winks, ed., *The Oxford History of the British Empire* V (Oxford, 1999), pp. 219.

17 D. A. Low, *Congress and the Raj: Facets of the Indian Struggle, 1917–47* (London, 1977).

18 Gyanendra Pandey, *The Ascendancy of Congress in Uttar Pradesh, 1926–34: A Study in Imperfect Mobilisation* (Delhi, 1978).

19 Sumit Sarkar, *Swadeshi Movement in Bengal, 1903–1908* (New Dehli, 1973).

20 B. Chandra, *Communalism in Modern India* (Delhi, 1984).
21 James, *Raj,* op. cit., p. 521.
22 Memorandum by General Smuts, 1921 PRO CO 886/10.
23 P. J. Cain and A. G. Hopkins, *British Imperialism: Crisis and Deconstruction, 1914–1990* (London, 1993), p. 110.
24 Howard M. Sachar, *The Emergence of the Modern Middle East, 1914–18* (New York, 1969), pp. 43–4.
25 Robert Holland, 'The British Empire and the Great War, 1914–1918', in Brown and Louis, *The Oxford History of the British Empire* IV, op. cit., p. 133.
26 Glen Balfour-Paul, 'Britain's Informal Empire in the Middle East', in Brown and Louis, *The Oxford History of the British Empire* IV, op. cit., p. 494.
27 Ibid., p. 134.
28 Justin McCarthy, *The Ottoman Peoples and the End of Empire* (London, 2001), pp. 136, 145–6.
29 Ibid., pp. 146–7.
30 Glen Balfour-Paul, 'Britain's Informal Empire' op. cit., p. 502.
31 Directive 28, Fuehrer Headquarters, 25 April 1941, in Hugh Trevor-Roper, *Hitler's War Directives* (London, 1964), p. 117.
32 See John Darwin, 'Imperialism in Decline: Tendencies in British Imperial Policy between the Wars' *Historical Journal* 23 (1980), p. 664.
33 Cited in P. J. Marshall, ed., *The British Empire* (Cambridge, 1996) p. 81.
34 See R. F. Holland, *Britain and the Commonwealth Alliance, 1918–1939* (London, 1981).
35 David Reynolds, *Britannia Overruled: British Policy and World Power in the Twentieth Century* (London and New York, 1991), pp. 206–10; Paul Kennedy, *The Rise and Fall of the Great Powers: Economic Change and Military Conflict from 1500 to 2000* (London, 1989), pp. 355–413.
36 Kennedy, *Rise and Fall,* op. cit., pp. 409–10, 413.
37 Cain and Hopkins, *British Imperialism,* op. cit., II, pp. 308–9.
38 Marshall, *British Empire,* op. cit., p. 81.
39 Patrick O'Brien, 'The Costs and Benefits of British Imperialism, 1846–1914' *Past and Present* 120 (1988), p. 188.
40 Lance E. Davis and Robert A. Huttenback, *Mammon and the Pursuit of Empire: The Political Economy of British Imperialism, 1860–1912* (Cambridge, 1986), pp. 161–5; Paul Kennedy, 'The Costs and Benefits of British Imperialism' *Past and Present* 125 (1989), p. 189.
41 Bernard Porter, *The Lion's Share: A Short History of British Imperialism, 1850–1983* (2nd edn, London, 1984), p. 260.
42 Ibid., p. 262.
43 *Parliamentary Debates*, 5th Series, 187 (1925), p. 80.
44 Ibid., 118 (1919), p. 2174.
45 Porter, op. cit., p. 281.

46 *Parliamentary Debates*, 5th Series, 144 (1921), p. 1555, cited in Porter, op. cit., p. 282.
47 Cain and Hopkins, op. cit., II p. 79.
48 Richie Ovendale, *Appeasement and the English-Speaking World: Britain, the United States, the Dominions and the Policy of Appeasement, 1937–39* (Cardiff, 1975).
49 David French, *The British Way in Warfare, 1688–2000* (London, 1990), p. 185.
50 Ibid., p. 189.
51 Porter, op. cit., pp. 301–2.
52 David Fromkin, *A Peace to End All Peace: Creating the Modern Middle East, 1914–1922* (London, 1989), p. 19.

12 What effect did the Second World War have on British imperialism?

1 Keith Jeffrey, 'The Second World War', in Judith M. Brown and Wm Roger Louis, eds, *The Oxford History of the British Empire: The Twentieth Century* IV (Oxford, 1999), p. 306.
2 Judith M. Brown, *Modern India: The Origins of an Asian Democracy* (2nd edn, Oxford, 1994), p. 324.
3 S. Gopal, 'Modern India' *Historical Association Pamphlet* G 66 (1967), p. 20.
4 Ibid., p. 22.
5 Ayesha Jalal, *The Sole Spokesman: Jinnah, the Muslim League and the Demand for Pakistan* (Cambridge, 1985), pp. 57–60.
6 Judith M. Brown, 'India', in Brown and Louis, *The Oxford History of the British Empire* IV, op. cit., p. 435.
7 Martin Kitchen, *The British Empire and Commonwealth: A Short History* (Basingstoke, 1996), p. 349.
8 Brown, *Modern India*, op. cit., p. 321.
9 R. J. Moore, *Escape from Empire: The Attlee Government and the Indian Problem* (Oxford, 1983).
10 Ken Bradley, *Hellfire Pass Memorial, Thailand-Burma Railway* (5th edn, Bangkok, 1997), p. 5.
11 Toyin Falola and A. D. Roberts, 'West Africa', in Brown and Louis, *The Oxford History of the British Empire* IV, op. cit., p. 518.
12 Rosaleen Smyth, 'Britain's African colonies and British propaganda during the Second World War' *Journal of Imperial and Commonwealth History* 14 (1985), p. 76.
13 Jeffrey, 'Second World War', op. cit., p. 307.
14 Ernest Barker, *The Ideas and Ideals of the British Empire* (Cambridge, 1942), pp. 163–4.
15 'The Colonial Empire' *Parliamentary Papers (House of Commons)* 1946–47, x, 415–16.

16 G. O. Olusanya, *The Second World War and Politics in Nigeria* (Lagos, 1973), p. 60, cited in Jeffrey, 'Second World War', op. cit., p. 314.

17 Cited in Ritchie Ovendale, 'The Empire-Commonwealth and the Two World Wars', in Robin W. Winks, ed., *The Oxford History of the British Empire* V (Oxford, 1999), p. 361.

18 S. R. Ashton and S. E. Stockwell, eds., *Imperial Policy and Colonial Practice*, 1925–1945 I (London, 1996), p. 197. Stanley's speech of 13 July 1943 is in *Hansard* CCCXCI (House of Commons), p. 48.

19 Paul Kennedy, *The Rise and Fall of the Great Powers: Economic Change and Military Conflict, 1500–2000* (London, 1989), p. 473.

20 Elizabeth Monroe, *Britain's Moment in the Middle East, 1914–1971* (2nd edn, London, 1981), p. 148.

21 The misunderstanding stemmed from Churchill's concern that if it came to a *choice* between defending Singapore or Burma, Burma must take priority. Noel Barber, *Sinister Twilight: The Fall and Rise Again of Singapore* (London, 1969), p. 103.

22 Adrian Stewart, *The Underrated Enemy: Britain's War with Japan, December 1941-May 1942* (London, 1987), p. 12. There was some feeling that the refusal of the Australian government to allow a division to disembark at Rangoon cost the British the control of Burma, but Churchill was more understanding, stating that it was 'natural' that the Australians should look to their own defence in such circumstances. Martin Gilbert, *Road to Victory: Winston Churchill, 1941–45* (London, 1986), VII, p. 65.

23 Lt. Col. Bruno Bauer, *The History of World War II* (Leicester, 1984), p. 215.

24 John Darwin, *Britain and Decolonisation: The Retreat from Empire in the Post-War World* (Basingstoke, 1988), p. 46.

25 Carl Bridge, ed., *Munich to Vietnam: Australia's Relations with Britain and the Unites States since the 1930s* (Victoria, 1991), pp. 2, 38–51.

26 John Gallagher, 'The Decline, Revival and Fall of the British Empire', in Anil Seal, ed., *The Decline, Revival and Fall of the British Empire: The Ford Lectures and Other Essays by John Gallagher* (Cambridge, 1982), pp. 73–153.

13 Decolonisation after 1945: how did British imperialism come to an end?

1 J. D. Hargreaves, *The End of Colonial Rule in West Africa* (London, 1979), pp. 3–8; P. Gifford and Wm Roger Louis, eds, *The Transfer of Power in Africa: Decolonisation, 1940–1960* (Yale, 1982), pp. 515, 569.

2   Paul Kennedy, *Strategy and Diplomacy, 1870–1945* (London, 1984), pp. 201–3.
3   M. E. Chamberlain, *Decolonisation* (2nd edn, London, 1999) p. 3; D. George Boyce, *Decolonisation and the British Empire, 1775–1997* (London, 1999), pp. 1, 269–70.
4   E. Stokes, *English Utilitarians and India* (Oxford, 1959), p. 46.
5   M. Lynn, 'British Policy, Trade, and Informal Empire in the Mid-Nineteenth Century', in Andrew Porter, ed., *The Oxford History of the British Empire* III (Oxford, 1999), p. 105.
6   Chamberlain, op. cit., p. 17.
7   W. David McIntyre, *British Decolonisation, 1946–1997* (London, 1998), p. 24.
8   Ibid., p. 26.
9   Ibid., p. 27.
10 Robin Neillands, *Fighting Retreat* (London, 1996), p. 223.
11 Obafemi Awolowo, *Path to Nigerian Freedom* (London, 1947), p. 30.
12 Chamberlain, op. cit., p. 47.
13 Edward Paice, *Lost Lion of Empire* (London, 2001), pp. 305–8 and 436, n.18.
14 Convention of Associations Papers, Rhodes House (Oxford) Mss. Afr. S. 594, cited in ibid., p. 309.
15 Neillands, op. cit., p. 191.
16 'Africa, the next ten years', 3 June 1959, AF (59) 28, Public Record Office, CAB 134/1355.
17 Wm Roger Louis and Ronald Robinson, 'The Imperialism of Decolonization' *Journal of Imperial and Commonwealth History* 22 (1994), pp. 462–511.
18 C. Barnett, *The Lost Victory* (London, 1995), pp. xii–xiii and 45.
19 Harold Macmillan to the Houses of Parliament, Cape Town, 3 February 1960, cited in A. N. Porter and A. J. Stockwell, eds, *British Imperial Policy and Decolonisation, 1938–1964* II (Basingstoke, 1987–9), pp. 524–5.
20 John Gallagher, *The Decline, Revival and Fall of the British Empire* (Cambridge, 1982), p. 74.
21 R. Robinson, 'Andrew Cohen and the Transfer of Power in Tropical Africa', in W. G. Morris-Jones and G. Fischer, eds, *Decolonisation and After: The British and French Experience* (London, 1980), p. 56.
22 D. Birmingham, *The Decolonisation of Africa* (London, 1995), p. 91.
23 D. A. Low, *Eclipse of Empire* (Cambridge, 1991), p. xii.
24 J. Darwin, *Britain and Decolonisation: The Retreat from Empire in the Post-War World* (London, 1988) p. 17, and John Darwin, *The End of the British Empire: The Historical Debate* (London, 1991), pp. 5–7.
25 S. Howe, *Anti-Colonialism in British Politics, 1918–1964* (Oxford, 1993), p. 323.

26 McIntyre, op. cit., pp. 83–4.
27 H. T. Bourdillon, 10 May 1948, cited in McIntyre, op. cit., p. 29.

14 What was the cultural legacy of imperialism?

1 Bernard Porter, *The Lion's Share: A Short History of British Imperialism, 1850–1983* (2nd edn, London, 1984), pp. 284–5.
2 John M. MacKenzie, ed., *Imperialism and Popular Culture* (Manchester, 1986), p. 9.
3 Stephen Constantine, 'Bringing the Empire Alive: The Empire Marketing Board and Imperial Propaganda, 1926–33', in ibid., p. 192.
4 Cited in Robin Neillands, *Fighting Retreat* (London, 1996), p. 49.
5 Jan Morris, *Farewell the Trumpets: An Imperial Retreat* (London, 1978), p. 29.
6 *Minute on British Policy in India by the Viceroy Lord Dufferin*, November 1888, p. 7. L/P&J/3/86 OIOC.
7 T. O. Ranger, 'Invention of Tradition in Colonial Africa', in Eric Hobsbawm and Terence Ranger, eds, *The Invention of Tradition* (Cambridge, 1983), pp. 221–2.
8 Martin Green, *Dreams of Adventure, Deeds of Empire* (New York, 1977).
9 Jeffrey Richards, 'Boys Own Empire: Feature Films and Imperialism in the 1930s', in MacKenzie, *Imperialism and Popular Culture*, op. cit., p. 153.
10 Thomas R. Metcalfe, 'Imperial Towns and Cities', in Peter Marshall, ed., *The British Empire* (Cambridge, 1996), p. 237.
11 Charles Allen, *Plain Tales from the Raj* (London, 1975), p. 129.
12 E. F. Knight, *Where Three Empires Meet* (London, 1900), pp. 357–8.
13 Allen, *Plain Tales*, op. cit., p. 129.
14 James Bryce, *Impressions of South Africa* (London, 1897), pp. 384–5.
15 L. C. B. Seaman, *Post-Victorian Britain, 1902–1951* (London, 1966), p. 129.
16 John M. MacKenzie, *Propaganda and Empire: The Manipulation of British Public Opinion, 1880–1960* (Manchester, 1984) p. 4.
17 Bernard S. Cohn, 'Representing Authority in Colonial India', in Ranger and Hobsbawm, *The Invention of Tradition*, op. cit., p. 207.
18 David Cannadine, 'The British Monarchy, c.1820–1977', in Ranger and Hobsbawm, ibid., p. 139.
19 Ibid., p. 149.
20 Fritz Stern, *The Politics of Cultural Despair: A Study in the Rise of Germanic Ideology* (New York, 1965), cited in Neil McMaster, *Racism in Europe, 1870–2000* (London, 2001), p. 28.

21 Allen, *Plain Tales,* op. cit., pp. 185–6.
22 Ibid., p. 190.
23 Robert Roberts, *The Classic Slum* (Manchester, 1971), p. 142.
24 Allen, *Plain Tales,* op. cit., p. 257.
25 Ibid., p. 258.
26 Ibid., p. 261.
27 Ibid., p. 261.
28 Elizabeth Pearl, ed., *A History of the Jews in England* (London, 1990), pp. 108–32.

Select Bibliography

General

Books

Abernethy, David, *The Dynamics of Global Dominance: European Overseas Empires, 1415–1980* (2000)

Armitage, David, *The Ideological Origins of the British Empire* (2000)

Bayly, C. A., *Imperial Meridian: The British Empire and the World, 1780–1830* (1989)

Beloff, Max, *Imperial Sunset*: I *Britain's Liberal Empire, 1897–1921* (1969)

——, *Imperial Sunset*: II *Dream of Commonwealth, 1921–42* (1989)

Boyce, D. George, *Decolonisation and the British Empire, 1775–1997* (1999)

Brown, Judith M., and Wm Roger Louis, eds., *The Oxford History of the British Empire* IV *The Twentieth Century* (1999)

Canny, Nicholas, ed., *The Oxford History of the British Empire* I *The Origins of Empire* (1998)

Clayton, A., *The British Empire as a Superpower 1919–1939* (1986)

Ferro, Marc, *Colonization: A Global History* (1997)

Hobsbawm, Eric, *The Age of Empire* (1989)

Holland, R. F., *European Decolonization 1918–1981: An Introductory Survey* (1985)

Hyam, Ronald, *Britain's Imperial Century; 1815–1914* (2nd edn, 1993)

James, Lawrence, *The Rise and Fall of the British Empire* (1995)

Judd, Denis, *Empire: The British Imperial Experience* (1996)

Kennedy, Paul, *The Rise and Fall of the Great Powers, 1500–2000* (1989)

Louis, W. R., ed., *Imperialism. The Robinson-Gallagher Controversy* (1976)

Marshall, P. J., ed., *The Cambridge Illustrated History of the British Empire* (1996)

——, ed., *The Oxford History of the British Empire* II *The Eighteenth Century* (1999)

McDonough, Frank, *The British Empire, 1815–1914* (1994)

McIntyre, W. David., *The Commonwealth of Nations: Origins and Impact, 1869–1971* (1977)

Porter, Andrew, ed., *Atlas of British Overseas Expansion* (1991)

——, ed., *The Oxford History of the British Empire* III *The Nineteenth Century* (1999)

Porter, Bernard, *The Lion's Share: A Short History of British Imperialism, 1850–1970* (1975; 3rd edn, 1996)
Smith, Simon C., *British Imperialism, 1750–1970* (1999)
Winks, Robin, ed., *The Oxford History of the British Empire*: v *Historiography* (1999)
——, *British Imperialism: Gold, Guns, Glory* (New York, 1963)

Articles and chapters

Atmore, A. E., 'The Extra-European Foundations of British Imperialism: Towards a Reassessment', in C. C. Eldridge, ed., *British Imperialism in the Nineteenth Century* (1984) pp. 106–25
Bayly, C. A., 'The First Age of Global Imperialism, *c.*1760–1830', *JICH 26* (1998)
Benyon, John, 'Overlords of Empire? British "Proconsular Imperialism" in Comparative Perspective', *JICH* 19, 2 (1991): 164–202.
Cain, P. J. and A. G. Hopkins, 'Gentlemanly Capitalism and British Expansion Overseas: I The Old Colonial System, 1688–1850', and 'II New Imperialism, 1850–1914', *Economic History Review* (1986): 501–25, and (1987): 1–26
Cain, P. J. and A. G. Hopkins, 'The Political Economy of British Expansion Overseas, 1750–1914', *Economic History Review* 33, 4 (1980): 9–23
Darwin, John, 'Imperialism and the Victorians: The Dynamics of Territorial Expansion', *English Hisorical Review* CXII (1997): 614–42.
Hyam, Ronald, 'British Imperialism in the Late Eighteenth Century', *Historical Journal* X (1967)
Hyam, Ronald, 'The primacy of Geo-Politics: The Dynamics of British Imperial Policy, 1763-1963'. *JICH 27* (1999): 27–52
Louis, Wm Roger and R. E. Robinson, 'The Imperialism of Decolonization', *JICH* 22, 3 (1994): 462–51
Porter, Andrew, "Gentlemanly Capitalism" and Empire: The British Experience Since 1750?' *JICH* 18, 3 (1990): 265–95
Robinson, Ronald, 'Non-European Foundations for a Theory of Collaboration', in R. Owen and B. Sutcliffe eds, *Studies in the Theory of Imperialism* (1972)
Robinson, R. E., and J. A. Gallagher, 'The Imperialism of Free Trade', *Economic History Review* 2nd ser. VI, 1 (1953): 1–15

Definitions and the nature of imperialism

Baumgart, Winfried, *Imperialism: The Idea and Reality of British and French Colonial Expansion, 1880–1914* (1982)
Bayly, C. A., 'The Second British Empire', in Robin Winks, ed., *The Oxford History of the British Empire* V Historiography (1999)
Cohen, B. J., *The Question of Imperialism* (1973)

Etherington, Norman, *Theories of Imperialism, War, Conquest and Capital* (1984)

Fieldhouse, David, *The Colonial Empires: A Comparative Survey from the Eighteenth Century* (1982)

Harlow, Vincent, *The Founding of the Second British Empire, 1763–1793* II (1964)

Kemp, Tom, *Theories of Imperialism* (1967)

Marshall, P. J., 'The First and the Second British Empires: a Question of Demarcation', *History* LIX (1964)

Mommsen, Wolgang J., *Theories of Imperialism* (1977)

Porter, A., *European Imperialism* (1994)

Marxist interpretations of imperialism

Bagchi, Amiya Kumar, *The Political Economy of Development* (1982)

Brewer, Anthony, *Marxist Theories of Imperialism: A Critical Survey* (1990)

Frank, Andre Gunder, 'The Development of Underdevelopment' *Monthly Review* 18, 4 (1966)

——, *ReOrient: Global Economy in the Asian Age* (1988)

Kiernan, V., *Marxism and Imperialism* (1974)

Lenin, V.I., *Imperialism: The Highest Stage of Capitalism* (1916)

Luxemburg, Rosa, *The Accumulation of Capital* (reprtd 1951)

Sweezy, P. M., *The Theory of Capitalist Development* (1964)

Wallerstein, Immanuel, *The Capitalist World System*: III *1730–1850, The Second Era of the Great Expansion of the Capitalist World Economy* (1980)

Slavery, humanitarianism and anti-slavery, *c*.1700–1900

Anstey, Roger, *The Atlantic Slave Trade and British Abolition, 1760–1810* (1975)

Cairns, H. A. C., *Prelude to Imperialism: British Reactions to Central African Society, 1840–1890* (1965)

Davis, David Brion, *Slavery and Human Progress* (1984)

Drescher, Seymour, *Capitalism and Anti-Slavery: British Mobilization in Comparative Perspective* (1986).

Gallagher, J. A., 'Fowell Buxton and the new African Policy', *Cambridge Historical Journal* X (1950): 36–58

Miers, Suzanne, *Britain and the Ending of the Slave Trade* (1975)

Porter, Andrew, 'Trusteeship, Anti-Slavery and Humanitarianism', in Porter, ed., *Oxford History of the British Empire*: III, *The Nineteenth Century* (1999)

——, 'Religion, Missionary Enthusiasm, and Empire', in ibid.

Porter, Bernard, *Critics of Empire: Liberal and Radical Attitudes to Empire, 1895–1914* (1968)

Rosselli, John, *Lord William Bentinck: The Making of a Liberal Imperialist, 1774–1839* (1974)

Walvin, James, *Making the Black Atlantic: Britain and the African Diaspora* (2000)

British rule in India

Bayly, C. A., *Empire and Information: Intelligence Gathering and Social Communication in India, 1780–1870* (1997)

——, *Indian Society and the Making of the British Empire* (1988)

Chatterjee, Kumkum, *Merchants, Politics and Society in Early Modern Bihar, 1730–1820* (1996)

Frykenburg, Robert E., *Guntur District, 1788–1858: A History of Local Influence and Central Authority in South India* (1965)

Gillard, David, *The Struggle for Asia, 1828–1914* (1977)

Guha, Ranajit, *A Rule of Property for Bengal* (1963)

Hopkirk, Peter, *The Great Game* (1990)

Marshall, P. J., *Bengal, The British Bridgehead: Eastern India, 1740–1828* (1988)

Nandy, Ashis, *The Intimate Enemy: Loss and Recovery of Self Under Colonialism* (1983)

Peers, Douglas, *Between Mars and Mammon: Colonial Armies and the Garrison State in India,* 1819–1835 (1995)

Robb, Peter, 'Ideas in Agrarian History: Some Observations on the British and Nineteenth-Century Bihai', in David Arnold and Peter Robb, eds, *Institutions and Ideologies* (1993)

Stokes, Eric, *The English Utilitarians and India* (1959)

Viswananthan, Gauri, *Masks of Conquest: Literary Study and British Rule in India,* (1989)

Washbrook, D. A., 'Progress and Problems in South Asian Economic History, 1720–1860' *Modern Asian Studies* (1988)

The Indian Mutiny/Rebellion of 1857–8

Bhadra, Gautam, 'Four Rebels of Eighteen Fifty-Seven', in Ranajit Guha, ed., *Subaltern Studies* IV (1985)

Buckler, F. W., 'The Political Theory of the Indian Mutiny', in M. N. Pearson, ed., *Legitimacy and Symbols: The South Asian Writings of F. W. Buckler* (1985)

Edwardes, Michael, *Red Year: The Indian Rebellion of 1857* (1973)

Metcalfe, Thomas R., *The Aftermath of Revolt: India, 1857–1870* (1964)

Mukherjee, R., *Awadh in Revolt, 1857–8* (1984)
Palmer, J. A. B., *The Mutiny Outbreak at Meerut in 1857* (1966)
Stokes, Eric, *The Peasant and the Raj: Studies in Agrarian Society and Peasant Rebellion in Colonial India* (1978)

British imperialism and the Indian economy

Bose, Sugata, *Peasant Labour and Colonial Capital: Rural Bengal since 1770* (1993)
——, ed., *South Asia and World Capitalism* (1990)
Brown, Judith M., *Modern India: The Making of a Modern Asian Democracy* (1985)
Charlesworth, Neil, *British Rule and the Indian Economy* (1982)
——, *Peasants and Imperial Rule: Agriculture and Agrarian Society in the Bombay Presidency, 1850–1935* (1985)
Misra, Maria, *Business, Race and Politics in British India, c.1850–1960* (1999)
Morris, M. D., 'Towards a Reinterpretation of Nineteenth-Century Indian Economic History', *Journal of Economic History* (1963)
Tomlinson, B. R., *The Economy of Modern India: 1860–1970* (1993)
Siddiqi, Asiya, *Agrarian Change in a Northern Indian State, Uttar Pradesh, 1819–1833* (1973)
Washbrook, D. A., 'Economic Depression and the Making of "Traditional" Society in India, 1820–1855', *Transactions of the Royal Historical Society* (1993)
——, 'Progress and Problems: South Asian Economic and Social History, 1720–1860', *Modern Asian Studies* (1988)

Britain and the scramble for Africa

Flint, John E., 'Britain and the Scramble for Africa', in Robin Winks, ed., *The Oxford History of the British Empire* v *Historiography* (1999)
Forster, S., W. J. Mommsen and Ronald Robinson, eds., *Bismarck, Europe and Africa* (1989)
Gifford, P., and W. R. Louis, eds, *Britain and Germany in Africa: Imperial Rivalry and Colonial Rule* (1967)
——, eds, *France and Britain in Africa: Imperial Rivalry & Colonial Rule* (1971)
Hargreaves, J. D., *West Africa Partitioned*: 2 vols, I *The Loaded Pause, 1885–1889* (1974), II *The Elephants and the Grass* (1985)
Kanya-Forstner, A. S., *The Conquest of the Western Sudan: A Study in French Military Imperialism* (1969)
Oliver, R., and G. N. Sanderson, eds, *The Cambridge History of Africa*: Vol. 6 *c.1870–c.1905* (1980)

Pakenham, Thomas, *The Scramble for Africa* (1991)

Robinson, R., and J. Gallagher with A. Denny, *Africa and the Victorians* (1961; 2nd edn, 1981)

Schreuder, D. M., *The Scramble for Southern Africa, 1877–1895* (1980)

The occupation of Egypt, 1882

Al-Sayyid-Marsot, Afaf Lufti, 'The British Occupation of Egypt from 1882', in A. Porter, ed., *The Oxford History of the British Empire* III *The Nineteenth Century* (1999)

Chamberlain, M. E., 'Sir Charles Dilke and the British Intervention in Egypt in 1882: Decision-Making in a Nineteenth Century Cabinet', *British Journal of International Studies* 2 (1976): 231–45

Hopkins, A. G., 'The Victorians and Africa: The British Occupation of Egypt in 1882', *Journal of African History* (1986)

Mowat, R. C., 'From Liberalism to Imperialism: The Case of Egypt, 1875–1887', *Historical Journal* (1973)

Owen, Roger, 'Egypt and Europe: From French Expedition to British Occupation', in R. Owen and B. Sutcliffe, eds, *Studies in the Theory of Imperialism* (1972)

——, 'Robinson and Gallagher on Middle East Nationalism: The Egyptian argument', in W. R. Louis (ed.), *Imperialism: The Robinson Gallagher Controversy* (1975)

Ramm, Agatha, 'Great Britain and France in Egypt, 1876–1882', in P. Gifford and W. R. Louis, eds, *France and Britain in Africa* (1971)

Robinson, R. E., and J. Gallagher, with Alice Denny, *Africa and the Victorians* (1961)

Scholch, Alexander, *Egypt for the Egyptians: The Socio-Political Crisis in Egypt, 1878–1882* (orig. 1972; Eng. transl. 1981)

——, 'The Men on the Spot and the English Occupation of Egypt', *Historical Journal* (1976)

The 'Imperialism of Free Trade' and Informal Empire.

Cain, P. J. and A. G. Hopkins, *British Imperialism: Innovation and Expansion* (1993)

Dean, B., "British Informal Empire: The case of China', *Journal of Commonwealth and Comparative Politics* 14 (1976): 64–81

Edwards, E. W., *British Diplomacy and Finance in China, 1895–1914* (1987)

Fairbank, J. K., *Trade and Diplomacy on the China Coast, 1842–1854* (1953)

Ferns, H. S., *Britain and Argentina in the Nineteenth Century* (1960)

Gallagher, J., and R. Robinson, 'The Imperialism of Free Trade', *Economic History Review* VI (1953): 1–15

Greenberg, M, *British Trade and the Opening of China, 1800–1842* (1951)

Louis, W. R., ed., *Imperialism: The Robinson and Gallagher Controversy* (1970)

Lowe, P., *Britain and the Far East* (1981)

Lynn, M., 'British Policy, Trade, and Informal Empire in the Mid-Nineteenth Century', in A. Porter, ed., *The Oxford History of the British Empire* III *The Nineteenth Century* (1999)

MacDonagh, O., 'The Anti-Imperialism of Free Trade', *Economic History Review* XIV (1962)

Mathew, W. M, 'The Imperialism of Free Trade: Peru 1820–1870' *Economic History Review* XXI (1968)

McLean, D., 'Finance and "Informal Empire" before the First World War', *Economic History Review* (1976)

——, *War, Diplomacy and Informal Empire: Britain and the Republics of La Plata,* 1836–1853 (1995)

Miller, R., *Britain and Latin America in the Nineteenth and Twentieth Centuries* (1993)

Platt, D. C. M., 'The Imperialism of Free Trade: Some Reservations', *Economic History Review* XXI (1968)

——, 'Further Objections to an "Imperialism of Free Trade"', *Economic History Review* XXVI (1973)

——, *Finance, Trade, and Politics in British Foreign Policy, 1815–1914* (1968)

Semmel, B., *The Rise of Free Trade Imperialism* (1970)

Winn, P., 'British Informal Empire in Uruguay in the Nineteenth Century' *Past and Present* (1976)

Economics and imperialism

Bayly, C. A., *Imperial Meridian* (1989)

Davis, L., and R. Huttenback, *Mammon and the Pursuit of Empire: The Political Economy of British Imperialism, 1860–1912* (1986)

Edelstein, M., *Overseas Investments in the Age of High Imperialism* (1982)

Fieldhouse, David, *Economics and Empire* (1973)

——, 'The Metropolitan Economics of Empire', in Judith M. Brown and Wm Roger Louis, eds, *The Oxford History of the British Empire* IV *The Twentieth Century* (1999)

Floud, R., and D. McCloskey, eds, *The Economic History of Britain since 1700* II *1860–1939* (1994)

Hobsbawm, Eric, *Industry and Empire* (1968)

Hopkins, A. G., 'Review Article: Accounting for the British Empire', *JICH* 16 (1988)

Kennedy, P., 'Debate: The Costs and Benefits of British Imperialism, 1846–1914', *Past and Present* 120 (1988)

O'Brien, P. K., 'Reply', *Past and Present* 120 (1988)

——, 'Inseparable Connections: Trade, Economy, Fiscal State and the Expansion of Empire, 1688–1815', in P. J. Marshall, ed., *The Oxford History of the British Empire* II *The Eighteenth Century* (1998)

——, 'Imperialism and the Rise and Decline of the British Economy, 1688–1989', *New Left Review* 238 (1999)

Offer, A., 'The British Empire, 1870–1914: A Waste of Money?', *Economic History Review* 46 (1993)

——, 'Costs and Benefits, Propesrity and Security, 1870–1914', in A. N. Porter, ed., *The Oxford History of the British Empire* III *The Nineteenth Century* (1999)

'Gentlemanly Capitalism'

Cain, P. J. and A. G. Hopkins, 'Gentlemanly Capitalism and British Expansion Overseas I: The Old Colonial System, 1688–1850', *Economic History Review* 39 (1986): 501–25

——, 'Gentlemanly Capitalism and British Expansion Overseas II: New Imperialism, 1850–1945', *Economic History Review* 40 (1987): 1–26

——, *British Imperialism* 2 vols, (1993)

Daunton, M., 'Gentlemanly Capitalism and British Industry, 1820–1914' *Past and Present* 122 (1989): 119–58

Dumett, R., *Gentlemanly Capitalism and British Imperialism: The New Debate on Empire* (1988)

Porter, A. N., 'Gentlemanly Capitalism and Empire: The British Experience since 1750?', *JICH* 18 (1990): 265–95

The colonies of settlement c.1788–1850

Atkinson, A., *The European in Australia* I *The Beginnings* (1997)

Blainey, Geoffrey, *The Tyranny of Distance* (1966)

Bumsted, J. M., *The Peoples of Canada* I (1992)

Burroughs, P., *Britain and Australia 1831–1855* (1967)

Cameron, J. M. R., *Ambition's Fire: The Agricultural Colonization of Western Australia* (1981)

Devine, T. M., *Scottish Emigration and Scottish Society* (1992)

Eddy, J. J., *Britain and the Australian Colonies, 1818–1831*(1969)

Fletcher, Brian H., *Colonial Australia before 1850* (1976)

Hargreaves, Alec. G., 'European Identity and the Colonial Frontier', *Journal of European Studies* 12 (1982): 167–79

Harper, Marjory, 'British Migration and the Peopling of the Empire', in A. Porter, ed., *The Oxford History of the British Empire* III *The Nineteenth Century* (1999)

Hirst, J. B., *Convict Society and Its Enemies* (1983)
Johnston, H. J. M., *British Emigration Policy, 1815–1830: Shovelling out Paupers* (1972)
Kline, B. E., 'British Emigration and New Identities', in P. J. Marshall, ed., *The Cambridge Illustrated History of the British Empire* (1996)
Kociumbas, Jan, *The Oxford History of Australia* 2 *1770–1860* (1992)
Mackay, David, *A Place of Exile: The European Settlement of New South Wales* (1985)
MacMillan, D. S., *Scotland and Australia 1788–1850* (1967)
Martin, Ged, *The Founding of Australia* (1978)
Morrell, W. P., 'Colonists and Aborigines in Early Australian Settlements', *New Zealand Journal of History* 12 (1978): 50–61
Reynolds, Henry, *The Other Side of the Frontier: Aboriginal Resistance to the European Invasion of Australia* (19)
Shaw, A. G. L., *Convicts and the Colonies* (1966)
Thompson, Leonard, *A History of South Africa* (1990)
White, Richard, *Inventing Australia: Images and Identity, 1688–1980* (1981)

Self-Government

Janet Ajzenstat *The Political Thought of Lord Durham* (1988)
Buckner, P. L., *The Transition to Responsible Government* (1985)
Burroughs, P., 'Colonial Self-Government', in C. Eldridge, ed., *British Imperialism in the Nineteenth Century* (1984)
Careless, J. M. S., *The Union of the Canadas* (1967)
Craig, G. M., *Upper Canada, 1784–1841 (1963)*
——, ed., *The Durham Report (1963)*
Martin, G., *The Durham Report and British Policy* (1972)
——, 'The Influence of the Durham Report', in R. Hyam and G. Martin, *Reappraisals in British Imperial History* (1975)
Ward, J. M., *Colonial Self-Government: The British Experience, 1759–1856* (1976)

Military imperialism

Anderson, D., and D. Killingray, *Policing the Empire* (1991)
Bond, B. J., *British Military Policy between the Two World Wars* (1980)
French, D., *The British Way in Warfare, 1688–2000* (1990)
Gordon, D. C., *The Dominion Partnership in Imperial Defence, 1870–1914* (1965)
Headrick, Daniel R., *The Tools of Empire: Technology and European Imperialism in the Nineteenth Century* (1981)
Heathcote, T. A., *The Indian Army, 1860–1940* (1974)
——, *The Military in British India* (1995)

Howard, M., *The Continental Commitment: The Dilemma of British Defence Policy in the Era of Two World Wars* (1972)

Kennedy, Paul, *The Rise and Fall of British Naval Mastery* (1976 etc.)

McIntyre, D., *The Rise and Fall of the Singapore Naval Base, 1919–1942* (1984)

Moor, J. A., and H. L. Wesserling, eds, *Imperialism and War: Essays on Colonial War in Asia and Africa* (1989)

Moreman, T. R., *The Army in India and the Development of Frontier Warfare, 1848–1947* (1998)

Omissi, David, *Air Power and Colonial Control, The Royal Air Force: 1919–1939* (1990)

——, *The Sepoy and the Raj: The Indian Army, 1860–1940* (1994)

Spiers, E. M., *The Late Victorian Army, 1868–1902* (1992)

Strachan, H., 'The Early Victorian Army and the Nineteenth-Century Revolution in Government', *English Historical Review* XCV (1980): 782–809

——, 'Lord Grey and Imperial Defence', in I. F. W. Beckett and J. Gooch, eds, *Politicians and Defence: Studies in the Formulation of British Defence Policy, 1845–70* (1981)

Vandervort, Bruce, *Wars of Imperial Conquest in Africa* (1998)

The South African War (1899–1902) and South Africa

Denoon, D. J. D., *A Grand Illusion: The Failure of Imperial Policy in the Transvaal Colony, 1900–1905* (1973)

Flint, J. E., *Cecil Rhodes* (1976)

Hyam, Ronald, *Elgin and Churchill at the Colonial Office, 1905–1908* (1965)

Le May, G. H., *British Supremacy in South Africa, 1899–1907* (1965)

Marais, J. S., *The Fall of Kruger's Republic* (1961)

Marks, S., and S. Trapido, 'Lord Milner and the South African State', *History Workshop* VIII (1979): 50–80

Marks, S., 'Southern and Central Africa, 1886–1910', in R. Oliver and G. N. Sanderson, eds, *Cambridge History of Africa* 6 (1985) ch. 8

Porter, A. N., 'The South African War (1899–1902): Context and Motive Reconsidered', *Journal of African History* XXXI (1990): 43–57

Saunders, Christopher, and Iain R. Smith, 'Southern Africa, 1795–1910', in A. Porter, ed., *The Oxford History of the British Empire* III *The Nineteenth Century* (1999)

Smith, Iain R., *The Origins of the South African War, 1899–1902* (1995)

Spies, S. B., *Methods of Barbarism?* (1977)

Thompson, L. M., *The Unification of South Africa, 1902–1910* (1960)

Warwick, P., *Black People and the South African War* (1980)

Collaboration and resistance in India, 1860–1914

Arnold, David, 'Bureaucratic Recruitment and Subordination in Colonial India, The Madras Constabulary, 1859–1947', in Ranajit Guha, ed., *Subaltern Studies*, (1985)
Cohn, Bernard S., 'Representing Authority in Victorian India', in Eric Hobsbawm and Terence Ranger, eds, *The Invention of Tradition* (1983)
Gallagher, J., Gordon Johnson and Anil Seal, eds, *Locality, Province and Nation: Essays on Indian Politics, 1870–1940* (1973)
Gopal, S., *British Policy in India. 1852–1905* (1965)
Metcalfe, T. R., *The Aftermath of Revolt: India, 1857–1870* (1964)
Moore, R. J., *Liberalism and Indian Politics, 1872–1922* (1966)
O'Hanlon, Rosalind, 'Recovering the Subject: Subaltern Studies and Histories of Resistance in Colonial South Asia', *Modern Asian Studies* 22 (1988): 189–224
Omissi, David, *The Sepoy and the Raj* (1994)
Sarkar, Sumit, *Modern India, 1880–1947* (1983)
Washbrook, D. A., *The Emergence of Provincial Politics: The Madras Presidency, 1870–1920* (1976)
Yang, Anand, *The Limited Raj: Agrarian Relations in Colonial India, Saran District, 1793–1920* (1989)

Colonial discourse and post-colonial theory

Asad, Talal, 'Two European Images of non-European Rule', in Talal Asad, ed., *Anthropology and the Colonial Encounter* (1973)
Brantlinger, Patrick, *British Literature and Imperialism, 1830–1914* (1988)
Cohn, Bernard S., 'Representing Authority in Victorian India', in Eric Hobsbawm and Terence Ranger, eds, *The Invention of Tradition* (1983)
Dewey, Clive, 'Images of the Village Community: A Study in Anglo-Indian Ideology', *Modern Asian Studies* (1972)
Fanon, Frantz, *Black Skins, White Masks* (1952)
Green, Martin, *Dreams of Adventure, Deeds of Empire* (1979)
Inden, Ronald, 'Orientalist Constructions of India', *Modern Asian Studies* (1986)
Lewis, Bernard, *Islam and the West* (1995)
MacKenzie, John M., *Orientalism: History, Theory and the Arts* (1995)
Raskin, Jonah, *The Mythology of Imperialism* (1971)
Said, Edward, *Culture and Imperialism* (1993)
——, *Orientalism* (1978)
Spivak, G., 'Can the Subalton Speak?', in Cary Nelson and Lawrence Grossberg, eds, *Marxist Interpretations of Culture* (1988) pp. 271–313.

Washbrook, D. A., 'Orients and Occidents: Colonial Discourse Theory and the Historiography of the British Empire', in Robin Winks, ed., *The Oxford History of the British Empire* v Historiography (1999)

Race and imperialism

Biddis, M., ed., *Images of Race* (1979)
Bolt, C., *Victorian Attitudes Towards Race* (1971)
Kiernan, V. G., *The Lords of Humankind: European Attitudes towards the Outside World in the Imperial Age* (1972)
Lorimer, D., *Colour, Class and the Victorians: English Attitudes to the Negro in the Mid-Nineteenth Century* (1978)
Mason, P., *Prospero's Magic: Some Thoughts on Class and Race* (1962)
Semmel, B., *The Governor Eyre Controversy* (1962)

Gender and imperialism

Amies, Marion, 'The Victorian Governess and Colonial Ideals of Womanhood', *Victorian Studies* 31, 4 (1988): 537–65
Ballhatchet, K., *Race, Sex and Class under the Raj: Imperial Attitudes and their Critics, 1793–1905* (1993)
Bristow, J., *Empire Boys: Adventures in a Man's World* (1991)
Brownfoot, J., 'Sisters under the Skin: Imperialism and the Emancipation of Women In Malaya, c.1891–1941', in J. Mangan, ed., *Making Imperial Mentalities* (1990)
Burton, Amanda, *Burdens of History: British Feminists, Indian Women and Imperial Culture, 1865–1914* (1994)
Callaway, H., *Gender, Culture and Empire: European Women in Colonial Nigeria* (1987)
——, 'Purity and Exotica in Legitimating the Empire: Cultural Constructions of Gender, Sexuality, and Race', in T. O. Ranger and O. Vaughan, eds, *Legitimacy and the State in Twentieth-Century Africa* (1993)
Chaudhuri, N., and Margaret Strobel, eds, *Western Women and Imperialism: Complicity and Resistance* (1991)
Davin, A., 'Imperialism and Motherhood', *History Workshop* v (1978): 9–65
Dawson, G., *Soldier Heroes: British Adventure, Empire and the Imaging of Masculinity* (1994)
Foley, T. P., *Gender and Colonialism* (1995)
Hunt, N. R., and other eds, *Gendered Colonialism in African History* VIII (1996): 365–92
Hyam, Ronald, 'Empire and Sexual Opportunity', *JICH* 14, 2 (1986): 34–90

——, *Empire and Sexuality: The British Experience* (1990)
Knapman, C., *White Women in Fiji, 1835–1930: The Ruin of Empire* (1986)
McClintock, Anne, *Imperial Leather: Race, Gender and Sexuality in the Colonial Contest* (1995)
Midgley, Clare, ed., *Gender and Imperialism* (1998)
O'Hanlon, R., 'Gender in the British Empire', in Judith M. Brown and Wm Roger Louis, eds, *The Oxford History of the British Empire* IV *The Twentieth Century* (1999)
Sinha, Mrinalini, *Colonial Masculinity: The Manly Englishman and the Effeminate Bengali in the Late Nineteenth Century* (1995)
Stoler, A. L., 'Making Empire Respectable: The Politics of race and Sexual Morality in Twentieth-Century Colonial Cultures', *American Ethnologist* XVI (1989): 634–60.
Strobel, Margaret, *European Women and the Second British Empire* (1991)

The First World War

Andrews, E. M., *The Anzac Illusion: Anglo-Australian Relations during World War* I (1994)
Brown, R. C., and R. Cook, *Canada, 1896–21: A Nation Transformed* (1974)
Darwin, J., *Britain, Egypt and the Middle East: Imperial Policy and the Aftermath of War,* 1918–22 (1981)
Gallagher, J., 'Crisis of Empire', *Modern Asian Studies* (1981)
Jeffrey, K., *The British Army and the Crisis of Empire, 1918–22* (1984)
Kendle, J. E., *The Round Table Movement and Imperial Union* (1975)
Louis, W. R., *Great Britain and Germany's Lost Colonies, 1914–1919* (1967)
Mansergh, N., *The Commonwealth Experience* I *The Durham Report to the Anglo-Irish Treaty* (2nd edn 1982)
Stockwell, A. J., 'The War and the British Empire', in J. Turner, ed., *Britain and the First World War* (1988)
Wigley, P. G., *Canada and the Transition to Commonwealth: British Canadian Relations, 1917–1926* (1979)

Imperialism and colonial nationalism

Bumsted, J. M., *The Peoples of Canada: A Post-Confederation History* (1992)
Denoon, Donald, *Settler Capitalism: The Dynamics of Dependent Development in the Southern Hemisphere* (1983)
Eddy, J., and D. Schreuder, eds, *The Rise of Colonial Nationalism* (1988)

Friedberg, A. L., *The Weary Titan: Britain and the Experience of Relative Decline, 1895–1905* (1988)

Green, E. H. H., *The Crisis of Conservatism: The Politics, Economics and Ideology of the British Conservative Party, 1880–1914* (1994)

Kendle, J. E., *The Colonial and Imperial Conferences, 1887–1911* (1975)

Norris, Ronald, *The Emergent Commonwealth: Australian Federation, Expectations and Fulfilment, 1889–1910* (1975)

Offer, Avner, *The First World War: An Agrarian Interpretation* (1989)

Trainor, Luke, *British Imperialism and Australian Nationalism* (1994)

Britain and the self-governing colonies, 1918–45

Carlton, D., 'The Dominions and the Gathering Storm', *JICH* 6, 2 (1978)

Constantine, Stephen, 'Migrants and Settlers', in Judith M. Brown and Wm R. Louis, eds, *The Oxford History of the British Empire* IV, *The Twentieth Century* (1999)

Darwin, J., 'Imperialism in Decline? Tendencies in British Imperial Policy between the Wars', *Historical Journal* 23, 3 (1980): 657–79

——, 'A Third British Empire? The Dominion Idea in Imperial Politics', in Judith M. Brown and Wm R. Louis, eds, *The Oxford History of the British Empire* IV *The Twentieth Century* (1999)

Davenport, R., *A Modern History of South Africa* (4th edn 1987)

Dawson, R., *The Development of Dominion Status, 1900–36* (1936)

Francis, Mark, *Governors and Settlers: Images of Authority in the British Colonies, 1820–1860* (1992)

Hall, D., 'The Genesis of the Balfour Declaration of 1926', *Journal of Commonwealth Political Studies* 1, 3 (1963)

Hancock, W. K., *Survey of Commonwealth Affairs* 1 *Problems of Nationality, 1918–1936* (1937)

——, *Survey of Commonwealth Affairs* 2 *Problems of Economic Policy, 1918–1939* (1940)

Harkness, D., *The Restless Dominion: The Irish Free State and the British Commonwealth of Nations, 1921–31* (1960)

Holland, R. F., *Britain and the Commonwealth Alliance, 1918–39* (1981)

Huttenback, Robert A., 'No Strangers Within the Gates: Attitudes and Polices Towards the Non-White Residents of the British Empire of Settlement', *JICH* 8, (1979): 30–55

Martin, G., 'The Irish Free State and the Evolution of the Commonwealth, 1921–49', in G. Martin and R. Hyam, *Reappraisals in British Imperial History* (1975)

McIntyre, S., *The Oxford History of Australia* 4 *The Succeeding Age, 1901–42* (1986)

Newbury, C. W., 'Labour Migration: The Imperial Phase', *JICH* 3 (1975)

Ovendale, R., *'Appeasement' and the English-Speaking World: Britain, the Dominions, the United States and the Policy of Appeasement, 1937–39* (1975)

Britain and colonial Africa, 1900–40

Afigbo, A. E., *The Warrant Chiefs* (1972)
Asad, T., ed., *Anthropology and the Colonial Encounter* (1973)
Bush, B., *Imperialism. Race and Resistance: Africa and Britain, 1919–1945* (1999)
Cell, John, 'Colonial Rule', in Judith M. Brown and Wm R. Louis, eds, *The Oxford History of the British Empire* IV *The Twentieth Century* (1999)
Chanock, M., *Law, Custom and Social Order: The Colonial Experience in Malawi and Zambia* (1985)
Fields, K., *Revival and Rebellion in Colonial Central Africa* (1985)
Gann, L. H., and P. Duignan, eds, *Colonialism in Africa* 5 vols (1969–75)
Havinden, M., and D. Meredith, *Colonialism and Development* (1993)
Kirk-Greene, A. H. M., 'The Thin White Line: The Size of the British Colonial Service in Africa', *African Affairs* (1980)
Mafeje, A. E., 'The Ideology of 'Tribalism', *Journal of Modern African Studies* (1971)
Mann, K., and R. Roberts, *Law in Colonial Africa* (1991)
Ranger, T. O., 'The Invention of Tradition in Colonial Africa', in T. Ranger and E. Hobsbawm, eds, *The Invention of Tradition* (1983)
——, 'Race and Tribe in Southern Africa – European Ideas and European Acceptance', in R. Ross, ed., *Racism and Colonialism* (1982)
——, 'The Invention of Tradition Revisited: The Case of Colonial Africa', in T. Ranger and O. Vaughan, eds, *Legitimacy and the State in Africa* (1993)
Roberts, A., *The Colonial Moment in Africa: Essays on the Movement of Minds and Materials,* 1900–1940 (1990)
Robinson, K. E., *The Dilemmas of Trusteeship: British Colonial Policy Between the Wars* (1965)
Southall, A., 'The Illusion of Tribe', *Journal of Asian and African Studies* (1970)
Vail, L., *The Creation of Tribalism in Southern Africa* (1989)

West Africa

Crowder, M., 'Indirect Rule – British and French Style' *Africa* 34 (1964)
——, *West Africa Under Colonial Rule* (1968, reprtd 1984)

Falola, Toyin, and A. D. Roberts, 'West Africa', in Judith M. Brown and Wm R. Louis, eds, *The Oxford History of the British Empire* IV *The Twentieth Century* (1999)

Philips, A., *The Enigma of Colonialism: British Policy in West Africa* (1989)

Tibenderana, P. K., 'The Role of the British Administration in the Appointment of the Emirs of Northern Nigeria' *Journal of African History* (1987)

East Africa

Berman, B., and J. Lonsdale, *Unhappy Valley: Conflict in Kenya and Africa*: 1 *State and Class* (1992) parts 1–3

Brett, E. A., *Colonialism and Underdevelopment in East Africa: The Politics of Economic Change* (1973)

Harlow, V., and E. M. Chilver, eds, *History of East Africa* 2 (1965)

Kennedy, D., *Islands of White: Settler Society and Culture in Kenya and Southern Rhodesia, 1890–1939* (1987)

Maxon, R., *Struggle for Kenya. The Loss and Reassertion of Imperial Initiative, 1912–1923* (1993)

Ochieng, W. R., ed., *A Modern History of Kenya, 1895–1980* (1989)

Oliver, Roland, and G. Matthew, with A. Smith, eds, *History of East Africa* 1 (1963)

Sorrenson, M., *The Origins of European Settlement in Kenya* (1968)

Wylie, D., 'Confrontation over Kenya: The Colonial Office and its Critics, 1918–40', *Journal of African History* 18 (1970)

Zwanenberg, R., *Colonial Capitalism and Labour in Kenya, 1919–1939* (1975)

Britain and the Middle East, 1914–45

Balfour-Paul, G., *The End of Empire in the Middle East* (1991)

Daly, M. W., *Imperial Sudan: The Anglo-Egyptian Condominium, 1934–1956* (1991)

Darwin, J., *Britain, Egypt and the Middle East: Imperial Policy in the Aftermath of War, 1918–1922* (1981)

Johnson, D., ed., *Sudan* 2 vols, (1998)

Kent, J., ed., *Egypt* 3 vols, (1998)

Kent, M., *Moguls and Mandarins: Oil, Imperialism and the Middle East in British Foreign Policy, 1900–1940* (1993)

Louis, W. R., *The British Empire in the Middle East, 1945–51* (1984)

Monroe, E., *Britain's Moment in the Middle East, 1914–1971* (rev. edn 1971)

Pieragostini, K., *Britain, Aden, and South Arabia* (1991)

Robinson, Francis, 'The British Empire and the Muslim World', in Judith M. Brown and Wm R. Louis, eds, *The Oxford History of the British Empire* IV *The Twentieth Century* (1999)

Palestine

Cohen, M., *Palestine: Retreat from the Mandate* (1978)
——, *Palestine and the Great Powers, 1945–1948* (1982)
——, *Palestine to Israel: From Mandate to Independence* (1988)
Louis, W. R., and R. W. Stookey, eds, *The End of the Palestine Mandate* (1986)
Schlaim, A., *The Politics of Partition: King Abdullah, the Zionists, and Palestine, 1921–1951* (1990)
Wasserstein, B., *The British in Palestine: The Mandatory Government and the Arab-Jewish Conflict, 1917–1929* (1991)
Zweig, R. W., *Britain and Palestine during the Second World War* (1986)

South-East Asia

Chandler, David K., and David J. Steinberg, eds, *In Search of South East Asia: A Modern History* (1970, rev. edn 1987)
Hall, Richard, *Empires of the Monsoon* (1996)
Jeshrun, Chandran, *The Contest for Siam, 1899–1902: A Study in Diplomatic Rivalry* (1977)
Osborne, Milton J., *South East Asia: An Introductory History* (1979, 6th edn 1995)
Terwiel, B. J., *A History of Modern Thailand, 1767–1942* (1983)
Tinker, Hugh, *South Asia: A Short History* (1966)
Wyatt, David K., *Thailand: A Short History* (1984)

The British Empire and the Second World War

Ashton, S. R., and S. E. Stockwell, eds, *Imperial Policy and Colonial Practice, 1925–1945* 2 vols, (1996)
Jackson, A., *Botswana, 1939–45: An African Community at War* (1999)
Jeffery, Keith, 'The Second World War', in Judith M. Brown and Wm R. Louis, eds, *The Oxford History of the British Empire* IV *The Twentieth Century* (1999)
Lee, J. M., ' "Forward thinking" and War: The Colonial Office during the 1940s', *JICH* VI, 1 (1977): 64–70
Louis, W. R., *Imperialism at Bay, 1941–1945: The United States and the Decolonization of the British Empire* (1977)
Moore, R. J., *Churchill, Cripps, and India, 1939–1945* (1979)

Rathbone, R., and D. Killingray, *Africa and the Second World War* (1986)

Smyth, R., 'Britain's African colonies and British propaganda during World War Two', *JICH* IV, 1 (1985): 65–82

Thorne, C., *The Issue of War* (1978)

——, *Allies of a Kind The United States, Britain and the War against Japan, 1941–45* (1978)

Wolton, S., *Lord Hailey, the Colonial Office and the Politics of Race and Empire in the Second World War* (2000)

Culture and imperialism

Armitage, David, 'Making the Empire British: Scotland in the Atlantic World, 1542–1707, *Past and Present* (1997)

Colley, Linda, *Britons: Forging the Nation, 1707–1837* (1992)

Cunningham, H., 'The Language of Patriotism, 1750–1914', *History Workshop Journal* (1981)

Fletcher, Laaden, 'Early British Colonial School Inspectors: Agents of Imperialism?', *History of Education* 11 (1982): 281–310

Kiernan, V., 'Working Class and Nation in Nineteenth-Century Britain', in M. Comforth, ed., *Rebels and their Causes* (1978)

MacKenzie, J. M., ed., *Imperialism and Popular Culture* (1986)

——, *Propaganda and Empire* (1984)

——, *Popular Imperialism and the Military, 1850–19.50* (1992)

Morris, J., 'The Popularisation of Imperial History', *JJCH* (1973)

Murdoch, Alexander, *British History, 1660–1832: National Identity and Local Culture* (1998)

Orwell, George, *Burmese Days*

Pelling, Henry, *Popular Politics and Society in Late Victorian England* (1968)

Price, R., *An Imperial War and the British Working Class* (1972)

Samuel, Raphael, ed., *Patriotism: The Making and Unmaking of British National Identity* 3 vols (1989)

Stedman Jones, G., 'Working Class Culture and Working Class Politics in London, 1890–1900', *Journal of Social History* (1974)

Stembridge, Stanley R., *Parliament, the Press and the Colonies, 1846–1880* (1982)

Stoddart, B., 'Sport, Cultural Imperialism and Colonial Response in the British Empire', *Comparative Studies in Society and History* 30 (1988)

Summerfield, P., 'The Effingham Arms and the Empire', in E. and S. Yeo, eds, *Popular Culture and Class Conflict, 1590–1914* (1981)

Imperialism and anti-imperialism in British politics

Butler, R. M., 'Imperial questions in British Politics, 1868–80', in *Cambridge History of the British Empire* III (1959)

Eldridge, C. C., *England's Mission: The Imperial Idea in the Age of Gladstone and Disraeli, 1868–90* (1973)

Hall, Catherine, 'Rethinking Imperial Histories: The Reform Act of 1867', *New Left Review* (1994)

Harcourt, F., 'Disraeli's Imperialism, 1866–68: A question of timing', *Historical Journal* XXXIII (1980): 87–109

——, 'Gladstone: Monarchism and the "New" Imperialism, 1868–74', *JICH* 14 (1985)

Koebner, R., and H. D. Schmidt, *Imperialism: The Story and Significance of a Political Word* (1964)

Madden, A. F., 'Changing Attitudes and Widening Responsibilities, 1895–1914', in *Cambridge History of the British Empire* III (1959)

Marsh, P. J., *Joseph Chamberlain: Entrepreneur in Politics* (1994)

Porter, B., *Critics of Empire* (1968)

Robinson, R. E., 'Imperial Problems in British Politics, 1880–95' in *Cambridge History of the British Empire* III (1959)

Semmel, B., *Imperialism and Social Reform: English Social-Imperial Thought, 1895–1914* (1960)

Shannon, Richard, *The Crisis of Imperialism* (1976)

Thompson, Andrew, 'The Language of Imperialism and the Meanings of Empire: Imperial Discourse and British Politics, 1895–1914', *Journal of British Studies* (1997)

——, *Imperial Britain: The Empire in British Politics, c.1880–1939* (2000)

Colonial development

Ashton, S. R., and A. E. Stockwell, eds, *Imperial Policy and Colonial Practice* 2 vols (1996)

Butler, L. A., 'The Ambiguities of British Colonial Development Policy, 1938–1948', in A. Gorst, Johnman and W. Scott Lucas, eds, *Contemporary British History* (1991)

Butler, L. J., *Industrialisation and the British Colonial State: West Africa, 1939–1951* (1997)

——, 'Reconstruction, Development and the Entrepreneurial State: The British Colonial Model, 1939–1951', *Contemporary British History* 13 (1999)

Constantine, S., *The Making of British Colonial Development Policy, 1914–40* (1984)

Cowen, M., 'Early Years of the Colonial Development Corporation: British State Enterprise Overseas during Late Colonialism', *African Affairs* 83 (1984): 63–75.

Cell, J., *Hailey: A Study in British Imperialism, 1872–1969* (1992)

Falola, T., *Development Studies and Colonial Policy* (1987)

Havinden, M., and D. Meredith, *Colonialism and Development: Britain and its Tropical Colonies, 1850–1960* (1993)

Hopkins, A. G., *An Economic History of West Africa* (1973)

Ingram, B., and C. C. Simmons, *Development Planning and Decolonization in Nigeria, 1938–64* (1996)

Lee, J. M., and M. Petter, *The Colonial Office, War and Development Policy: Organisation and Planning of a Metropolitan Initiative, 1939–1945* (1982)

Low, D. A., and A. Smith, eds, *History of East Africa* 3 (1976)

Meredith, D., 'The British Government and Colonial Economic Policy, 1919–1939', *Economic History Review* XXVIII (1975): 484–99

Morgan, D. J., *The Official History of Colonial Development* 5 vols (1980)

Index